History
of
The Sherman Law

History

of

The Sherman Law

of

The United States of America

By

Albert H. Walker
OF THE NEW YORK BAR

BeardBooks
Washington, D.C.

PREFACE.

The discoveries and inventions of the nineteenth century were the causes of its great increases in commerce and of its high multiplications of contracts and of corporations. Those increases and multiplications operated to multiply yet more highly those opportunities for personal acquirement of disproportionate wealth which the most strong and the most cunning men in every age are eager to seize and to employ. As the end of the nineteenth century drew near, prophetic statesmen could foresee that this procession of causes, unless checked by law, would ultimately operate to put into the hands of a small minority of men most of the property which labor could evolve from the surface or from the bosom of the earth. And those statesmen could also see that one good way to check that process was by a law to prevent the crafty and strong minority from combining to extort high prices for commodities from the weaker and uncombined majority of the people. At the end of the year 1889 there was no such law on the statute books of the United States, and never had been. But such a law was then proposed by Senator John Sherman, and with his almost Rooseveltian energy was so pressed upon the attention of Congress that it was enacted with only one opposing vote in either house, and was approved by President Harrison on July 2, 1890, and has ever since been known as the Sherman law.

That law has never been amended, and is not likely to be repealed or altered. It has been adjudicated in nearly a hundred judicial decisions, and has been held by the Supreme Court to be clearly constitutional and broadly comprehensive. Nearly all the statesmen whose votes enacted it have left the Congress, to return no more. Their votes represented the national will of their time, and the law which they enacted is clearly concordant with the national will of the twentieth century. The Sherman law is a Magna Charta among the statutes of the United States. And this history of that law has been written to condense, upon three hundred and twelve pages, the light relevant thereto, which was originally diffused through some thousands of pages of speeches of statesmen and of decisions and opinions of judges.

A. H. W.

Park Row Building,
    Manhattan, New York.
September 28, 1910.

TABLE OF CONTENTS.

CHAPTER I.

CHAPTER II.

CHAPTER III.

CHAPTER IV.

CHAPTER V.

CHAPTER VI.

CHAPTER VII.

CHAPTER VIII.

CHAPTER IX.

CHAPTER X.

CHAPTER XI.

INDEX OF EXPLAINED CASES.

CHAPTER I.

John Sherman during his life passed through a career of public service, which in continuous length and great value has never been equaled by any other American. That career began when he took the oath of office as a member of Congress in December, 1855, and it continued without any interruption until he resigned the office of Secretary of State forty-three years later at the time of the Spanish War in 1898. During thirty-two of the intervening years he was a United States Senator from Ohio, and was a member of the Senate Committee on Finance during the whole of that time, and during many of those years was the chairman of that committee. His service in the Senate and on its Finance Committee consisted of two parts of sixteen years each, which parts were divided by his service of four years as Secretary of the Treasury in the Cabinet of President Hayes. During nearly thirty years, ending with his transfer from the Senate to the Cabinet of President McKinley in March, 1897, he was generally and, indeed, uniformly reputed to be the ablest and most influential financial statesman in this country. Among his financial achievements, as indeed among all the financial achievements known to the history of the United States, a very high place was immediately reached and will be permanently retained by his initiation, advocacy and execution of the bill to resume specie payments, after the many years through which they were suspended, from the time of the Civil War until the middle of the administration of President Hayes.

It was this influential statesman who, after thirty-four years of consecutive service, at the beginning of the first session of the Fifty-first Congress, on December 4, 1889, introduced Senate Bill No. 1 of that Congress, which bill he entitled, "A bill to declare unlawful, trusts and combinations in restraint of trade and production."[1]

That Sherman bill was never enacted into law, but Senator Sherman in drawing and introducing that bill, and afterward in powerfully advocating its passage upon the floor of the Senate, initiated and carried far forward the movement which resulted, in the summer of 1890, in the passage by both houses of Congress, and the approval by President Harrison, of a more elaborate and comprehensive statute, which in the meantime was drawn by Senator George F. Hoar of Massachusetts, and was substituted for the Sherman bill with the cordial approval of Senator Sherman. Inasmuch as Senator Sherman was the originator of the proposed legislation and was its leading advocate in Congress, the resulting statute has always been known as the Sherman law; although the language of that law was written by Senator Hoar, and was adopted by both houses of Congress without any amendment, as a more comprehensive and accurate expression of the Congressional purpose, than the briefer bill which had been written by Senator Sherman himself, and introduced by him on December 4, 1889.

That Sherman bill of 1889, though never enacted into law, deserves to be read, analyzed and understood because its provisions, when considered in connection with the four months of consideration which it received in the Senate, furnish several valuable guides to the Congressional intention which was finally expressed in the Sherman law of July 2, 1890. For this reason it is the plan of the present chapter to reprint the Sherman bill

[1] Congressional Record, Fifty-first Congress, first session, page 96.

of December 4, 1889, and to present a brief and proper analysis of its provisions, and to follow that presentation in a brief though comprehensive account of the Senate debates which were based upon that bill, and of the action of the Senate which resulted from those debates.

The Sherman bill of December 4, 1889, was as follows:

"Be it enacted by the Senate and House of Representatives of the United States of America in Congress assembled:

Sec. 1. That all arrangements, contracts, agreements, trusts, or combinations between persons or corporations made with a view or which tend to prevent full and free competition in the importation, transportation or sale of articles imported into the United States, or in the production, manufacture, or sale of articles of domestic growth or production, or domestic raw material that competes with any similar article upon which a duty is levied by the Unitetd States, or which shall be transported from one State or Territory to another, and all arrangements, contracts, agreements, trusts or combinations between persons or corporations, designed or which tend to advance the cost to the consumer of any such articles, are hereby declared to be against public policy, unlawful and void.

Sec. 2. That any person or corporation, injured or damnified by such arrangement, contract, agreement, trust or combination, may sue for and recover in any court of the United States of competent jurisdiction, of any person or corporation a party to a combination described in the first section of this act, the full consideration or sum paid by him for any goods, wares and merchandise included in or advanced in price by said combination.

Sec. 3.   That all persons entering into any such arrangement, contract, agreement, trust or combination, described in section 1 of this act, either on his own account or as an agent or attorney for another, or as an officer, agent or stockholder of any corporation, or as a trustee, committee or in any capacity whatever, shall be guilty of a high misdemeanor, and on conviction thereof in any district or circuit court of the United States, shall be subject to a fine of not more than $10,000, or to imprisonment in the penitentiary for a term of not more than five years, or both such fine and imprisonment, in the discretion of the court.   And it shall be the duty of the District Attorney of the United States of the district in which such persons reside, to institute the proper proceedings to enforce the provisions of this act."[2]

A primary analysis of this Sherman bill results in showing that its substantive section is Section 1; and that Section 2 provides for a civil remedy for violations of Section 1; and that Section 3 provides a criminal remedy for violations of Section 1.

An analysis of Section 1 results in showing that that section would prohibit all combinations between a plurality of persons or corporations, to prevent or even to diminish competition, either in the importation, transportation or sale of imported articles; or in the manufacture or other production, or the sale of any article of domestic production which competes with any similar article upon which a duty is levied by the United States; or which shall be transported from one state or territory into another.   And that section would also prohibit all combinations between a plurality of persons or corporations, designed to advance, or which would tend to advance the cost to the consumer of any of the articles designated

[2] Congressional Record, Fifty-first Congress, first session, page 1765.

in the section. Thus the section prohibited all combinations to diminish competition or advance prices in respect of the importation, transportation or sale of imported articles, and in respect of the production or sale of such domestic articles as compete with similar dutiable articles, and in respect of the transportation of any articles from one state or territory to another.

Any proper judgment of the provisions of Section 1 of this Sherman bill must begin with a comparison of those provisions with the Constitution of the United States, to ascertain whether it would be adequately based upon that fundamental law. Such a comparison will result in finding that the only constitutional foundation for those provisions resides in the third paragraph of Section 8 of Article 1 of the Constitution, which section and which paragraph provide that Congress has power "to regulate commerce with foreign nations and among the several States and with the Indian tribes."

It was Senator Sherman's opinion that that commerce clause of the Constitution justified all parts of Section 1 of the Sherman bill. He thought that it justified its regulation of the importation into the United States and transportation or sale in any state or states of imported articles, on the ground that that provision was a regulation of commerce with foreign nations. And he thought that its regulation of the manufacture or other production or sale of domestic articles that competed with any similar dutiable articles was also justified as a regulation of commerce with foreign nations. And he thought that its regulation of transportation of any articles from one state or territory to another was justified as a regulation of commerce among the several states.

Passing at present over the question whether Senator Sherman was right or was wrong in any or all of these opinions, relevant to the relations between the Sherman bill and the commerce clause of the Constitution, it is apparent that he wished to prohibit all decreases of competition and all increases of prices in respect of the transportation and also the sale of as many classes or articles as possible, so far as such decrease of competition or increase of prices might result from combinations between a plurality of persons; and that section 1 of his bill was so comprehensively drawn as to provide for such prohibition in respect of all articles of commerce, except such domestic articles as would not compete with any dutiable article, and would not be transported from one state or territory into another.

Thus it is apparent that Section 1 of the Sherman bill did not propose to regulate any transaction except what might result from combinations between a plurality of persons or corporations; but that it did propose to regulate all combinations of persons or corporations in respect of all transportation and all sales of articles in this country, except such articles of domestic origin as would not compete with dutiable articles, and as would be used up in the same state or territory in which they originated, respectively.

An analysis of Section 2 of the Sherman bill will show at once that it proposed to enable any person or corporation injured by any transaction forbidden in Section 1, to recover from any person or corporation belonging to the combination causing the injury, whatever money might have been paid by the injured party to any member of the combination for any articles included in or advanced in price by the combination.

An analysis of Section 3 of the Sherman bill will show that it contemplated crime as personal, and that it proposed to punish by a heavy fine or a long imprisonment, every person who in any capacity might participate in any combination prohibited by Section 1.

As soon as the Sherman bill was introduced, it was referred to the Senate Committee on Finance, of which

Senator Morrill of Vermont at that time was chairman, but of which Senator Sherman was the most active member.

On January 14, 1890, Senator Sherman reported the Sherman bill to the Senate from the Finance Committee, and on February 27, 1890, he moved the Senate to proceed to its consideration. That motion having been adopted, Senator George of Mississippi took the floor and made an elaborate speech upon the subject.[3]

Senator George began his speech by saying that he regarded legislation on the subject of this bill as probably the most important to be considered by the Fifty-first Congress, for which reason he had prepared with particular care the remarks which he proposed to submit to the Senate in opposition to the bill as it then stood, and which remarks he said would discuss the question of its constitutionality and also the question of its efficiency.

On the first of these heads, Senator George took the ground that the bill was unconstitutional for several reasons, including the fact that it proposed to regulate not only interstate and foreign commerce, but also to regulate, under some circumstances, manufacture or other production within individual states, of some classes of commodities. On the second head he took the ground that the bill was inefficient, because while it proposed to prohibit "arrangements, contracts, agreements, trusts or combinations" that prohibition was confined, as Senator George thought, to plans to decrease competition or increase prices, and did not include any overt acts done in pursuance of those plans. In accordance with this view, Senator George argued that representatives of corporations or other persons might go to Canada or to any other foreign country, and there make their arrange-

---

[3] Congressional Record, Fifty-first Congress, first session, page 1765.

ments, contracts, agreements, trusts or combinations to decrease competition or increase prices without violating the bill, because the bill if enacted into law would not be in force in Canada; and that having thus made their plans, they might return to the United States and execute those plans here without violating that bill, because that bill did not prohibit any overt acts which might be done in pursuance of such plans.

Mr. George was a very able lawyer and a member of the Judiciary Committee of the Senate; and his speech of February 27, 1890, on this subject was so elaborate and so weighty as to convince many Senators that the Sherman bill required to be materially amended before being passed into law.

The Senate resumed consideration of the Sherman bill on March 21, 1890;[4] whereupon Senator Sherman stated that upon further consideration, the Committee on Finance had decided to present a substitute for that bill. That substitute proposed to strike out all the bill after the enacting clause, and to insert the following:

"Sec. 1.   That all arrangements, contracts, agreements, trusts, or combinations between two or more citizens or corporations, or both, of different States, or between two or more citizens or corporations, or both, of the United States and foreign states, or citizens or corporations thereof, made with a view or which tend to prevent full and free competition in the importation, transportation, or sale of articles imported into the United States, or with a view or which tend to prevent full and free competition in articles of growth, production or manufacture of any State or Territory of the United States with similar articles of the growth, production, or manufacture of any other State or Territory, or in the transportation or sale of like articles, the production of any State

[4] Congressional Record, Fifty-first Congress, first session, page 2455.

or Territory of the United States, into or within any other State or Territory of the United States; and all arrangements, trusts, or combinations between such citizens or corporations, made with a view or which tend to advance the cost to the consumer of any such articles, are hereby declared to be against public policy, unlawful and void. And the Circuit Courts of the United States shall have original jurisdiction of all suits of a civil nature at common law or in equity arising under this section, and to issue all remedial process, orders, or writs proper and necessary to enforce its provisions. And the Attorney General and the several district attorneys are hereby directed, in the name of the United States, to commence and prosecute all such cases to final judgment and execution.

Sec. 2. That any person or corporation, injured or damnified by such arrangement, contract, trust or combination defined in the first section of this act, may sue for and recover in any court of the United States of competent jurisdiction, without respect to the amount involved, of any person or corporation a party to a combination described in the first section of this act, twice the amount of damages sustained and the costs of the suit, together with a reasonable attorney's fee."

A comparison of this amended Finance Committee bill with the original Sherman bill, shows that the Committee on Finance attempted therein to strengthen the constitutional foundation of its first section by confining its prohibitions to arrangements, contracts, agreements, trusts or combinations between citizens or corporations or both, of different states or territories of the United States and foreign countries; on the theory that Congress had more power to regulate the doings of combinations of citizens or corporations of different states or countries than it had to regulate the doings of combinations of citizens or

corporations, all of whom might belong to the same state.
And such a comparison will also show that the Finance
Committee now proposed to confer upon the Circuit
Courts of the United States original jurisdiction in equity
to enforce the provisions of the first section by means of
writs of injunction; and also to make it the duty of the
Attorney General of the United States and of the several United States district attorneys throughout the
United States, to commence and prosecute, in the name
of the United States, all such actions in equity, and also
all proper actions at common law for enforcing the provisions of the first section. And such a comparison will
also show that the Finance Committee proposed to substitute a remedy for double damages, with a reasonable
attorney's fee, for the other civil remedy which Section
2 of the original Sherman bill provided for the benefit
of whatever persons or corporations might be injured by
violations of Section 1. And such a comparison will also
show that the Finance Committee proposed to omit all
criminal proceedings and penalties from among its provisions for the enforcement of Section 1 of the bill.

The Finance Committee substitute for the Sherman
bill being thus before the Senate for consideration, Senator Reagan of Texas offered a substitute for the committee substitute, and which Reagan substitute was as follows:

"Sec. 1. That all persons engaged in the creation
of any trust, or as owner, or part owner, agent or manager of any trust employed in any business carried on
with any foreign country, or between the States, or between any State and the District of Columbia, or between any State and any Territory of the United States,
or any owner or part owner, agent or manager of any
corporation using its powers for either of the purposes
specified in the second section of this act, shall be deemed

guilty of a high misdemeanor, and on conviction thereof, shall be fined in a sum not exceeding $10,000, or imprisoned at hard labor in the penitentiary not exceeding five years, or by both of said penalties, in the discretion of the court trying the same.

Sec. 2. That a trust is a combination of capital, skill or acts by two or more persons, firms, corporations or association of persons, or of any two or more of them for either, any or all of the following purposes:

First. To create or carry out any restrictions in trade.

Second. To limit or reduce the production, or to increase or reduce the price of merchandise or commodities.

Third. To prevent competition in the manufacture, making, purchase, sale or transportation of merchandise, produce or commodities.

Fourth. To fix a standard or figure whereby the price to the public shall be in any manner controlled or established of any article, commodity, merchandise, produce or commerce intended for sale, use or consumption.

Fifth. To create a monopoly in the making, manufacture, purchase, sale or transportation of any merchandise, article, produce or commodity.

Sixth. To make, or enter into, or execute, or carry out any contract, obligation or agreement of any kind or description, by which they shall bind or shall have bound themselves not to manufacture, sell, dispose of or to transport any article or commodity, or article of trade, use, merchandise or consumption, below a common standard figure, or by which they shall agree in any manner to keep the price of such article, commodity or transportation at a fixed or graduated figure, or by which they shall in any manner establish or settle the price of any article, commodity or transportation between themselves or between themselves and others, so as to preclude free and unrestrained competition among themselves and others in the sale and transportation of any such article or commodity, or by which they shall agree to pool, combine or unite in any interest they may have in connection with the sale or transportation of any such article or commodity, that its price may in any manner be so affected.

Sec. 3.   That each day any of the persons, associations or corporations aforesaid shall be engaged in violating the provisions of this act, shall be held to be a separate offense."

The Finance Committee substitute for the original Sherman bill and the Reagan substitute for both being thus before the Senate, Senator Sherman, on March 21, 1890, made an elaborate speech upon the general subject.[5]

Speaking of Section 1 of the original Sherman bill, Senator Sherman said: "This section will enable the courts of the United States to restrain, limit and control such combinations as interfere injuriously with our foreign and interstate commerce to the same extent that the state courts habitually control such combinations as interfere with the commerce of the state;" and that "The first section being a remedial statute, would be construed liberally with a view to promote its object.   It defines a civil remedy and the courts will construe it liberally; they will prescribe the precise limits of the constitutional power of the Government.   They will distinguish between lawful combinations in aid of production, and unlawful combinations to prevent competition and in restraint of trade; they can operate on corporations by restraining orders and rules.   They can declare the particular combination null and void, and deal with it according to the nature and extent of the injuries," and

[5] Congressional Record, Fifty-first Congress, first session, page 2456.

that "This bill does not seek to cripple combinations of capital and labor; the formation of partnerships or corporations; but only to prevent and control combinations made with a view to prevent competition or for the restraint of trade, or to increase the profits of the producer at the cost of the consumer."

Speaking of the wrongs which the Sherman bill proposed to remedy, Senator Sherman said: "Associated enterprise and capital are not satisfied with partnerships and corporations competing with each other, and have invented a new form of combination commonly called 'trusts,' that seeks to avoid competition by combining the controlling corporations, partnerships and individuals engaged in the same business, and placing the power and property of the combination under the government of a few individuals, and often under the control of a single man called a trustee, a chairman or a president. The sole object of such a combination is to make competition impossible. It can control the market, raise or lower prices as will best promote its selfish interests, reduce prices in a particular locality and break down competition, and advance prices at will where competition does not exist. Its governing motive is to increase the profits of the parties composing it. The law of selfishness uncontrolled by competition, compels it to disregard the interest of the consumer. It dictates terms to transportation companies. It commands the price of labor without fear of strikes, for in its field it allows no competitors. Such a combination is far more dangerous than any heretofore invented, and when it embraces the great body of all the corporations engaged in a particular industry in all the states of the Union, it tends to advance the price to the consumer of any article produced. It is a substantial monopoly injurious to the public, and by the rule of both the common law and the civil law is null and void and the just subject of restraint by the courts;

of forfeiture of corporate rights and privileges and, in some cases, should be denounced as a crime, and the individuals engaged in it should be punished as criminals. It is this kind of a combination we have to deal with now."

"If the concentrated powers of this combination are entrusted to a single man, it is a kingly prerogative, inconsistent with our form of government, and should be subject to the strong resistance of the state and national authorities. If we will not endure a king as a political power, we should not endure a king over the production, transportation and sale of any of the necessaries of life. If we would not submit to an emperor, we should not submit to an autocrat of trade, with power to prevent competition and to fix the price of any commodity. If the combination is confined to a state, the state should apply the remedy; if it is interstate and controls any production in many states, Congress must apply the remedy. If the combination affects interstate transportation or is aided in any way by a transportation company, it falls clearly within the power of Congress, and the remedy should be aimed at the corporation embraced in it, and should be swift and sure."

"Now, Mr. President, what is this bill? A remedial statute to enforce, by civil process in the courts of the United States, the common law against monopolies. How is such a law to be construed? Liberally, with a view to promote its object. What are the evils complained of? They are well depicted by the Senator from Mississippi in this language, and I will read it as my own with quotation marks:

"These trusts and combinations are great wrongs to the people. They have invaded many of the most important branches of business. They operate with a double-edged sword. They increase beyond reason the cost of the necessaries of life and business, and they decrease the cost of the raw material, the farm products of the country. They regulate prices at their will, depress the price of what they buy, and increase the price of what they sell. They aggregate to themselves great enormous wealth by extortion, which makes the people poor. Then making this extorted wealth the means of further extortion from their unfortunate victims, the people of the United States, they pursue unmolested, unrestrained by law, their ceaseless round of peculation under the law, till they are fast producing that condition of our people in which the great mass of them are servitors of those which have this aggregated wealth at their command."

Senator Sherman thereupon proceeded to argue that his bill was constitutionally based upon that clause which provides that "Congress shall have power to regulate commerce with foreign nations and among the several States and with the Indian Tribes." Thereupon he proceeded as follows:

"What is the extent of this power? What is the meaning of the word commerce? It means the exchange of all commodities between different places or communities. It includes all trade and traffic, all modes of transportation by land or by sea, all kinds of navigation, every species of ship or sail, every mode of transit, from the dog-cart to the Pullman car, every kind of motive power, from the mule or the horse to the most recent application of steam or electricity applied on every road, from the trail over the mountain or the plain to the perfected railway or steel bridges over great rivers or arms of the sea. The power of Congress extends to all this commerce, except only that limited within the bounds of a state."

Senator Sherman closed his long and eloquent argument in support of his bill with the following peroration:

"In no respect does the work of our fathers in framing the Constitution of the Unitetd States appear more like the work of the Almighty Ruler of the Universe, rather than the conception of human minds, than by the powers conferred by it upon the branches of the Federal Government. Many of these powers have remained dormant, unused, but plainly there, awaiting the growth and progress of our country, and when the time comes and the occasion demands, we find in that instrument provided for thirteen states, containing four millions of people, all the powers necessary to govern a continental empire of forty-two states, with sixty-five millions of people, the largest in manufactures, the second in wealth, and the happiest in its institutions of all the nations of the world."

"While we should not stretch the powers granted to Congress by strained construction, we cannot surrender any of them; they are not ours to surrender; but whenever occasion calls, we should exercise them for the benefit and protection of the people of the United States. And, sir, while I have no doubt that every word of this bill is within the powers granted to Congress, I feel that its defects are in its moderation, and that its best effect will be a warning that all trade and commerce, all agreements and arrangements, all struggles for money or property, must be governed by the universal law that the public good must be the test for all."

Senator Vest of Missouri next addressed the Senate, beginning thus:

"Mr. President, no one can exaggerate the importance of the question before the Senate, or the intensity of feeling which exists in the country in regard to it. I take it there will be no controversy with the Senator from Ohio, as to the enormity of the abuses that have grown up under the system of trusts and combinations which now prevail in every portion of the Union."

"This bill, if it becomes a law, must go through the crucible of a legal criticism which will avail itself of the highest legal talent throughout the entire Union. It will go through a furnace, not seven times, but seventy-seven times heated."

Thereupon Senator Vest proceeded to indorse the adverse argument of Senator George, and to take with him the ground that the original Sherman bill, and, indeed, the Finance Committee substitute therefor, were unconstitutional and also inefficient.

Senator Vest closed by saying: "This is a subject so elaborate, so important, so overwhelming, that it should be approached with the greatest caution and treated with the greatest care. I sympathize with the object of the Senator from Ohio. I am willing to vote for any bill which I think as a law would stand judicial criticism and construction. I hope that some member of the majority will move to refer this question to the Judiciary Committee."[6]

Senator Hiscock of New York next addressed the Senate. He began by saying that he sympathized with much that had been said by the Senator from Ohio, and agreed with all he had said against trusts and combinations, and was willing to join with him in every effort that promised to defeat them. But Senator Hiscock added and elaborately argued that the Sherman bill was not suitable, in his judgment, to accomplish that end.[7]

Senator Reagan of Texas was the next speaker, and he began as follows: "Mr. President, with some of the criticisms made upon the bill reported by the Senator from Ohio, I agree. I think the country is debtor to that distinguished Senator for his efforts to furnish a remedy for a great and dangerous evil."

[6] Congressional Record, Fifty-first Congress, first session, page 2467.
[7] Congressional Record, Fifty-first Congress, first session, page 2467.

Senator Reagan then proceeded to explain and advocate his own substitute for the Sherman bill, claiming
that it was clearly constitutional in all its parts and
would be fully effective in its operation; whereas, he
thought that some of the provisions of the Sherman bill
were unconstitutional, and that that bill, as a whole, was
not comprehensive enough to be completely effective.[8]

Senator Allison of Iowa next followed with an argument in reply to some portions of the argument of Senator Vest; but which portions attended to the relations
between the trusts and the tariff, rather than to the
Sherman bill itself.[9]

Senator Teller of Colorado next took the floor. He
said: "There is not a civilized country anywhere in the
world that is not more or less cursed with trusts. A trust
may not always be an evil. A trust for certain purposes which may simply mean a combination of capital
may be a valuable thing to the community and to the
country. There have been trusts in this country that
have not been injurious. But the general complaint
against trusts is that they prevent competition." Having
thus stated his view of the wrongs to be remedied, Senator Teller stated that he was inclined to vote for the
Sherman bill, though he did not think it strong enough
to accomplish the result at which it was aimed, and which
appeared to be desired by the Senate.[10]

The debate on the Sherman bill was resumed on March
24, 1890,[11] beginning with a speech by Senator Turpie

[8] Congressional Record, Fifty-first Congress, first session,
page 2469.
[9] Congressional Record, Fifty-first Congress, first session,
page 2470.
[10] Congressional Record, Fifty-first Congress, first session,
pages 2471 and 2560.
[11] Congressional Record, Fifty-first Congress, first session,
page 2556.

of Indiana, who said: "The purpose of the bill of the Senator from Ohio is to nullify the agreements and obligations of the trusts; of these fraudulent combinations. I favor it. There is another purpose, to give to parties injured a civil remedy in damages for injury inflicted. I am in favor of that. Those are the two principal measures embraced in that bill. I am willing to go much further, and I think Senators generally will also. There can be no objection to the proposition to nullify trust contracts. There can be no objection to giving a civil remedy for those injured thereby; and there ought to be still less objection to punishing penally those who are guilty of these fraudulent combinations."

"There may be some difficulty in defining this offense; to describe it is impossible. It is like the penal offense of fraud. The courts have never attempted to define that. There may be no description, there can be none altogether applicable to fraudulent commercial trusts; they vary so much and are so multiform in their character; yet the definition here attempted will, if it do nothing else, lead us to a better form and to a more explicit definition or description of the offense here meant to be denounced. The moment we denounce these trusts penally, the moment we declare these fraudulent trusts combinations to be conspiracies, to be felonies or misdemeanors, that moment the courts are bound to carry out the intention and purpose of the legislation, and even to favor that purpose and intention, that the will of the people may prevail and not perish. I have no doubt that when this law comes into practical operation it will receive a construction and definition very useful to us. It will be aided by courts and juries. It will be aided by advocates on both sides, in stating different views of construction; and, above all, it will be supported and upheld by public opinion, expressed in a

2

denunciation of those evils which this kind of legislation
would avert and avoid."[12]

Senator Pugh of Alabama followed with his argument
upon this subject, beginning with the following paragraph:

"Mr. President, the existence of trusts and combinations to limit the production of articles of consumption,
entering into interstate and foreign commerce, for the
purpose of destroying competition in production, and
thereby increasing prices to consumers, has become a
matter of public history, and the magnitude and the op-
pressive and merciless character of the evils resulting
directly to consumers, and to our interstate and foreign
commerce from such organizations, are known and admitted everywhere, and the universal inquiry is, what
shall be done that can be done by Congress to prevent
or mitigate these evils and intolerable exactions."

Thereupon Senator Pugh proceeded to argue in support of the constitutionality and propriety of the original
Sherman bill.[13]

Senator Stewart of Nevada then delivered the only
remarks which were made in either house of Congress
in opposition to the proposed anti-trust legislation. Without making any comprehensive argument upon the point,
he said: "I do not find any warrant in the Constitution
for this particular class of legislation." His speech consisted mainly in contending that the true remedy against
"trusts" organized among capitalists, manufacturers and
railroad companies, would be found in counter combinations among the people.[14] Senator Stewart did not explain in what way such counter combinations among the

[12] Congressional Record, Fifty-first Congress, first session,
page 2558.

[13] Congressional Record, Fifty-first Congress, first session,
page 2558.

[14] Congressional Record, Fifty-first Congress, first session,
page 2565.

people could be made effective; but he must have meant
to recommend boycotting for that purpose, because it
must have been plain to him, as it is to us, that boycotting is the only means by which the people could resist
combinations of railroad companies to charge excessive
freight rates, or combinations of manufacturing companies to charge excessive prices for commodities. The
Senate did not appear to take Senator Stewart's argument on this subject seriously, for no other Senator mentioned it in his own speech, or took any time to con-
trovert any such view.

Senator Hoar of Massachusetts made the last argument of the day relevant to the proposed anti-trust legislation. In that argument he criticised the Sherman bill
in several respects. His first criticism was that in his
opinion that bill was aimed at less than all of the offend-
ers who ought to be subject to its penalties. And his
second criticism was that the bill failed to provide any
effective remedy for its violation, except so far as it gave
power to private citizens to bring suits for private
damages.[15]

The Senate next resumed consideration of the Sherman bill on March 25, 1890,[16] the pending question being
upon the amendment which had been submitted by Senator Reagan of Texas, and which he now proposed to
add to the Sherman bill, instead of making it a substitute
therefor, as he had originally intended.

Thereupon Senator George of Mississippi moved to
refer the Sherman bill and all proposed substitutes therefor and amendments thereto, to the Judiciary Committee,
and he proceeded to support that motion by an elaborate
argument. He justified his motion to transfer jurisdic-

[15] Congressional Record, Fifty-first Congress, first session,
page 2567.

[16] Congressional Record, Fifty-first Congress, first session,
page 2597.

tion over the subject from the Finance Committee to the Judiciary Committee by emphasizing the great importance of the subject, and by criticising the Sherman bill as being, in his judgment, an inadequate remedy for the great and flagrant wrongs at which it was aimed. On the first of these points Senator George said: "It is a sad thought to philanthropists that the present system of production and exchange is having that tendency, which is sure at some not very distant day to crush out all small men, all small capitalists, all small enterprises. So now the American Congress and the American people are brought face to face with this sad, this great problem. Is production, is trade, to be taken away from the great mass of the people and concentrated in the hands of a few men who, I am obliged to add, by the policies pursued by our Government, have been enabled to aggregate to themselves large, enormous fortunes?"[17] Under the second head Senator George criticised the Sherman bill for assuming that Congress had jurisdiction over trusts or combinations, whether they affected interstate or foreign commerce or not; and he then proceeded to review that bill and the proposed amendments thereto, and concluded by saying that he thought the whole subject ought to be referred to the Committee on Judiciary.[18]

Thereupon an extended debate occurred, which was nominally based upon Senator George's motion to refer, by which actually included many statements relevant to the merits and demerits of the various bills, substitutes and amendments proposed to be referred.[19] The Senators who participated in that debate were numerous, and

[17] Congressional Record, Fifty-first Congress, first session, page 2598.

[18] Congressional Record, Fifty-first Congress, first session, page 2600.

[19] Congressional Record, Fifty-first Congress, first session, page 2600.

when the vote upon the motion to refer was taken, that motion was rejected by twenty-eight nays to fifteen yeas.[20]

The motion to refer to the Judiciary Committee having been thus defeated, the Senate undertook to perfect the bill in Committee of the Whole, and to that end the Senate voted by thirty-four yeas to twelve nays to add the entire Reagan substitute to the Sherman bill.

When the Reagan substitute represented the ideas of Senator Reagan only, its character threw no conclusive light upon the purpose of the Senate. But when the Senate decided by a vote of nearly three to one to add the Reagan substitute to the Sherman bill, that substitute at once became highly indicative of the Senatorial purpose relevant to anti-trust legislation. For this reason it is useful to analyze the Reagan substitute with a view to ascertain and state precisely what were its elements, and that is the interesting work to which it is now in order to turn attention.

Section 1 of the Reagan amendment was a penal provision, aimed at all persons engaged in the creation or in the management of any "trust," where that trust was employed in any international or interstate "business;" and that section provided that all such persons should be deemed guilty of high misdemeanor, and on conviction thereof should be fined not exceeding $10,000, or imprisoned at hard labor not exceeding five years, or should be punished by both of said penalties, at the discretion of the court.

To make section 1 of this amendment effective, it was necessary to define the pivotal word "trust," which that section contained; and section 2 of the Reagan amendment was devoted to that purpose. That section declared that a "trust" is a combination of capital, skill or acts

[20] Congressional Record, Fifty-first Congress, first session, page 2611.

by two or more persons, firms, corporations or associations of persons made for any or all of many specified
purposes, namely: 1, to produce any restriction in
trade; 2, to limit or reduce production of any commodity;
3, to increase or reduce the price of any commodity; 4,
to prevent competition in the manufacture, transportation,
purchase or sale of any commodity; 5, to fix a standard
whereby the price of any commodity would be established or controlled; 6, to create a monopoly in the manufacture, purchase, sale or transportation of any commodity; 7, to enter into or to execute any contract, not
to manufacture, sell or transport any commodity below
a standard figure or to keep the price of any commodity
at a fixed or graduated figure, or to establish the price
of any commodity, or the price of transporting any commodity, so as to preclude unrestrained competition in the
sale or transportation of any commodity, or to pool, combine or unite in any interest, relevant to the sale or transportation of any commodity, whereby its price might in
any manner be affected.

This abridgment of Section 2 of the Reagan amendment shows more briefly, but not more clearly, than
does that section itself, that in adopting that amendment
to the Sherman bill, the Senate expressed its purpose to
regulate international and interstate commerce, in such
thorough detail as to prohibit every combination of capital, skill or acts which might be made for the purpose of
securing unity of action between previous competitors
in any kind of international or interstate commerce.

Section 3 of the Reagan amendment provided that each
day any persons, associations or corporations might be
engaged in violating Section 1 or Section 2, should be
held to be a separate offense.

The Reagan amendment to the Sherman bill having
been adopted, but the bill as amended not yet having

been voted upon, the Senate again resumed consideration of the subject on March 27, 1890.[21] It was on this day that Senator Edmunds of Vermont, the chairman of the Judiciary Committee, first took part in the debate, and he spoke at some length and made many cogent statements and arguments, including the following:[22]

"I am in favor of the scheme in its fundamental desire and motive—most heartily in favor of it—directed to the breaking up of great monopolies, which get hold of the whole or some parts of particular business in the country, and are enabled therefore to command everybody, laborer, consumer, producer and everybody else, as the Sugar Trust and the Oil Trust. I am in favor, most earnestly in favor, of doing anything that the Constitution of the United States has given Congress power to do, to repress and break up and destroy forever the monopolies of that character; because in the long run, however seductive they may appear in lowering prices to the consumer, for the time being, all human experience and all human philosophy has proved that they are destructive of the public welfare and come to be tyrannies, grinding tyrannies."

Having thus emphatically stated his opinion of the propriety and necessity of the object of the Sherman bill, Senator Edmunds stated that he thought that bill to be broader than the constitutional foundation therefor, in that it proposed to do more than to regulate foreign and interstate commerce, and that therefore it was impossible for him to vote for that bill.

Senator Platt of Connecticut, while not dissenting from the purpose of the Sherman bill to properly regulate international and interstate commerce, by suppressing unfair combinations of persons or corporations engaged in

[21] Congressional Record, Fifty-first Congress, first session, page 2723.
[22] Congressional Record, Fifty-first Congress, first session, page 2726.

such commerce, thereupon made an argument against the
Sherman bill in the form then under consideration, because he thought the provisions of that bill were broader
than the constitutional powers of Congress to regulate
international and interstate commerce, and also because
he thought that that bill in that form transcended the
principles of public policy in attempting to suppress some
agreements which ought not to be suppressed.[23]

Senator Walthall of Mississippi thereupon moved to
refer the original Sherman bill and the Reagan amendment which had been adopted and several other amendments, which had been offered but not adopted, to the
Committee on Judiciary, with instructions to report within
twenty days; and although the previous motion of Senator George to refer the subject to the Committee on
Judiciary had some days previous been defeated, so many
noteworthy criticisms of that bill had in the meantime
been made in the course of the debate, that the motion
of Senator Walthall was agreed to on March 27, 1890,
by a vote of thirty-one yeas to twenty-eight nays.[24]

[23] Congressional Record, Fifty-first Congress, first session,
page 2729.
[24] Congressional Record, Fifty-first Congress, first session,
page 2729.

CHAPTER II.

On April 2, 1890, Senator Edmunds reported back the original Sherman bill and all its amendments, accompanied by a new substitute for all of them. That substitute consisted of eight sections, and it was identical in every section and in every word with the Sherman law as it was afterward passed by both houses of Congress, and was approved by President Harrison on July 2, 1890.[1]

Senator Edmunds, in presenting that new substitute to the Senate, did not state the name of its author, but he stated that it had been agreed to by all the members of the Judiciary Committee. Inasmuch as the new substitute had the same general purpose as that of the original Sherman bill of December 4, 1889, and inasmuch as Senator Sherman was the author and had always been the leading advocate of the proposed anti-trust legislation, the substitute for his bill which was reported from the Judiciary Committee, continued to be known as the Sherman bill. Indeed, the name of the man who wrote the Judiciary Committee substitute was never mentioned in either house of Congress during the three months which passed between the day when Senator Edmunds reported that substitute from the Judiciary Committee and the day whereon it was approved by President Harrison. Senator Edmunds resigned his Senatorship in 1891, and has never since been in public life; but he is still living, and on February 1, 1910, wrote a letter to Mr. Charles P. Howland, in which he stated that the Sherman bill was not finally framed by Mr. Sherman, but was put in

[1] Congressional Record, Fifty-first Congress, first session, page 2901.

the very form in which it now stands on the statute books by one of the members of the Judiciary Committee, and was agreed to unanimously by all the members of that committee after the most careful discussion and consideration.   Senator Edmunds did not state in that letter the name of that member of the Judiciary Committee who wrote the Sherman bill, in the sections and words in which it now appears in the statute book; and the identity of the author of that act has never become generally known.   Indeed, that point was probably never published until thirteen years after the Sherman law was enacted, when it was published in the "Autobiography of Seventy Years," by George F. Hoar.[2] In that record of his long and distinguished career, Senator Hoar expressly stated that he was the author of the Judiciary Committee substitute for the Sherman bill, and that that substitute was finally passed, without any change, by both houses of Congress, as indeed it also appears in the Congressional Record to have been.

The history of Congressional legislation from its beginning in 1789 until now, probably presents no other instance of a statute so important, and relevant to a subject of such scope and complexity, being written by one man, exactly as it was passed by both houses of Congress, and approved by the President.   But when Senator Hoar wrote the Sherman law he was sixty-four years old, and through a career of more than twenty years at the Massachusetts Bar, followed by a career of more than twenty years in the two houses of Congress, he had developed his remarkable original ability for clear statement, into an intellectual power on that point, which was not equalled by that of any other man in Congress.   It was the exercise of this remarkable power by Senator Hoar that produced in the spring of 1890 the following admirable specimen of statute writing:

[2] Autobiography, Volume II, page 364.

Be it enacted by the Senate and House of Representatives of the United States of America in Congress assembled:

Section 1. Every contract, combination in the form of trust or otherwise, or conspiracy, in restraint of trade or commerce among the several States, or with foreign nations, is hereby declared to be illegal. Every person who shall make any such contract, or engage in any such combination or conspiracy, shall be deemed guilty of a misdemeanor, and, on conviction thereof, shall be punished by a fine not exceeding five thousand dollars, or by imprisonment not exceeding one year, or by both said punishments, in the discretion of the court.

Sec. 2. Every person who shall monopolize, or attempt to monopolize, or combine or conspire with any other person or persons to monopolize any part of the trade or commerce among the several States, or with foreign nations, shall be deemed guilty of a misdemeanor, and, on conviction thereof, shall be punished by fine not exceeding five thousand dollars, or by imprisonment not exceeding one year, or by both said punishments, in the discretion of the court.

Sec. 3. Every contract, combination in form of trust or otherwise, or conspiracy, in restraint of trade or commerce in any Territory of the United States, or the District of Columbia, or in restraint of trade or commerce between any such Territory and another, or between any such Territory or Territories and any State or States or the District of Columbia, or with foreign nations, or between the District of Columbia and any State or States or foreign nations, is hereby declared illegal. Every person who shall make any such contract or engage in any such combination or conspiracy, shall be deemed guilty of a misdemeanor, and, on conviction thereof, shall be punished by fine not exceeding five thousand dollars, or by imprisonment not exceeding one year, or by both said punishments, in the discretion of the court.

Sec. 4.   The several circuit courts of the United States are hereby invested with jurisdiction to prevent and restrain violations of this act; and it shall be the duty of the several district attorneys of the United States, in their respective districts, under the direction of the Attorney-General, to institute proceedings in equity to prevent and restrain such violations. Such proceedings may be by way of petition setting forth the case and praying that such violation shall be enjoined or otherwise prohibited. When the parties complained of shall have been duly notified of such petition the court shall proceed, as soon as may be, to the hearing and determination of the case; and pending such petition and before final decree, the court may at any time make such temporary restraining order or prohibition as shall be deemed just in the premises.

Sec. 5.   Whenever it shall appear to the court before which any proceeding under section 4 of this act may be pending, that the ends of justice require that other parties should be brought before the court, the court may cause them to be summoned, whether they reside in the district in which the court is held or not; and subpœnas to that end may be served in any district by the marshal thereof.

Sec. 6.   Any property owned under any contract or by any combination, or pursuant to any conspiracy (and being the subject thereof) mentioned in section one of this act, and being in the course of transportation from one State to another, or to a foreign country, shall be forfeited to the United States, and may be seized and condemned by like proceedings as those provided by law for the forfeiture, seizure and condemnation of property imported into the United States contrary to law.

Sec. 7.   Any person who shall be injured in his business or property by any other person or corporation by reason of anything forbidden or declared to be unlawful by this act may sue therefor in any Circuit Court of the United States in the district in which the defendant resides or is found, without respect to the amount in controversy, and shall recover threefold the damages by him sustained, and the costs of suit, including a reasonable attorney's fee.

Sec. 8. That the word "person" or "persons" wherever used in this act shall be deemed to include corporations and associations existing under or authorized by the laws of either the United States, the laws of any of the Territories, the laws of any State, or the laws of any foreign country.

The Senate began on April 8, 1890, its consideration of the Hoar substitute for the Sherman bill.[3] That consideration was begun on the motion of Senator Hoar, who thereupon said that he would not undertake to explain the bill, because it was already well understood.

Senator Sherman thereupon said that, after having fairly and fully considered the substitute prepared by the Committee on Judiciary for his own bill, he would vote for it.

Senator Vest of Missouri then stated that though Section 7 of the Judiciary Committee substitute did not go so far as he thought desirable in its direction, he was satisfied that public interest required the passage of the bill as it came from the Judiciary Committee, and that he sincerely hoped that it would be passed without amendment and without delay. Thereupon the Judiciary Committee substitute was unanimously adopted by the Senate as in Committee of the Whole; and the bill was reported to the Senate, as amended by the substitution of the Ju-

[3] Congressional Record, Fifty-first Congress, first session, page 3145.

diciary Committee substitute for the Sherman bill and for all other propositions upon the subject.

Senator Reagan of Texas thereupon moved to amend Section 7 of the Judiciary Committee substitute by inserting therein after the word "found" the words "or any state court of competent jurisdiction," so as to give to state courts concurrent jurisdiction with United States courts, of actions brought by private persons for damages inflicted upon them by violators of the proposed law. But the impracticability of that Reagan amendment was so clearly pointed out by Senator Edmunds and other Senators, that it was defeated by a vote of thirty-six nays to thirteen yeas.[4]

Senator George of Mississippi thereupon proposed to add to Section 7 of the Judiciary Committee substitute, a lengthy addition, the object of which was to provide that a plurality of persons who might be separately injured by one violator of the proposed law, might join as plaintiffs in one suit against that violator to recover their separate damages for that injury.[5] But Senator Edmunds made so strong an argument against that George amendment, that it was rejected without calling for the yeas and nays.[6]

Senator Reagan of Texas thereupon moved to amend Section 3 of the Judiciary Committee substitute by adding thereto the proviso, "That each day's violation of any of the provisions of the act should be held to be a separate offense." But that amendment was rejected without debate and without calling for the yeas and nays.[7]

[4] Congressional Record, Fifty-first Congress, first session, page 3151.
[5] Congressional Record, Fifty-first Congress, first session, page 3148.
[6] Congressional Record, Fifty-first Congress, first session, page 3151.
[7] Congressional Record, Fifty-first Congress, first session, page 3151.

Senator Kenna, of West Virginia, thereupon asked
Senator Edmunds to explain the meaning of the word
"monopolize" in Section 2 of the Judiciary Committee
substitute. In explanation of this request, Senator Kenna
asked whether that word would cover the conduct of a
citizen who might secure the entire demand for some
particular commodity by virtue of his superior skill or
facilities for producing that article, and without any attempt to interfere with anybody else in trying to
produce similar articles. Senator Edmunds answered to
this question in the negative, and supported that answer
by stating that the word "monopolize" has a meaning in
the dictionaries and in the law which confines its scope
to conduct which includes some attempt made by the
monopolist to impede competitors and to prevent them
from having an equal opportunity with himself to engage
in the particular business sought to be monopolized.

Senator Hoar expressed his agreement with the
opinion of Senator Edmunds on this point, and stated
that all the members of the Judiciary Committee agreed
that the word "monopoly" is a technical term known to
the common law and that in that law it signifies "the
sole engrossing to a man's self, by means which prevent
other men from engaging in fair competition with him."

Senator Kenna thereupon inquired of Senator Hoar
whether such a monopoly as he had defined is prohibited
at common law, and Senator Hoar replied that he so
understood. Senator Kenna thereupon asked why the
bill should denounce a monopoly already illegal at common law; to which Senator Hoar replied that there is
not any common law of the United States, and that the
common law prevailing in the separate states of the
Union cannot, as such, be enforced by the Federal courts
by means of any penalty or punishment.[8]

[8] Congressional Record, Fifty-first Congress, first session,
page 3151.

Senator Gray, of Delaware, thereupon moved to amend Section 2 of the Judiciary Committee substitute by cancelling the words "monopolize or attempt to monopolize or," so as to confine that section to combinations of persons to monopolize or attempt to monopolize, and make it omit to prohibit monopolization by one person acting alone.[9]

Senator Edmunds opposed Senator Gray's motion by saying: "I assure my friend that although we may be mistaken (we do not pretend to know all the law) we were not blind to the very suggestions which have been made and we thought we had done the right thing in providing in the very phrase we did, and that if one person alone should monopolize or attempt to monopolize, it was just as offensive to the public interest as if two would combine to do it." Thereupon, without any further statement or argument upon the question, the amendment of Senator Gray was rejected.[10]

The president *pro tempore* then asked if there were any further amendments to be offered to the Judiciary Committee substitute, and no such amendments being offered, that substitute, which had already been concurred in in Committee of the Whole, was concurred in by the Senate.

The president *pro tempore* then stated the question to be whether the bill should pass; upon which question Senator Edmunds called for the ayes and nays. And the Sherman bill, in the form of the Hoar substitute, was thereupon passed by fifty-two ayes to one nay. The only negative vote was given by the undistinguished Senator Blodgett, of New Jersey, who had taken no part whatever in any of the debates on the subject and who

[9] Congressional Record, Fifty-first Congress, first session, page 3152.

[10] Congressional Record, Fifty-first Congress, first session, page 3152.

did not state any reason for his vote. While the vote was being taken announcement was made by several Senators that several other Senators who were absent would have voted yea if they had been present; but no announcement was made that any Senator would have voted nay if he had been present.[11]

The bill having been thus passed its title was amended so as to read: "A Bill to protect trade and commerce against unlawful restraints and monopolies."[12]

The title of the original Sherman bill was "A Bill to declare unlawful trusts and combinations in restraint of trade and production," but that title was not suitable for the Hoar substitute as passed by the Senate, because that substitue did not purport to regulate production, but only to regulate trade and commerce. Though the Sherman bill was thus reconstructed in the Senate in respect of its title as well as in respect of all of its enactments, it retained its original number of Senate Bill No. 1 when it was passed by the Senate on April 8, 1890.

That Senate Bill No. 1, having been received by the House, was on April 11, 1890, taken from the speaker's table and referred to the House Committee on Judiciary.[13]

On April 25, 1890, Mr. Culberson, of Texas, the father of the present Senator Culberson, of Texas, who was then a member of the House Committee on Judiciary, reported favorably from that Committee on that Senate Bill No. 1, without any amendment.[14]

On May 1, 1890, Mr. McKinley, of Ohio, afterward

[11] Congressional Record, Fifty-first Congress, first session, page 3152.
[12] Congressional Record, Fifty-first Congress, first session, page 3153.
[13] Congressional Record, Fifty-first Congress, first session, page 3326.
[14] Congressional Record, Fifty-first Congress, first session, page 3857.

President of the United States, presented a report from the Committee on Rules, which report provided that the House should immediately proceed to consider Senate Bill No. 1, relating to trusts. That report being immediately adopted by the House, that bill was read for information and Mr. Culberson thereupon proceeded to advocate it during a speech of forty-five minutes.[15]

Mr. Culberson stated during that speech that there was no opposition in the Judiciary Committee to that bill and that the bill did not attempt to exercise any doubtful authority, but was confined to subjects over which there was no question of the legislative power of Congress.

Though Mr. Culberson did not attempt to foresee or foretell all of the transactions which the courts would find to be within the prohibitions of the bill he did mention some which he thought would be violative thereof. Among those which he mentioned was a case in which a manufacturer or a wholesale dealer might sell commodities to a retail dealer, accompanied with a written contract that the retail dealer should not sell those articles below a certain price fixed by the manufacturer or wholesaler. On that point, he stated, that he understood that the Standard Oil Company habitually made contracts with merchants which obliged them not to sell oil below a certain price, except where it might become necessary to do so, to drive some competitor out of business by underselling that competitor; in which case the Standard Oil Company would shoulder the temporary loss caused by such underselling. Mr. Culberson stated that such a contract as that would violate the proposed law.[16]

Mr. Culberson, in speaking of Section 2 of the bill,

[15] Congressional Record, Fifty-first Congress, first session, pages 4086 to 4089.

[16] Congressional Record, Fifty-first Congress, first session, page 4089.

stated that that section prohibited monopolizing any part of a particular business, as well as monopolizing the whole of a particular business.[17]

In explaining Section 6 of the bill, Mr. Culberson stated that that section would apply to any particular case covered thereby as soon as the property mentioned therein was delivered to a common carrier for shipment to any state, and also whenever that property was found *in transitu* from one state to another.

Mr. Henderson, of Iowa, who was afterward Speaker of the House, having received permission to do so, interrupted Mr. Culberson's speech by the following statement and question:

"This is a matter in which I feel deeply interested and I would like to be informed upon this point. I think it has been well settled by the investigation of a Congressional committee within the last year that a trust or combination of a few men in Chicago, Illinois, has been able to reduce the price of western cattle from one-third to one-half, controlling as they do the stock yards, the cattle yards and the transportation in Chicago; and it seems at the same time they have been enabled to keep up the price of every beefsteak that is used in this country. Now I want to ask the gentleman from Texas, who has carefully considered this matter in his committee, whether this bill, in his judgment, reaches that difficulty or not." To this question Mr. Culberson replied by saying: "I believe it will if it is construed as we think it ought to be construed by the courts."

Mr. Henderson thereupon asked, "Does the bill go as far as Congress has the power to go to strike at that damnable system?" To which Mr. Culberson replied: "That is the opinion of the Committee."[18]

[17] Congressional Record, Fifty-first Congress, first session, page 4090.

[18] Congressional Record, Fifty-first Congress, first session, page 4091.

Mr. Wilson, of West Virginia, who was afterward chairman of the Committee on Ways and Means of the House, and still later was a member of the cabinet of President Cleveland, followed Mr. Culberson with a long speech in support of the bill and in denunciation of "trusts," saying:

"A combination or pool is a voluntary association depending upon the good faith of the parties associating and carrying with it those elements of weakness and disintegration that necessarily belong to a voluntary association. A 'trust' is a legal consolidation of properties, a legal concentration of control."[19]

Thereupon Mr. Wilson proceeded to make an historical sketch of the origin and development of "trusts," and showed that the combination by that means of a plurality of corporations, constituted the most effective and dangerous combinations at which the bill was aimed.

Mr. Taylor, of Ohio, chairman of the House Committee on Judiciary, followed Mr. Wilson with an argument in support of the bill,[20] saying among other things that the subject had been before the country for months, and that the bill had been duly considered and unanimously approved by the Judiciary Committee of the House. Mr. Taylor closed his speech with the following paragraphs:

"I am opposed to trusts, foreign or domestic; they toil not, neither do they spin, and yet they accumulate their numberless millions from the toil of others. They lay burdens, but bear none. The beef trust fixes arbitrarily the daily price of cattle, from which there is no appeal, for there is no other market. The farmers get from one-third to one-half of the former value of their cattle, and yet beef is as costly as ever. Even if the conscience of the retailer is touched and he reduces his price, the trust

[19] Congressional Record, Fifty-first Congress, first session, page 4092.

[20] Congressional Record, Fifty-first Congress, first session, page 4098.

steps on him and refuses to sell to him, or undersells him till he is ruined.

"This monster robs the farmer on the one hand and the consumer on the other. This bill proposes to destroy such monopolies, such destructive tyrants, and goes as far in that direction as Congress has power to go under the Constitution. It describes and condemns the wrong, fixes the penalty, both civil and criminal, and gives the United States courts new jurisdiction. It is clearly drawn, is practical and will prove efficacious and valuable."

Mr. Cannon, of Illinois, followed Mr. Taylor with a short argument in favor of the bill, in which he said of the bill that "It defines combinations and conspiracies in restraint of trade among the several states and with foreign countries, and declares them illegal. It makes such combination or conspiracy a misdemeanor, punishable by fine or imprisonment. It gives to any person injured by such combination an action for damages and he can recover three times the damages sustained, with costs and a reasonable attorney's fee. It invokes the equity side, the great restraining power of the court, and it makes it the duty of United States district attorneys under the direction of the Attorney General, to go upon the equity side of the court and invoke the strong hand of the Chancellor, backed by the whole power of the United States, and cause the same to be laid upon any person or corporation in the United States that is violating or about to violate the provisions of this act, and compel him to halt, to refrain from or to cease violating the same. It forfeits to the United States any property owned under any contract, or by any combination, which is used in violation of the provisions of the act. Gentlemen say they do not know how the courts will construe the act. It is for us to enact the law, and for courts to construe and enforce it. If we do our duty, it is reasonable to believe that the co-ordinate branch of the Government will do its duty. I believe this is a valuable bill, and I shall vote for it with pleasure."[21]

Mr. Heard, of Missouri, followed with a speech advocating the bill, saying: "The bill, as it is now presented to us, has the sanction of an almost unanimous vote in the Senate and the unanimous approval of the Judiciary Committee of the House. In the Senate, at the beginning of the present session, the bill for which the one now before us is a substitute had the distinction of being the first one introduced in that body. After being considered by the Finance Committee and favorably reported therefrom it was most ably discussed and its defects, as they then appeared, were pointed out, whereupon it was referred to the Judiciary Committee, composed of some of the ablest lawyers of the country, who happily being led by the light of extended investigation and full discussion, reached by unanimous agreement the result presented in this bill."[22]

Mr. Rogers, of Arkansas, followed Mr. Heard with a speech in favor of the bill, saying among many other things: "So high a body as the Committee on Finance of the Senate of the United States, headed by Senator Sherman, whose large and long experience, as well as great ability is known to all, formulated the original of this measure. After nearly ten days of nearly consecutive debate in the Senate, participated in by some of the ablest lawyers of the country, that bill was referred to the Judiciary Committee of the Senate and in that Committee this bill originated. I believe its author is entitled to the thanks of the country."[23]

[21] Congressional Record, Fifty-first Congress, first session, page 4099.

[22] Congressional Record, Fifty-first Congress, first session, page 4100.

[23] Congressional Record, Fifty-first Congress, first session, page 4101.

Mr. Fithian, of Illinois, followed with an elaborate speech in favor of the bill and in denunciation of "trusts," saying: "It is sufficient for me to know that they exist, that they are an evil, that they are destroying the legitimate commerce of the country, that they enhance the price of commodities to the people beyond an honest profit, and that they are a crime against the Government and against the people. These cases are sufficient to call for the intervention of the power of the Government for their suppression."

Many other speeches having been made in favor of the bill and none against it, Mr. Culberson called for the previous question on its passage. But pending that motion, Mr. Bland, of Missouri, was permitted to offer, and did offer, the following amendment thereto:[24]

"Every contract or agreement entered into for the purpose of preventing competition in the sale or purchase of a commodity transported from one state or territory to be sold in another, or so contracted to be sold, or to prevent competition in transportation of persons or property from one state or territory into another, shall be deemed unlawful within the meaning of this act; provided that the contracts here enumerated shall not be construed to exclude any other contract or agreement declared unlawful in this act."

Thereupon this Bland amendment was adopted by the House without debate and without opposition; and then the bill as amended was passed without opposition.[25]

On May 2, 1890, Senate Bill No. 1, with the Bland amendment thereon, was received from the House by

[24] Congressional Record, Fifty-first Congress, first session, page 4104.

[25] Congressional Record, Fifty-first Congress, first session, page 4104.

the Senate and was referred to the Committee on Judiciary.[26]

On May 12, 1890, Senator Hoar reported back Senate Bill No. 1 with an amendment to the House amendment, which amendment consisted in so changing the House amendment as to make it read as follows:

"Every contract or agreement entered into for the purpose of preventing competition in transportation of persons or property from one state or territory to another shall be deemed unlawful within the meaning of this act."

Thereupon Senator Hoar explained that the Bland amendment proposed by the House contained two points. First, it provided that any contract or agreement entered into for the purpose of preventing competition in the sale or purchase of a commodity transported from one state or territory to another shall be prohibited; and second, that contracts to prevent competition in the transportation of persons or property from one state to another should be prohibited. Senator Hoar stated that the Committee on Judiciary objected to the first of these provisions, but approved the second one, though they supposed the second provision was already covered by the bill, because transportation is commerce as truly as sales are commerce.[27]

On May 13, 1890, Senator Hoar moved to recommit the bill with the Senate amendment to the House amendment to the Judiciary Committee, and that motion was adopted.[28]

On May 16, 1890, Senator Edmunds reported the bill

[26] Congressional Record, Fifty-first Congress, first session, page 4123.

[27] Congressional Record, Fifty-first Congress, first session, page 4560.

[28] Congressional Record, Fifty-first Congress, first session, page 4599.

back from the Judiciary Committee with the House amendment amended so as to read as follows:

"That every contract or agreement entered into for the purpose of preventing competition in transportation of persons or property from one state or territory into another, so that the rates of such transportation may be raised above what is just and reasonable, shall be deemed unlawful within the meaning of this act."

Senator Edmunds thereupon moved that the Senate agree to the House amendment as thus amended and insist upon its amendment to the House amendment, and ask for a conference between the two Houses. That motion being agreed to, the Vice-President appointed Senator Edmunds, Senator Hoar and Senator Vest as conferees on the part of the Senate.[29]

In the House on May 17, 1890, Mr. Taylor, of Ohio, chairman of the Judiciary Committee, moved that the House non-concur in the Senate amendment to the House amendment and agree to the conference asked by the Senate, which motion was agreed to by the House.[30] And on May 21, 1890, the Speaker appointed Mr. Taylor, of Ohio, Mr. Stewart, of Vermont, and Mr. Bland, of Missouri, conferees on the part of the House.[31]

On June 11, 1890, the Conference Committee agreed to amend the Bland amendment so as to read as follows:

"Every contract or agreement entered into for the purpose of preventing competition in the transportation of persons or property from one state or territory into another, so that the rates of said transportation may be

[29] Congressional Record, Fifty-first Congress, first session, page 4753.

[30] Congressional Record, Fifty-first Congress, first session, page 4837.

[31] Congressional Record, Fifty-first Congress, first session, page 5113.

raised above what is just and reasonable, shall be deemed unlawful within the meaning of this act, and nothing in this act shall be deemed or held to impair the powers of the several states in any of the matters in this act mentioned."[32]

Thereupon a long debate ensued upon the question of agreeing to the conference report.[33]

That debate was resumed on June 12, 1890, and was followed by a rejection of the conference report.[34]   That rejection was followed by a motion of Mr. Stewart, of Vermont, that the House ask for a further conference and instruct its conferees to recede from the House amendment, which motion was agreed to by a vote of one hundred and six ayes to ninety-six nays.[35]   And on June 14, 1890, the Speaker appointed Mr. Taylor, of Ohio, Mr. Stewart, of Vermont, and Mr. Culberson, of Texas, as conferees on the part of the House.

On June 16, 1890, the president *pro tempore* laid before the Senate the foregoing action of the House, whereupon Senator Edmunds moved the Senate to agree to the conference asked for by the House. That motion being agreed to, the president *pro tempore* appointed Senator Edmunds, Senator Hoar and Senator Vest conferees on the part of the Senate.[36]

On June 18, 1890, Senator Edmunds presented to the Senate the report of the Conference Committee, which was to the effect that both Houses should recede from their respective amendments to the Senate bill, and that

[32] Congressional Record, Fifty-first Congress, first session, page 5950.
[33] Congressional Record, Fifty-first Congress, first session, pages 5950 to 5961.
[34] Congressional Record, Fifty-first Congress, first session, page 5981.
[35] Congressional Record, Fifty-first Congress, first session, page 5983.
[36] Congressional Record, Fifty-first Congress, first session, pages 6116 and 6117.

report was immediately agreed to without debate and without opposition.[37]

On June 20, 1890, Mr. Stewart, of Vermont, submitted to the House the same conference report which Senator Edmunds had submitted to the Senate.[38] Thereupon a short debate occurred in which Mr. Culberson, of Texas, and Mr. Bland, of Missouri, stated that though they had been in favor of the Bland amendment, they were still in favor of the bill after the rejection of that amendment. During the same debate Mr. Kerr, of Iowa, called attention to the fact that this was the first bill that was ever passed by an American Congress undertaking to regulate trusts in this country.

The debate was closed by Mr. Stewart, of Vermont, saying: "The provisions of this trust bill are just as broad, sweeping and explicit as the English language can make them to express the power of Congress on this subject under the Constitution of the United States."[39]

Thereupon Mr. Stewart demanded the previous question upon the adoption of the conference report, and the previous question was ordered.

Thereupon Mr. Heard, of Missouri, demanded that the vote upon the adoption of the conference report be taken by ayes and nays, and the ayes and nays were accordingly ordered. The vote being thus taken, the conference report was adopted and the bill was passed by the House by a vote of two hundred and forty-two ayes to no nays on June 20, 1890.[40]

[37] Congressional Record, Fifty-first Congress, first session, page 6208.

[38] Congressional Record, Fifty-first Congress, first session, page 6312.

[39] Congressional Record, Fifty-first Congress, first session, page 6314.

[40] Congressional Record, Fifty-first Congress, first session, page 6314.

On June 23, 1890, the enrolled Senate Bill No. 1 was signed by the Speaker of the House;[41] and on June 24, 1890, it was signed by the Vice-President of the United States.[42]

President Harrison, on July 2, 1890, approved and signed Senate Bill No. 1, namely: "An Act to protect trade and commerce against unlawful restraints and monopolies."[43]

[41] Congressional Record, Fifty-first Congress, first session, page 6410.

[42] Congressional Record, Fifty-first Congress, first session, page 6425.

[43] Congressional Record, Fifty-first Congress, first session, page 6922.

CHAPTER III.

The Sherman law, when it was approved by President Harrison July 2, 1890, was like the Constitution of the United States when it was framed in 1787, in that it was expressed in brief, broad and comprehensive language, requiring some judicial construction and many diversified applications to different cases for its practical development into generally recognized law. The statesmen who framed the Constitution of the United States realized that it required and would receive such judicial development and application, from period to period, further into the future than they could see; but that foresight did not deter Hamilton and Madison and Jay from writing those celebrated papers which, when afterward collected, came to be known as the "Federalist," and which were published contemporaneously with the Constitution, to set forth their views of its meaning and its scope. No corresponding contemporaneous publication accompanied the enactment of the Sherman law; but it is possible and will be useful for us to submit that statute to such a prima facie analysis now as would have been practicable then. And such an analysis seems suitable, if indeed not almost necessary, to subsequent consideration of the numerous decisions of the Federal Courts which have been rendered relevant to the Sherman law during the twenty years which have passed since its enactment.

The Sherman statute is divided into eight sections.
Sections 1, 2 and 3 are devoted to defining or describ-
ing the wrongs to be prevented, to be punished or to
be remedied, and to the punishment of those wrongs.
Sections 4 and 5 relate to prevention of those wrongs.
Section 6 relates to punishment for those wrongs by
way of forfeiture, in addition to those punishments by
way of fine and imprisonment which are provided for in
Sections 1, 2 and 3. Section 7 relates to a remedy for
those wrongs, provided for the benefit of persons injured
thereby. Section 8 is a short section which simply defines
the words "person" or "persons" wherever they are
used in the act.

A more detailed analysis of the Sherman statute may
begin with the first sentence of Section 1. Whenever
a clear and complete view is acquired of the significance
of that sentence, that view will constitute a key by means
of which all the other parts of the statute may be opened
and explored. That first sentence of Section 1 comprises
the following thirty-two words:

"Every contract, combination in the form of trust or
otherwise, or conspiracy, in restraint of trade or commerce among the several states or with foreign nations,
is hereby declared to be illegal."

This sentence may, for the purpose of analysis, be
paraphrased into a still briefer sentence, such as the following:

"Every combination in restraint of interstate or international commerce is hereby prohibited."

This paraphrase appears to be equivalent to the statutory language because the word "combination" covers
all forms and varieties of "contract," and all kinds
and all conditions of "conspiracy;" and because the
words "in the form of trust or otherwise," express only
what is expressed, or at least implied, by the word

"every;" and because the word "commerce" covers all the meaning of the word "trade;" and because the words "interstate or international" concisely cover all the meaning of the words "among the several states or with foreign nations;" and because the word "prohibited" is synonymous in signification with the phrase "declared to be illegal."

This paraphrase of the first sentence of Section 1 of the Sherman statute conveys a meaning which is clear, precise and undebatable in all its words except two. Those words are "restraint" and "commerce." And in ascertaining that those two words are the only debatable words in our paraphrase, we have also ascertained that they are the only debatable words in the first sentence of Section 1 of the statute. To construe those two words is to construe that sentence. And to construe that sentence is to take the first and only really difficult step toward construing the whole statute.

Now let us undertake to construe the word "commerce" before we attempt to construe the word "restraint," because "commerce" is the substantive matter in respect of which "restraint" is prohibited, and because therefore the ascertainment of the meaning of the word "commerce" is a necessary step to be taken in ascertaining the meaning of the word "restraint."

The dictionaries generally define "commerce" as "exchange of property;" and that definition includes selling and buying for money. When the proposed Sherman law was under consideration in the House of Representatives Mr. Bland of Missouri entertained the idea that the word "commerce" does not include transportation of property from place to place without any change of ownership, and therefore he thought that that bill did not prohibit combinations in restraint of interstate or international transportation of commodities. So thinking, he offered in the House the Bland amendment, which amendment proposed to expressly prohibit every contract made to prevent competition in transportation of persons or property from one state or territory into another.[1]   Indeed, that amendment was adopted by the House as expressing its intention to include transportation of persons or property as well as sales and purchases of property, among the subjects of the bill. When the Bland amendment reached the Senate that portion of it was there adopted as being expressive of the Senatorial intention,[2] though Senator Hoar explained with apparent general approval that that expression was unnecessary, inasmuch as the word "commerce" covers transportation as truly as it covers buying and selling of commodities.[3]

The Senate and the House both afterward agreed to this view by agreeing to omit the Bland amendment from the statute,[4] and thus both Houses of Congress, in constructing and enacting the Sherman law, construed the word "commerce" in that law as including transportation of persons and property, as well as purchases and sales of commodities.

Three questions relevant to the statutory signification of the word "restraint" must be answered in order to ascertain that meaning. Those questions are the following:

1. Is the word "restraint" indicative of mutual restraint between the members of a combination, or is it indicative of extraneous restraint exercised by the com-

[1] Congressional Record, Fifty-first Congress, first session, page 4104.

[2] Congressional Record, Fifty-first Congress, first session, page 4753.

[3] Congressional Record, Fifty-first Congress, first session, page 4560.

[4] Congressional Record, Fifty-first Congress, first session, pages 6208 to 6314.

bination as a whole against one or more other parties, or is it indicative of both those kinds of restraints?

2. Is the word "restraint" indicative of all restraint, however indirect it may be, or is its meaning confined to direct restraint?

3. Is the word "restraint" indicative of all direct restraint, however slight, or is its meaning confined to such restraint as is extensive enough to be materially injurious to public or to private welfare?

The first of these questions is vastly important because there may be many combinations of corporations or persons which are organized and conducted for the express purpose of restraining mutual competition between themselves, but which were not organized and have not been conducted with a view to restrain extraneous competition between themselves and any other party. If the word "restraint" in the first sentence of Section 1 of the Sherman law is to be construed as confined to such extraneous restraint, then those combinations do not violate that law; whereas, if the word "restraint" is to be construed as including mutual restraint as well as extraneous restraint, then those combinations do violate that law.

This distinction between mutual restraint and extraneous restraint was not expressly discussed during the debates on the Sherman bill, or on the Hoar substitute, in either the Senate or the House. The only light which is to be gathered from those debates on that question is to be gathered from the statements which were made in the course of those debates relevant to the evils which those Senators and Representatives who made those statements were desiring to prevent or to remedy, or that light which can be gathered from amendments to the Sherman bill which at one time or another were provisionally agreed to by the Senate or by the House.

The first of these classes of sources of light includes

3

the elaborate speech which Senator Sherman made on
March 21, 1890.[3]   That speech plainly indicated that
Senator Sherman contemplated both mutual restraint of
competition between the members of a combination and
extraneous restraint of competition between such a combination and other parties as being the evils which required to be prevented or remedied by the proposed legislation.   It is true that much of what he said in his
speech applies only to such extraneous restraint of competition; but it is also true that many of the strongest
passages of his speech were uttered in condemnation of
restraint of mutual competition between the members of
a combination of corporations, partnerships or persons.
These statements are also fairly applicable to nearly all
the speeches which were made in the Senate relevant to
the proposed legislation during the pendancy of the original Sherman bill in that body, and none of those speeches
took the ground that the proposed prohibition of restraint of interstate or international commerce should
be confined to extraneous restraint, exercised by the combination as a whole, against other parties.

The second of these classes of sources of light upon
the intended meaning of the word "restraint" includes the
Reagan amendment, which was offered by Senator
Reagan of Texas on March 21, 1890,[4] and which was
provisionally adopted by the Senate March 25, 1890.[5]
That Reagan amendment was expressly aimed at all
trusts engaged in any interstate or international commerce, and it defined a "trust" in several ways, including
a combination of capital, skill or acts by two or more
persons, firms, corporations or associations to increase or

[3] Congressional Record, Fifty-first   Congress, first session,
page 2456.

[4] Congressional Record, Fifty-first   Congress, first session,
page 2455.

[5] Congressional Record, Fifty-first   Congress, first session,
page 2611.

reduce the price of any merchandise or commodity. This definition was plainly broad enough to cover restraint of mutual competition between the members of the combination as well as restraint of extraneous competition between a combination as a whole and other parties.

So also the Reagan amendment defined a "trust" as a combination of two or more persons, firms, corporations or associations by which they shall in any manner establish or settle the price of any article, commodity or transportation between themselves so as to preclude free and unrestrained competition among themselves in the sale of any such article or commodity.

Thus it appears to be entirely plain that in provisionally adopting the Reagan amendment the Senate intended to prohibit mutual restraint of competition between the members of a combination, engaged in interstate or international commerce, as well as extraneous restraint of competition between such a combination as a whole, and other parties.

The debates which occurred in the House upon the bill as it was finally passed by that body also indicate that those members who took part in that debate and who had this distinction in view between mutual restraint exercised by the members of the combination upon each other and extraneous restraint exercised by the combination as a whole upon other parties, intended and understood that the bill would prohibit both these kinds of restraint, and particularly such mutual restraint of competition in interstate and international commerce.

For example, Mr. Henderson of Iowa particularly mentioned the Beef Trust as being a proper subject to prohibition, because it restrained all mutual competition between its members. Having clearly indicated that he thought it necessary to prohibit mutual restraint of interstate commerce between the members of a combination, he asked Mr. Culberson of Texas whether the bill, in his judgment, would have that effect. To this question Mr. Culberson replied by saying: "I believe it will, if it is construed as we think it ought to be construed by the courts."[6]

Harmoniously with this opinion of Mr. Culberson, every member of the House who said anything to indicate that he was thinking of extraneous restraint of interstate commerce exercised by a combination as a whole against other parties, and was also thinking of mutual restraint on interstate commerce exercised by the members of a combination between themselves, expressed or implied the idea that both those kinds of restraint ought to be prohibited, and that the bill before the House was adapted to prohibit them both.

The very last speech which was made in either house relevant to the proposed legislation was made in the House by Mr. Stewart of Vermont immediately before the final passage of the bill in that body. During that short speech Mr. Stewart said: "The provisions of this trust bill are just as broad, sweeping and explicit as the English language can make them to express the power of Congress on this subject under the Constitution of the United States."[7] This statement amounts to a declaration that the bill in prohibiting combinations in restraint of international and interstate commerce was intended to cover combinations in mutual restraint by its members of such commerce, as well as combinations in extraneous restraint by those combinations of such commerce conducted by other parties.

No one analyzing the Sherman bill as it was approved by President Harrison July 2, 1890, could assume to dogmatically foretell whether the Supreme Court, in construing that law, would construe its pivotal word "re-

[6] Congressional Record, Fifty-first Congress, first session, page 4091.
[7] Congressional Record, Fifty-first Congress, first session, page 6314.

straint" to include extraneous restraint of other parties by a combination as a whole, and also to include mutual restraint exercised by that combination upon its own members, or would construe that word to be confined to one of these kinds of restraint. But those who attentively read the Congressional Record of those proceedings in the two houses of Congress which led from the Sherman bill of December 4, 1889, to the Sherman law of July 2, 1890, will inevitably learn that both houses intended that law to prohibit both those kinds of restraint of international and interstate commerce.

The second question relevant to the meaning of the word "restraint" would naturally be answered in favor of the view that that word in Section 1 of the Sherman law is confined to direct restraint and is not aimed at indirect restraint of interstate or international commerce. The reasons for this distinction reside in the fact that indirect restraint of such commerce may result from combinations of business men which were not organized and are not conducted for any such purpose, and where such restraint of interstate or international commerce as results from such combinations, results incidentally and involuntarily and without any consequent profit or advantage to the combination, and without any loss or disadvantage to other parties. The proposition that such an indirect restraint was not intended to be prohibited or penalized by the Sherman law, is indicated by the fact that those Senators and those Representatives who advocated that law in Congress aimed their arguments and censures at wilful, intentional and direct restraints of interstate and international commerce without visiting any censure upon such indirect and unintentional restraints as may result from some useful and meritorious combinations of persons or corporations engaged in interstate or international commerce.

Where particular cases of restraint of interstate or international commerce are claimed or are proved to have resulted from particular combinations of men or corporations, a difference of opinion may arise among judicially minded men on the questions whether that particular restraint was direct or indirect, for the line of division between direct and indirect operation of any particular cause is not always so precise as to be generally agreed upon by those who direct their attention to its ascertainment. In such a case as this it appears to be probable that the benefit of the doubt will be found to be due to the combination charged with the particular "restraint" in question, and that such restraint only as is clearly direct will be found to be covered by the prohibition of Section 1 of the Sherman law.

The third question relevant to the meaning of the word "restraint" should apparently be answered in favor of the view that its meaning in Section 1 of the Sherman law is confined to such restraint as is extensive enough to be materially injurious to public or to private welfare. For if every combination in direct restraint of interstate or international commerce were to be prosecuted and punished under the Sherman law, even where that restraint was too slight to have any noteworthy effect upon any public or private interest, it might result that the courts would be burdened with so many trivial cases brought as a result of mistaken or unworthy motives that they would not have time enough to adjudicate the really important litigations which would be brought or ought to be brought before them.

For these reasons it is apparent that when Congress in Section 1 of the Sherman law prohibited combinations in restraint of interstate and international commerce, it did not intend to make that law the foundation for trivial and vexatious suits.

The foregoing analysis of the first sentence of Section 1 of the Sherman law appears to conduct to the conclusion that that sentence was intended by Congress to have the meaning which it would have if it had been written in the following words:

"Every combination in mutual or extraneous, direct and material restraint of interstate or international commerce is hereby prohibited."

The second sentence of Section 1 of the Sherman law is so plain in all its parts as to require no interpretation or explanation, except to say that the words "such combination" in that sentence operate to so connect it with the first sentence as to make it apply to whatever combination shall have been found to be covered by the first sentence.

Section 2 of the Sherman law is so plain in all its language as to require no explanation or interpretation, except to define the word "monopolize," which is the pivotal word upon which the meaning of that sentence depends. Some people reading that word in that section will suppose it to signify complete acquirement, and indeed, that is the meaning of that word in the patent laws of the United States, as well as in some other departments of language. During the Senate debate upon the Hoar substitute for the Sherman bill, this meaning of the word "monopolize" occurred to Senator Kenna of West Virginia as perhaps being the meaning which that word would carry in that bill,[8] and he asked Senator Edmunds, the chairman of the Judiciary Committee, and Senator Hoar, the author of the substitute, to state their understanding of the meaning of that word in Section 2 of the proposed statute. To this inquiry Senator Ed-

[8] Congressional Record, Fifty-first Congress, first session, page 3151.

munds replied to the effect that the word "monopolize"
has a meaning in the law which includes the idea that
the monopolist in making a complete acquirement of the
thing monopolized did something to prevent others from
competing with him in reaching that complete acquirement. And Senator Hoar stated that all the members of
the Judiciary Committee agreed that the word "monopoly" is a technical term known to the common law,
and that in that law it means "the sole engrossing to a
man's self by means which prevent other men from engaging in fair competition with him."[9]

No Senator or Representative expressed any view different from that of Senators Edmunds and Hoar relevant to the meaning of the word "monopolize" in Section
2 of the Sherman law. Therefore we are justified in
provisionally holding that Section 2 of the Sherman law
does not prohibit a complete acquirement of the whole or
any part of interstate or international commerce, except
where that complete acquirement results from efforts of
the monopolizer to prevent other parties from competing
with him in achieving that complete acquirement.

It follows from this view of the meaning of the word
"monopolize" in Section 2 of the Sherman law, that that
section is not violated where a party completely acquires
a particular part of interstate or international commerce
by means of his superior skill or superior facilities for
carrying forward that part of the world's work. But it
also follows that where a particular monopolizer does or
does not possess or use superior skill and superior
facilities for doing the work monopolized, but does at-
tain a monopoly of that work by the aid of impediments
placed by him in the paths of his competitors, that monopolizer violates Section 2 of the Sherman law.

[9] Congressional Record, Fifty-first   Congress, first session,
page 3151.

Section 3 of the Sherman law is identical with Section 1, except that it applies to restraint of trade or commerce in any territory of the United States or in the District of Columbia, or between any two territories, or between any territory and any state, or between any territory and the District of Columbia, or between any territory and any foreign nation, or between the District of Columbia and any state or foreign nation; whereas Section 1 applies to restraint of trade or commerce between two or more states or between any one state and any foreign nation. It would have been possible to blend together all the provisions of Section 1 and Section 3, but inasmuch as commerce among the several states or with foreign nations amounts to many times more than all the commerce in which the people of the District of Columbia or of the territories are engaged, it was desirable to devote the first section of the bill entirely to interstate and international commerce in order to avoid the complexity of expression and enactment which would have resulted from an attempt to treat in that section the quite different and much smaller commerce which might occur within any one territory or within the District of Columbia, or might occur between any one territory and some other political division, or between the District of Columbia and some other political division.

Sections 4 and 5 of the Sherman law confer jurisdiction in equity upon the several Circuit Courts of the United States to prevent and restrain violation of the Sherman law in pursuance of petitions presented by the district attorneys of the United States under the direction of the attorney general of the United States on behalf of the United States. Those two sections contain a few special directions for the guidance of such proceedings, and so far as such directions are not expressed therein, those sections imply that such proceedings are to be covered by the rules of equity procedure which are in force in the several Circuit Courts of the United States.

Section 6 of the Sherman law is in the following language:

"Any property owned under any contract or by any combination, or pursuant to any conspiracy (and being the subject thereof) mentioned in section 1 of this act, and being in the course of transportation from one state to another, or to a foreign country, shall be forfeited to the United States and may be seized and condemned by like proceedings as those provided by law for the forfeiture, seizure and condemnation of property imported into the United States contrary to law."

Those proceedings which were provided by law on July 2, 1890, for the forfeiture, seizure and condemnation of property imported into the United States contrary to law, have been amended from time to time during the twenty years which have passed since then. But at that time, and always since that time, and now, the proceedings thus provided by law were and have been, and still are summary and severe. Such proceedings are prosecuted according to the customs laws, by the same district attorneys of the United States who are charged by section 4 of the Sherman law, with the enforcement of that statute by means of proceedings in equity to restrain its violation. It therefore follows that whenever it becomes the duty of a particular district attorney of the United States to institute proceedings in equity for the purpose of stopping a particular combination from continuing past violation of Section 1 of the Sherman law, it also becomes the duty of the same district attorney to institute and prosecute proceedings to accomplish the seizure, condemnation and forfeiture of whatever property was the subject of that combination and has been found in the course of transportation from one state to another, or to a foreign country. Moreover, such forfeiture proceedings, under Section 6 of the Sherman law, should always follow or accompany any indictment under Section 1 of that statute.

Section 7 of the Sherman law provides that any person injured in his business or his property by any other person or corporation as a result of any violation of the Sherman law may recover threefold the damages by him sustained and the costs of the suit, and a reasonable attorney's fee, by means of an action brought by him in any Circuit Court of the United States for the district in which the defendant resides or is found.

This section is so plain and precise in all its parts that it requires only to be attentively read in order to be understood.

Section 8 of the Sherman law simply provides that the words "person" or "persons" wherever used in that act shall be deemed to include corporations and associations existing under or authorized by law anywhere.

The foregoing detailed analysis of the Sherman statute fairly conducts to the conclusion that all parts of that statute are free from the necessity for judicial construction, except so far as some such necessity arises from one or another of only three words in the entire act. These words are "restraint" and "commerce" in Section 1, and "monopolize" in Section 2 of the act. The meaning which the courts would ascribe to those three words could not be foreseen with certainty when the Sherman law was enacted by Congress and approved by President Harrison. And though the statutory signification of the words "commerce" and "monopolize" can now be deduced from the judicial decisions which have been rendered relevant thereto during the last twenty years, important differences of interested opinion still exist relevant to the meaning and scope of the word "restraint," as that word occurs in Section 1 and also in Section 3 of the act. Inasmuch as the legality or illegality of a thousand now existing combinations in the United States depends upon the legal meaning and scope of these three words, and particularly upon the legal meaning and scope of the word "restraint" in the Sherman law, a complete exposition of the subject must include a review of all the relevant decisions which have been rendered and published by the Federal courts during the twenty years which have passed since the Sherman law was enacted.

CHAPTER IV.

The administration of President Harrison continued thirty-two months after he carried the Sherman law into the statute books by means of his presidential approval. During those thirty-two months his attorney general, William H. H. Miller, either by himself or through the solicitor general, William H. Taft, acting as attorney general, began five prosecutions under the Sherman law, with the results which will be set forth in the following review of those five cases respectively.

1. United States v. Jellico Mountain Coal Co. and others, 43 Fed. Rep 898 and 46 Fed. Rep. 432. This was an action in equity begun September 25, 1890, in the United States Circuit Court for the Middle District of Tennessee against the members of the "Nashville Coal Exchange," which Coal Exchange was composed of a number of coal-mining corporations in Kentucky and Tennessee, and a number of persons and partnerships dealing in coal in Nashville, Tennessee; the Coal Exchange being a combination which had been formed for the purpose of regulating the output of coal and fixing the prices thereof.

In this case the United States was represented by W. H. H. Miller, Attorney General; William H. Taft, Acting Attorney General, and John Ruhm, United States District Attorney for the Middle District of Tennessee. These gentlemen moved in October, 1890, that a preliminary injunction be granted against the defendants. But Judge Hammond, who was then United States District Judge for the Western District of Tennessee, and who was temporarily holding the United States Circiut Court for the Middle District of Tennessee, refused to grant that motion, though he reserved all expressions of opinion from the subject matter of the bill of complaint until the final hearing.

That final hearing was had in 1891, when the court was being held by Judge Key, who was then the United States District Judge for the Middle District of Tennessee, and who had long before been postmaster general in the Cabinet of President Hayes, and still earlier had been a United States Senator from Tennessee.

In pursuance of that final hearing, and on June 4, 1891, Judge Key decided the case against the defendants, holding that by their organization of the Nashville Coal Exchange and their operations under it before and at the time of the beginning of the suit, they were guilty of a violation of Sections 1 and 2 of the Sherman law of July 2, 1890, and should be enjoined from further violation of that law, as provided by the fourth section thereof. 46 Fed. Rep. 433.

The facts upon which the suit was based were undisputed and were made known to the court by means of a written contract, which had been made by the defendants and was being performed by them. That contract provided that every person, firm or corporation owning or operating coal mines and shipping coal to Nashville, and all coal dealers in Nashville, were to be eligible to membership in the combination which they named the "Nashville Coal Exchange," and that the coal mining members of the Exchange should not ship or sell any coal to Nashville, to any party not a member of the Exchange, and that the coal-selling members of the Exchange should not buy any coal from any one not a member of the Exchange. The contract also provided that the Exchange should establish from time to time the prices at which coal should be sold in Nashville; and that every member who might be found guilty of selling coal in Nashville at a less price than the price thus fixed by the Exchange should be fined for the benefit of the Exchange.

It was not proved in the case that all the persons, firms or corporations owning or operating coal mines and shipping coal to Nashville, nor that all the coal dealers in Nashville had joined the combination by becoming members of the Nashville Coal Exchange, and the contrary is implied in the report of the case. But it was proved that several mining companies in Kentucky and most of the coal dealers in Nashville had entered into the combination at the time of the final hearing; though some of them did not join until after the suit was brought, and some of them appeared to have withdrawn from the combination after the suit was brought and before the final hearing.

On the final hearing the attorneys for the United States included the United States District Attorney and the Assistant District Attorney and Mr. James Trimble, while three legal partnerships, composed of two lawyers each, represented the defendants.

The defendants' attorneys made the following statements of defense:

1. The Sherman law is unconstitutional because it confers jurisdiction in equity over controversies other than controversies between citizens of different states.

2. Section 4 of the Sherman law is unconstitutional in that it purports to give to United States Circuit Courts jurisdiction in equity to restrain the criminal offenses which are defined in Sections 1, 2 and 3; whereas the Constitution provides that the "trial of all crimes, except in cases of impeachment, shall be by jury."

3.   The defendants had not violated Sections 1 or 2 of the Sherman law, because what they had done did not constitute any restraint or monopolization of any interstate or international commerce.

The first of these defenses evidently had no foundation, except a misapprehension of defendants' counsel, for Section 2 of Article III of the Constitution provides that the judicial power shall extend to all cases in law and equity arising under the Constitution and the laws of the United States as well as providing that that jurisdiction shall extend to controversies between citizens of different states.

The second of these defenses was unsound because an action in equity to restrain the commission of a misdemeanor is not a trial of a crime. No judicial proceeding is a trial of crime unless it involves the possibility of punishment by fine or imprisonment or death in the event of conviction. Any violator of the Sherman law, when prosecuted under Sections 1, 2 or 3 of that act, is constitutionally entitled to a trial by jury, in the absence of which he might be convicted and punished without being found guilty by twelve good and true men, empanelled to decide the question of his guilt. That immunity from being convicted and punished for a crime otherwise than as a result of a trial by jury does not involve any immunity from any injunction issued by a court of equity without any jury trial to prevent the future continuance of a past misdemeanor and such an injunction was all that the United States asked for in this case.

The third defense was based upon the theory that those defendants who were miners of coal had done nothing relevant to coal outside of the State of Kentucky, and that those of the defendants who were sellers of coal had done nothing relevant to coal outside of the State of Tennessee, and that none of the defendants had transported any coal from one state to another. But this defense was overruled by Judge Key on the ground that the transportation of the coal from Kentucky to Nashville, Tennessee, was a necessary incident to the contract between the miners and the sellers of coal, and that the execution of that contract would have been impossible without that transportation, and that though the instrumentality of transportation did not belong to any of the defendants and was not controlled by any of them, it was operated by a common carrier from the coal miners in Kentucky to the coal sellers in Nashville.

The facts of this case did not necessitate or occasion any construction of the Sherman law upon any debatable point; for it was undeniable that the contract and the doings of the defendants operated not only as a mutual restraint of interstate commerce between them, but also operated as an extraneous restraint of interstate commerce against other parties. Those other parties included the independent coal dealers of Nashville who were prevented by the contract and the doings of the defendants from buying any coal from those of the defendants who were miners of coal. And those outside parties also included those independent miners of coal in Kentucky who were restrained by the contract and the doings of the defendants from selling any coal to those of the defendants who were coal dealers in Nashville.

So also the contract and doings of the defendants operated in direct restraint of interstate commerce to a material extent and could not possibly be said to be legal, either as being indirect in operation or negligible in amount.

Moreover, the contract and doings of the defendants undeniably constituted an attempt to monopolize the coal business between the city of Nashville in Tennessee and the state of Kentcky. For that contract and those doings were intended to operate and did operate to impede independent coal miners in Kentucky from selling coal in

Nashville, and also to impede independent coal sellers in Nashville from buying coal in Kentucky.

For these reasons Judg Key, in his opinion deciding the case, said: "It seems to me that the purpose and intentions of the association could hardly have been more successfully framed to fall within the provisions of the Act of July 2, 1890, had the object been to organize a combination, the business of which should subject it to the penalties of that statute."

In pursuance of this opinion, Judge Key ordered a writ of injunction to issue against all the defendants except those who were not members of the combination at the time the suit was brought, and except those who were not members of the combination at the time of Judge Key's decision.

2.   United States vs. Greenhut and others, 50 Fed. Rep. 469. This was an indictment in the United States District Court for the District of Massachusetts, in 1892, based upon alleged violation by the defendants of Section 2 of the Sherman law. The indictment stated that the defendants were officers of the Distilling & Cattle Feeding Company, a corporation chartered under the laws of Illinois, and having its principal place of business in Peoria, Illinois, and that, as such officers, they had purchased or leased seventy-eight theretofore competing distilleries within the United States, and that within a certain time specified they had managed and operated such distilleries, and had manufactured sixty-six million gallons of distilled spirits, and sold that product within the United States and part of it in the District of Massachusetts, at prices fixed by them, the whole being three-quarters of all the distilled spirits manufactured and sold within the United States during that period, and that all such acts (excepting the purchasing and leasing of the distilleries) were done with the intention to monopolize to the company the manufacture and sale of distilled spirits among the several states, to increase the usual prices at which distilled spirits were sold, to prevent and counteract further competition in the sale of distilled spirits and thereby to exact great sums of money from citizens of the several states who might purchase those distilled spirits.

The attorney for the United States in this case was Frank D. Allen, then United States District Attorney for the District of Massachusetts, while the defendants were represented by Richard Olney, who was afterward Attorney General and was still later Secretary of State in the administration of President Cleveland, and by Elihu Root, who was afterward Secretary of War in the cabinet of President McKinley and Secretary of State in the cabinet of President Roosevelt. The defendants were also represented by numerous other lawyers, as juniors to Mr. Olney and Mr. Root.

The defendant Greenhut filed a motion to quash the indictment, and all the other defendants demurred thereto on the ground that the indictment was insufficient in law and did not charge any offense created by any statute of the United States.

Judge Thomas C. Nelson, who was then United States District Judge for the District of Massachusetts, decided the case in favor of the defendants on those grounds, and because the indictment did not contain "a distinct averment in the words of the statute or in any equivalent language, that by means of the acts charged the defendants had monopolized, or had combined or conspired to monopolize trade and commerce among the several states or with foreign nations." Accordingly, Judge Nelson held the indictment to be insufficient under the rules of criminal pleading to be a foundation of a trial, and he ordered the indictment to be quashed and rendered a judgment upon the demurrer.

This indictment had already been held to be illegal by three Federal Judges when three of the defendants, who did not reside in Massachusetts, had been arrested elsewhere for trial there, and when they applied to the Federal judges in their own localities to protect them from transportation thither. Those three judges were District Judge Ricks, of the Northern District of Ohio, Circuit Judge Lacombe, of the Second Circuit, and Circuit Judge Jackson, of the Sixth Circuit. All of them discharged the petitioning prisoners from arrest on the ground that the indictment did not state facts enough to constitute a violation of the Sherman law. The three opinions are printed in 51 Fed. Rep. 205; and 51 Fed. Rep. 213; and 52 Fed. Rep. 104, respectively. The opinion of Judge Jackson, in the last of these books, was more comprehensive than the other two. He construed the word "restraint" in the Sherman law to mean "general restraint" and the word "monopoly" to mean "monopoly resulting from legal restriction."

3. United States vs. Nelson and others, 52 Fed. Rep. 646. This was an indictment of a considerable number of men who were dealers in lumber, and each of whom transacted such business in different states of the Union. The indictment was based upon alleged violation of Section 1 of the Sherman law, and was presented to the United States District Court for the District of Minnesota by a Grand Jury for that district, in 1892. There were twelve counts in the indictment, the first six of which charged the alleged offense in the language of the statute, and the last six of which set forth facts which were claimed by the United States District Attorney to constitute the offense.

The United States District Attorney for the District of Minnesota represented the United States in this case, while the defendants were represented by W. E. Hale, who filed a demurrer to all the counts of the indictment.

The facts upon which the indictment was based were all stated in the seventh count, and were as follows:

The defendants, on September 7, in Minneapolis, Minnesota, had agreed together that they would raise the price of pine lumber fifty cents per thousand in the states of Wisconsin, Minnesota, Iowa, Illinois and Missouri; and in pursuance of that agreement they did thus raise that price in those five states in which they transacted business.

Judge R. R. Nelson, who was then United States District Judge for the District of Minnesota, sustained this demurrer in October, 1892, on the ground that in his opinion the facts stated in the indictment did not constitute a violation of Section 1 of the Sherman law. That opinion was based upon the fact that the only restraint of interstate commerce charged in the indictment was mutual restraint between the defendants, and did not include any extraneous restraint by them against any other party. On that point Judge Nelson said: "An agreement between a number of dealers and manufacturers to raise prices, unless they practically control the entire commodity, cannot operate as a restraint upon trade. Competition is not stifled by such an agreement, and other dealers will soon force the parties to the agreement to sell at a reasonable price."

This case was the first one brought under the Sherman law, the decision of which involved any debatable question of the construction of that law. That debatable question was the question whether the restraint of interstate and international commerce which is prohibited by Section 1 of that law includes extraneous restraint of other parties by the combination of men or corporations exercising that restraint on the one hand; or whether, on the other hand, the prohibited "restraint" occurs whenever the parties to the combination restrain each other in respect of interstate or international commerce. The decision of Judge Nelson was that such purely mutual "restraint" does not constitute a violation of Section 1 of the Sherman law.

4. United States vs. Trans-Missouri Freight Association, 53 Fed. Rep. 440; 58 Fed. Rep. 58. This was a bill in equity filed in 1892 by the United States in the United States Circuit Court for the District of Kansas against eighteen railroad companies which were operating railroads west of the Missouri River, and which had organized themselves into the Trans-Missouri Freight Association.

The attorneys for the United States in this case were J. W. Ady and S. R. Peters, while the defendants were represented by nearly twenty attorneys, of whom the most distinguished was John M. Thurston, then general counsel for the Union Pacific Railway Company and afterward, during six years, a United States Senator from Nebraska.

The purpose of the bill was to obtain a decree dissolving that freight association and enjoining the eighteen railroad companies and each of them from performing the terms of a certain agreement which they had made to constitute that association, and which agreement was alleged in the bill to be a violation of the Sherman law of July 2, 1890.

That agreement had been in effect ever since April 1, 1889, more than a year before the Sherman law existed, and therefore nearly three years before this suit was brought. That fact of priority of the agreement to the statute was not held to be material to the litigation, because the bill was based upon what had been done after the enactment of the statute in pursuance of the agreement.

That Trans-Missouri agreement is printed in full on pages 456, 457, 458 and 459 of 53 Fed. Rep. Its avowed purpose was mutual protection of the railroad companies which were parties thereto, "by establishing and maintaining reasonable rates, rules and regulations on all freight traffic" which was to be conducted by those railroad companies throughout a specifically delineated and designated territory, which included nearly one-half of the whole surface of the United States, and extended from the Missouri River on the east to the Pacific Ocean on the west, and from the Dominion of Canada on the north to the Republic of Mexico on the south.

The case was heard about the middle of 1892 by Judge Riner, who was then the United States District Judge for the District of Wyoming, but who was temporarily holding the United States Circuit Court for the District of Kansas. That hearing was based upon the complainant's bill and the defendant's answer, without any replication and without any evidence, in pursuance of a well-known equity practice which may be followed where the complainant is satisfied that the defendant's answer is true in respect of its statements of fact. If, in such a case, the complainant omits to file any replication to that answer the case is heard upon the bill and answer, and on that hearing the answer is conclusively assumed to be true in its statements of fact. This practice in this case left nothing to be argued by counsel or decided by the court, except the question whether the facts stated in the answer constituted a violation of the Sherman law. Those facts included a copy of the Trans-Missouri agreement and a statement that the parties to that agreement had been acting under it and in accordance therewith ever since it went into effect on April 1, 1889.

Judge Riner construed that agreement to be a reasonable mutual regulation between the eighteen railroad companies of freight rates throughout the extensive territory covered by that agreement, and thereupon he decided that neither that agreement nor anything done under it constituted any violation of the Sherman law. He based that decision upon two independent grounds. One ground was that the Sherman law did not, in his opinion, apply to interstate transportation of commodities by common carriers. The other ground was that even if that law did apply to such interstate transportation, it should be construed as not applying to any reasonable regulation of freight rates between competing common carriers.

For either, and particularly for both of these reasons, Judge Riner decreed the bill of complaint to be dismissed, and it was dismissed. 53 Fed. Rep. 456.

An appeal from Judge Riner's decision and decree was promptly taken by the United States to the United States Circuit Court of Appeals for the Eighth Circuit, and in pursuance of that appeal the case was heard by that court before three judges, who were Judge Walter H. Sanborn, who then was and still is one of the Circuit Judges for the Eighth Circuit; Judge Oliver P. Shiras, who was then United States District Judge for the Northern District of Iowa, and Judge Amos M. Thayer, who was United States District Judge for the Eastern District of Missouri.

In 1893 Judge Sanborn delivered the opinion of the Circuit Court of Appeals, which affirmed the decree which Judge Riner had rendered in the Circuit Court in 1892. But Judge Shiras dissented from that affirmance and filed an elaborate opinion in support of his dissent.

Judge Sanborn did not base the affirmance of Judge Riner's decision, even partly, upon Judge Riner's view that the Sherman law had no application to restraint of interstate or international transportation of commodities by common carriers. But he did express the agreement of the majority of the judges of the Circuit Court of Appeals with Judge Riner's view that the prohibitions of Section 1 of the Sherman law are limited to *unreasonable* restraints of interstate or international commerce, and he stated the conclusion of the majority of the judges in the following paragraph:

"The result is that neither this contract nor the association formed under it can be held to be obnoxious to the provisions of the Anti-Trust Act, in view of the facts admitted by the pleadings in this suit, and in the absence of other evidence of their consequences and effect." 58 Fed. Rep. 83.

Judge Shiras expressed the result and conclusion of his own investigation of that question in the following paragraph at the end of his dissenting opinion, 58 Fed. Rep. 100:

"In my judgment, the right to insist upon free competition between railway companies engaged in carrying on interstate commerce is a right which belongs to the public, of which it cannot be deprived except by its own consent, and every contract or combination between these public corporations which tends to remove the business carried on by them from the influence of free competition tends to deprive the public of this right, of necessity tends to subject interstate commerce to burdens which are a restraint thereon, is inimical to the public welfare, is contrary to public policy, and in contravention of both the language and spirit of the anti-trust act of July 2, 1890."

An appeal was taken by the United States from the decision of the Circuit Court of Appeals for the Eighth Circuit in this case, to the Supreme Court of the United States. But, inasmuch as the prosecution and argument of that appeal was conducted during President Cleveland's administration, an explanation of the history and result of that appeal is now relegated to the next chapter of this book.

5. United States vs. Patterson and others, 55 Fed. Rep. 605. This was an indictment in the United States Circuit Court for the District of Massachusetts, returned in January, 1893, against the members of a combination formed for the purpose of controlling the price of cash registers. The indictment comprised eighteen counts, the first ten of which were based upon Section 1, and the last eight of which were based upon Section 2 of the Sherman law of July 2, 1890. The first half of each set of counts alleged the conspiracy without alleging any overt acts performed in pursuance of the conspiracy. The second half of each set of counts repeated the allegations of the first half, and added thereto allegations of overt acts. The defendants filed a demurrer to the indictment by H. W. Chaplin, their attorney; the United States being represented by Frank D. Allen, United States District Attorney for the District of Massachusetts.

That demurrer in February, 1893, was argued before Judge Putnam, who then was and still is one of the United States Circuit Judges for the First Judicial Circuit. At the time of that argument Mr. Allen filed an able and elaborate brief in support of the indictment on behalf of the United States; while Elihu Root and John D. Lindsay filed another elaborate brief in support of the indictment on behalf of certain private persons, and while Mr. Chaplin filed a still more elaborate brief on behalf of the defendants. Those three briefs are printed on pages 607 to 638 inclusive, of 55 Fed. Rep.; and they are all worthy to be read by those who have occasion and have time to study in detail such views of the Sherman law as were held and expressed by able men at the time of the Patterson case.

The decision of Judge Putnam was to sustain two counts in each of the two sets of counts of the indictment and to quash the other fourteen counts. The distinctions which Judge Putnam drew between the counts to be quashed and the counts to be sustained were based upon his construction of Sections 1 and 2 of the Sherman law, for according to that construction, some of the counts could stand, while the others could not. For this reason the significance of this Patterson case resides in the views which Judge Putnam took of the meaning of Sections 1 and 2 of the Sherman law. Those views were the following:

The words "trade" and "commerce" are synonymous in the Sherman law.

The word "monopolize" in the Sherman law means "engrossing or controlling the market."

The word "restraint" in the Sherman law does not include boycotts or strikes.

The word "restraint" does not include driving away competitors, except where that conduct operates to grasp, engross and monopolize the field, from which those competitors are driven away.

The first two of these Putnam views are still tenable; but the last two were afterward overruled by the Supreme Court, as will be explained hereafter, when certain decisions of that tribunal are reached for exposition.

Judge Putnam, in overruling the defendants' demurrer as to four counts in the indictment, gave leave to the defendants to answer or plead to those counts. But before defending themselves against the indictment any further the defendants extended their combination by receiving into its fold those competitors for interfering with whom the indictment had been found.

Thereupon the Attorney General, Mr. Richard Olney, who had succeeded to that office in the meantime, dropped the case and it was never prosecuted any further.

The five cases which have been explained in this chapter were all the cases which were brought anywhere on

behalf of the United States for violation of the Sherman
law during President Harrison's administration, except
two other cases which were brought near the end of that
administration, but were not adjudicated until after the
beginning of the second administration of President
Cleveland, and which two cases will be explained under
that head in the next chapter.

Four of the five cases which were adjudicated during
the administration of President Harrison were failures,
and the Jellico Mountain case, which succeeded, was so
plain a case that it could not fail.

During the thirty-two months of President Harrison's
administration which passed between his approval of the
Sherman law on July 2, 1890, and the end of his administration, on March 4, 1893, there existed many great
combinations, in the form of trusts, which were engaged
in restraint of interstate commerce contrary to Section
1 of the Sherman law, according to any construction of
that section. Among these were the Standard Oil Trust,
the Cotton Seed Oil Trust, the Beef Trust, the Sugar
Trust, the Whiskey Trust, the Cordage Trust, the Barbed
Fence Wire Trust and many others. It then was, and
long has been, claimed in Congress and among the
people that these trusts had acquired a power which
was dangerous to the whole country, and that their existence was directly antagonistic to its peace and prosper-
ity. These facts were so well known to have been true
during the administration of President Harrison that
they were mentioned in these terms by Mr. Justice Peckham when he was delivering one of the opinions of the
United States Supreme Court in 1897, and on page 319
of volume 166 of the reports of that tribunal.

Any careful historian of the Sherman law must naturally wonder why the Attorney General of the United
States, during the administration of President Harrison,
omitted to bring any prosecution under that law against

any of the great trusts which then existed and were generally believed to be violating that law, except one feeble indictment which he caused to be brought into the United States District Court for the District of Massachusetts against the Whiskey Trust, and which indictment was quashed for non-conformity to the rules of pleading in criminal cases, and one feeble case in equity, which he brought against the Knight Company and which, though afterward prosecuted in the Cleveland administration, was never prosecuted successfully.

The Attorney General of the United States throughout the administration of President Harrison was William Henry Harrison Miller, who had been practicing law in partnership with President Harrison in Indianapolis, Indiana, during the fifteen years last preceding the beginning of President Harrison's administration.

Though Section 4 of the Sherman law made it the duty of the Attorney General, through the several District Attorneys of the United States, "to institute proceedings in equity to restrain" all violations of that law, and although that law was undeniably being violated by many combinations in restraint of interstate and international commerce throughout the thirty-two months of President Harrison's administration which passed after the enactment and approval of that law, Attorney General Miller did not even mention the subject of that statute, or of his duty under it, in his annual report of December 1, 1890, nor in his annual report of December 1, 1891. He did devote a page to those subjects in his annual report of December 1, 1892. On that page he mentioned the unsuccessful prosecution of Greenhut and others, and explained that case and its result, though less fully than it has been explained in this chapter of this book. He also mentioned that two other cases had been brought in equity under the Sherman law in the Eastern District of Louisiana and the Eastern District of Penn-

sylvania, respectively, though neither of those cases had
reached any adjudication at that time. He did not, in his
report, state the name of either of those cases, but he
described them well enough to furnish a foundation for
their identification with the two cases which have already been mentioned herein as having been brought
near the end of the Harrison administration, but which
were not adjudicated until after the beginning of the
second administration of President Cleveland and which
are the first two cases explained under that head in the
next chapter.

Attorney General Miller appears never to have reported
to Congress anything else on this subject, except what
he stated in his annual report of December 1, 1892, in the
last paragraph of the page which he devoted to this subject in that report, and which paragraph was as follows:

"Investigations have been made in reference to other
alleged violations of this law by other alleged combinations of persons and corporations. As was to have been
expected, it has been found, in all cases investigated, that
great care and skill have been exercised in the formation
and manipulation of these combinations so as to avoid the
provisions of this statute, and, as has been seen in the
proceedings growing out of the indictments in Massachusetts, these efforts have not been without success. It
is hoped, however, that in the cases commenced, the validity of this statute and its applicability to the abuses which
have become very common in the business of the country
under the name of trusts may be demonstrated. If so,
the investigations made and the evidence accumulated in
cases where no proceedings have been commenced will
be valuable."

When he made this, his only report to Congress, relevant to what he had done toward enforcing the Sherman
law, Attorney General Miller could foresee that his duty
in that direction would end less than one hundred days

later, for he knew that on the fourth day of the following March President Harrison would be succeeded by President Cleveland and he would be succeeded by a new Attorney General. Under these circumstances his report to Congress cannot be construed to be a strong document on this subject, nor to constitute a record of strenuous performances of official duty.

Three litigations between private parties, relevant to the Sherman law, occurred during President Harrison's administration. Those three litigations were the following:

1. American Biscuit & Manufacturing Co. vs. Klotz and another, 44 Fed. Rep. 721. This was a bill in equity, filed in the latter part of 1890 in the United States Circuit Court for the Eastern District of Louisiana. The bill prayed that a receiver might be appointed by the court to take charge of a biscuit and candy factory in Louisiana which the defendants, composing the firm of B. Klotz & Company, had sold to the complainant for $301,000, which was paid by conveying to the sellers a portion of the stock of the complainant corporation, but which sale the defendants afterward repudiated without resort to any legal proceedings. They proceeded to hold possession of the factory adversely to the complainant, instead of continuing to hold that possession as agents of the complainant, as the defendants had done, for a time after the date of the sale.

The motion for the appointment of the receiver was heard by Circuit Judge Pardee and District Judge Billings, sitting together on this occasion. Those judges concurred in deciding the case on January 8, 1891, and in holding that while a case for a receiver was otherwise presented, the prayer for the receiver would be denied, on the ground that the purchase of the factory by the complainant was a part of a combination of thirty-five similar factories located in twelve different states of the Union, and that that combination appeared to be unlawful under the Sherman law of July 2, 1890, and also under the Anti-Trust law of Louisiana, which was enacted by the legislature of that state, and approved by the governor July 5, 1890; and on the ground that a court of equity would not, by the appointment of a receiver, aid the complainant to perfect its unlawful combination.

The Anti-Trust statute of Louisiana of July 5, 1890, was partly copied from the Sherman law, or rather from the Hoar draft of that law, which was reported to the United States Senate from its Judiciary Committee on April 2, 1890, and enacted without any change on July 2, 1890. The principal difference between the two statutes consisted in the fact that whereas the Sherman law prohibited restraint or monopolization of interstate or international commerce, the Louisiana statute prohibited restraint or monopolization of commerce within the limits of that state.

The most important sections of the Louisiana statute were as follows:

"Section 1. That every contract, combination in the form of trust, or conspiracy in restraint of trade or commerce, or to fix or limit the amount or quantity of any article, commodity, or merchandise to be manufactured, mined, produced, or sold in this state, is hereby declared illegal."

Sec. 3. That every person who shall monopolize, or attempt to monopolize, or combine or conspire with any other person or persons to monopolize, any part of the trade or commerce within the limits of this state, shall be deemed guilty of a misdemeanor, and, on conviction thereof, shall be punished by a fine not exceeding five thousand dollars, or by imprisonment not exceeding one

year, or by both said punishments, in the discretion of
the court.

The decision of the court in this case was made in
pursuance of one of the historic maxims of courts of
equity, namely, "He who comes into equity must do so
with clean hands."   In pursuance of this maxim, courts
of equity properly decline to enforce any unlawful contract.   It follows from this principle of equity jurisprudence that those who embark their property in combinations which violate the Sherman law are trusting
their property to their confederates, and cannot get any
assistance from any court of equity toward preventing
those confederates from cheating them.

2.   Bishop vs. American Preservers' Company, and
others, 51 Fed. Rep. 272.   This was an action at law
brought early in 1892, in the United States Circuit Court
for the Northern District of Illinois, for injuries alleged
to have been sustained by the plaintiff as a result of acts
done by the defendants, in violation of the Sherman law.
The declaration in the case stated that the plaintiff had
formerly been engaged in the business of manufacturing preserves of fruit in Chicago, and that he had entered into a combination or trust with the defendants,
Ryan and Dougherty, who had been engaged in similar
business ; and that the purpose of that combination was
to advance the prices of such preserves, and that the
name of it was the "American Preservers' Trust;" and
that afterward the managers of that combination took in
additional manufacturers of preserves and organized a
corporation under the laws of West Virginia, named the
"American Preservers' Company," to take the place of
the "American Preservers' Trust."   The declaration also
stated that after the plaintiff had transferred his factory
and business to that company, the company brought an
action of replevin in one of the state courts sitting in

4

Chicago, and took possession of that factory and its contents, away from the plaintiff, who had been managing it for awhile, as agent of the company or trust; and that the company had also brought an action at law in the United States Circuit Court against the plaintiff to recover $3,000, in pursuance of some right of action which the company or trust claimed to have against the plaintiff.

The defendants filed a demurrer to this declaration; and Judge Blodgett, who was then the United States District Judge for the Northern District of Illinois, decided that the demurrer was good in point of law, because the declaration was bad in point of law; and that its badness was due to the fact that the two suits which had been brought by the defendants against the plaintiff had not yet been decided, and that the bringing of them did not constitute any ground of legal complaint against the parties who brought them. On this point the court said that "The commencement of a suit at law is an assertion of a right, in a manner provided by law; and persons so commencing suits cannot be subjected to other actions for having done so. The remedy of the party so sued is in defending the suit, and, if he is successful in his defense he recovers costs, and sometimes damages."

3.   Blindell and others vs. Hagen and others, 54 Fed. Rep. 40. This was a bill in equity, filed about the beginning of 1893, in the United States Circuit Court for the Eastern District of Louisiana. The bill stated that the complainants belonged to the Kingdom of Great Britain, and were the owners of the steamship "Violante" which they used in transportation between New Orleans and Liverpool; and that the defendants were citizens of Louisiana, who had combined to prevent the complainants from obtaining in New Orleans a crew of mariners to serve on their ship, and that this interference of the defendants was restraining the business of international transportation of the complainants from the United States to Great Britain.

The bill prayed for an injunction to restrain the defendants from any further interference with the business of the complainants. This prayer was based upon two grounds, namely: (1) The Sherman law, and (2) the general rule of equity jurisprudence, which provides that equity has jurisdiction to restrain defendants from trespassing upon the rights of complainants, where the injured party has no plain and adequate remedy for such a trespass by means of an action at law.

The case was decided by Judge Billings, who was then the Unitetd States District Judge for the Eastern District of Louisiana. He decided the Sherman law was not applicable to the case, because that law gives no right to bring an action in equity, except to the United States, and confines actions brought under it by private parties to actions at law for triple damages and costs and attorney's fees.

Judge Billings also decided that the bill of complaint was properly based upon its second ground. But that decision had no relevancy to the Sherman law, and is mentioned here only to show that justice did not fail in this Blindell case.

The foregoing statements and explanations in this chapter show that nothing affirmative was accomplished in any court under the Sherman law during the first thirty-two months of its existence, ending March 4, 1893, except in the one case of the United States vs. Jellico Mountain Coal Company and others. Moreover, that was so plain a case that its decision did not involve any decision of any debatable question relevant to the Sherman law. So also, the particular combination in restraint of interstate commerce, which was suppressed in that case, was so limited in its field of operation that no extensive benefit resulted from its suppression.

For these reasons it is apparent that the Sherman law was never used to any considerable extent as an instrument for the promotion of justice or for the prevention of injustice, at any time prior to the end of the administration of President Harrison.

CHAPTER V.

The second administration of President Cleveland extended from March 4, 1893, to March 4, 1897. The first Attorney General during that administration was Richard Olney of Boston, Massachusetts, who held that office until he was appointed to be Secretary of State about the first of June, 1895. His successor was Judson Harmon of Cincinnati, who is now Governor of Ohio, and who continued to be Attorney General until the end of President Cleveland's administration in March, 1897. During the four years of that administration the number of cases which the United States prosecuted under the Sherman law was ten; and the history of that administration in respect of the Sherman law is substantially coincident with the history of those ten cases during those four years. Those ten cases were the following:

1. United States vs. Workingmen's Amalgamated Council of New Orleans and others, 54 Fed. 994, and 57 Fed. Rep. 85. This was an action in equity, which was begun in the United States Circuit Court for the Eastern District of Louisiana, shortly before the end of President Harrison's administration, but which was not adjudicated until March 25, 1893, after the beginning of President Cleveland's administration. The attorney for the United States was F. B. Earhart, then United States District Attorney for the Eastern District of Louisiana; while the defendants were represented by three or four attorneys. The object of the suit was

to get an injunction from the court against the defendants to prevent them from further prosecution of a general strike or cessation of labor, which had been ordered
and carried on by the "Amalgamated Council," and
which council was the general labor organization to
which the other defendants belonged. In support of its
prayer for such an injunction, the bill of complaint
stated that the strike sought to be enjoined was operating
to restrain general business in New Orleans, including
the interstate and international commerce which had
been flowing through that city.

The defendants interposed six defenses, namely: 1.
The strike had ended, and there was therefore no need
for an injunction. 2. The Sherman law was not applicable to combinations of laborers. 3. The defendants' answer being under oath and denying all the allegations
of the bill no injunction could issue in pursuance of the
bill. 4. The evidence in the case was insufficient to
prove the allegations of the bill. 5. The origin and purpose of the defendants' labor organization was innocent
and lawful. 6. The object of the strike had been to
compel employers to employ no laborers except those
belonging to the Union, which effort if accomplished
would not result in any restraint of commerce.

The motion for the injunction was heard by Judge
Billings, who was then the United States District Judge
for the Eastern District of Louisiana. He overruled all
six of the defendants' defenses, and granted the injunction prayed for in the bill. Only two of those defenses
related to the construction of the Sherman law; and
therefore there is no present occasion to explain the
other four defenses, or why Judge Billings overruled
them.

The two defenses which related to the Sherman law
were those numbered 2 and 6, respectively. In overruling the second defense, Judge Billings said:

"I think the Congressional debates show that the statute had its origin in the evils of massed capital; but when the Congress came to formulate the prohibition which is the yardstick for measuring the complainant's right to the injunction, it expressed it in these words: 'Every contract or combination in the form of trust, or otherwise, in restraint of trade or commerce among the several states or with foreign nations, is hereby declared to be illegal.' The subject had so broadened in the minds of the legislators, that the source of the evil was not regarded as material, and the evil in its entirety was dealt with. They made the interdiction include combinations of labor, as well as of capital; in fact, all combinations in restraint of commerce, without reference to the character of the persons who entered into them. It is true that this statute has not been much expounded by judges, but as it seems to me, its meaning, as far as relates to the sort of combinations to which it is to apply, is manifest, and that it includes combinations which are composed of laborers acting in the interest of labor."

In overruling the sixth defense, Judge Billings said:

"The combination setting out to secure and compel the employment of none but union men in a given business, as a means to effect this compulsion, finally enforced a discontinuance of labor in all kinds of business, including the business of transportation of goods and merchandise which were in transit through the City of New Orleans, from state to state, and to and from foreign countries. I do not think there can be any question but that that combination of the defendants was in restraint of commerce."

The defendants prosecuted an appeal from the decision of Judge Billings to the United States Circuit Court of Appeals for the Fifth Circuit; but that tribunal affirmed the decision of Judge Billings, as being fully justified by the case as presented to him, saying that all of the defendants' defenses were "well summarized, discussed and disposed of in the very able opinion of the judge of the Circuit Court."

2. United States vs. E. C. Knight Co. and others, 60 Fed. Rep. 306, and 60 Fed. Rep. 934, and 156 U. S. 1. This was an action in equity, which was begun in the United States Circuit Court for the Eastern District of Pennsylvania, in the last year of President Harrison's administration, but which was not adjudicated until it was first decided on January 30, 1894, by Judge Butler, who was then the United States District Judge for the Eastern District of Pennsylvania. The bill was based upon the fact that the American Sugar Refining Company, a New Jersey corporation, which had been producing about sixty-five per cent. of all the refined sugar produced in the United States, had purchased all the stock of the E. C. Knight Company, and of three other Pennsylvania corporations, and which four companies had been engaged in refining sugar in Philadelphia, where they had produced about thirty-three per cent. of all the refined sugar in the United States; and upon the fact that the American Sugar Refining Company had paid for the stock thus purchased by issuing to the selling stockholders some stock in the American Sugar Refining Company, which was newly issued for that purpose. It was proved in the case, that after that acquirement by the American Sugar Refining Company of the stock of the four Pennsylvania corporations, those corporations continued to refine sugar in their Philadelphia refineries, and indeed, increased their production thereof.

The attorneys for the United States in this case were Ellery P. Ingham, the United States District Attorney for the Eastern District of Pennsylvania, and his assistant, Robert Ralston; while the attorneys for the defendants were John G. Johnson and R. C. McMurtrie.

The attorneys for the United States claimed that the facts constituted a violation of Section 1 and also a violation of Section 2 of the Sherman law. The essential question involved in the case was the question whether those facts constituted a combination to restrain interstate or international commerce, or constituted an attempt to monopolize any interstate or international commerce, on the one hand; or, on the other hand, whether those facts related only to the manufacture of refined sugar in one city of one state, and therefore did not relate to any interstate or international commerce. Judge Butler decided this question in favor of the latter view, and thereupon ordered the bill to be dismissed.

An appeal was taken and prosecuted by the United States from this decision of Judge Butler to the United States Circuit Court of Appeals for the Third Circuit, but the decision of Judge Butler was affirmed by that tribunal on March 26, 1894, in an opinion which is reported on page 934 of Volume 60 of the Federal Reporter. That court on that occasion was held by Circuit Judges Acheson and Dallas, and District Judge Green. The case was argued for the United States by Ellery P. Ingham and Samuel F. Phillips; and by John G. Johnson for the defendants. The opinion of the court was delivered by Judge Dallas, and was to the effect that the doings of the defendants, which were complained of in the bill and proved in the evidence, related to the manufacture of refined sugar in one city of one state, and did not constitute any restraint of interstate or international commerce.

The United States took and prosecuted an appeal from the foregoing decision of the Circuit Court of Appeals for the Third Circuit, to the Supreme Court of the United States. That appeal was argued in that court on October 24, 1894, by Lawrence Maxwell, Jr., Solicitor General of the United States, and by Mr. Samuel F.

Phillips, as counsel; and was argued for the defendants by Mr. John C. Johnson.

Chief Justice Fuller on January 21, 1895, delivered the opinion of the Supreme Court, affirming the decision of the Circuit Court of Appeals, 156 U. S. 1. But Justice Harlan at the same time delivered a dissenting opinion, holding that the decision of the Circuit Court of Appeals was wrong. 156 U. S. 18.

This Knight case was the first case involving the Sherman law which was adjudicated in the Supreme Court, and the conflicting views of Chief Justice Fuller and Justice Harlan, which were developed in that case, are very important to be understood.

The views of Chief Justice Fuller are sufficiently set forth in the following extracts from his opinion:

"By the purchase of the stock of the four Philadelphia refineries with shares of its own stock, the American Sugar Refining Company acquired nearly complete control of the manufacture of refined sugar within the United States."

"The fundamental question is, whether conceding that the existence of a monopoly in manufacture is established by the evidence, that monopoly can be directly suppressed, under the act of Congress, in the mode attempted by this bill."

"The argument is that the power to control the manufacture of refined sugar is a monopoly over a necessary of life, to the enjoyment of which by a large part of the population of the United States, interstate commerce is indispensable, and that, therefore, the general government in the exercise of the power to regulate commerce may repress such monopoly directly, and set aside the instruments which have created it."

"Doubtless the power to control the manufacture of a given thing involves, in a certain sense, the control of its disposition; but this is a secondary and not the primary sense; and although the exercise of that power may result in bringing the operation of commerce into play, it does not control it, and affects it only incidentally and indirectly. Commerce succeeds to manufacture, and is not a part of it. The power to regulate commerce is the power to prescribe the rule by which commerce shall be governed, and is a power independent of the power to suppress monopoly. But it may operate in repression of monopoly, whenever that comes within the rules by which commerce is governed, or whenever the transaction is itself a monopoly of commerce."

"The fact that an article is manufactured for export to another state does not of itself make it an article of interstate commerce, and the intent of the manufacturer does not determine the time when the article passes from the control of the state and belongs to commerce."

"The contracts and acts of the defendants related exclusively to the acquisition of the Philadelphia refineries, and the business of sugar refining in Pennsylvania, and bore no direct relation to commerce between the states or with foreign nations."

"The Circuit Court declined, upon the pleadings and proofs, to grant the relief prayed and dismissed the bill, and we are of opinion that the Circuit Court of Appeals did not err in affirming that decree."

The pivotal point in the statement and argument of Chief Justice Fuller was where he said that "the contracts and acts of the defendants related exclusively to the acquisition of the Philadelphia refineries and the business of sugar refining in Pennsylvania, and bore no direct relation to commerce between the states or with foreign nations." 156 U. S. 17, lines 3 to 7.

This statement of the Chief Justice amounted to saying that there was no evidence that any of the defendants sold any sugar outside of the State of Pennsylvania; though the Chief Justice elsewhere in his opinion as-

sumed it to be probable that much of the sugar thus sold
in Pennsylvania was resold in other states by the first
purchasers thereof; and that the defendants knew, or
had reason to know, that much of the sugar sold by
them in Philadelphia would be transported to other states
and resold therein. The surprising point in this Knight
case resides in the fact that the United States appears
therein to have brought a suit against the defendants for
manufacturing sugar in Pennsylvania; whereas the suit
ought to have been brought for monopolistic selling in
many different states the sugar they manufactured in
Pennsylvania and also the sugar they manufactured in
New York.

The American Sugar Refining Company, when the
Knight case was begun in 1892, was a typical combination
in the form of a holding company, owning the capital
stock of several other corporations which were engaged
in manufacturing and selling refined sugar, as well as
being itself a manufacturing corporation engaged in
making and selling refined sugar. The entire scheme of
the American Sugar Refining Company included manufacturing refined sugar in particular states of the Union,
and included also monopolistic selling the refined sugar
thus made in many other states of the Union. In so far
as that business covered the monopolistic selling of refined
sugar in interstate commerce, it was undeniably a violation of Section 1 of the Sherman law, because that part
of its business was done in pursuance of a combination
in restraint of interstate commerce. But in so far as
the business consisted in manufacturing refined sugar in
particular states, it did not constitute any violation of
the Sherman law; because manufacturing is not commerce, and being necessarily localized, is not an interstate
transaction. But for some reason, which has never been
publicly explained, the attorneys for the United States
in the Knight case based that suit upon a portion only

of that portion of the American Sugar Refining Company's business which did not violate the Sherman law, instead of basing that suit upon the whole of that portion of that business which did violate the Sherman law. For that reason that suit failed in the Circuit Court, and in the Circuit Court of Appeals, and in the Supreme Court, as it should have been expected to do before it was begun.

Justice Harlan was so shocked at this failure of justice that he diligently sought out some course of reasoning upon which the suit might be sustained, even upon the ground upon which it was based. That diligent search resulted in his dissenting opinion of more than ten thousand words, which is printed on pages 18 to 46, inclusive, of Volume 156, of the United States Reports. That dissenting opinion was a very valuable contribution to the legal literature of the Sherman law, and covers a much wider range of discussion than the opinion of the majority of the court, which was delivered by Chief Justice Fuller. But in the midst of a remarkable exhibition and record of learning upon the general subject, Justice Harlan took direct issue with Chief Justice Fuller upon the pivotal point of the case. He did this by stating and contending that a suppression of competition between corporations theretofore engaged in manufacturing sugar in a particular state, and selling it in that state, constituted a restraint of interstate commerce, because it deprived citizens of other states of the right to go to that state and purchase sugar under competitive conditions, to be afterward transported by them to their own states and sold there. It was precisely to this effect that he wrote in his dissenting opinion:

"In my judgment the citizens of the several states composing the Union are entitled, of right, to buy goods in the state where they are manufactured, without being confronted by an illegal combination whose business extends throughout the whole country, and which prevents such buying except at prices arbitrarily fixed by it.   I insist that the free course of trade among the states cannot co-exist with such combinations."   156 U. S. 37, lines 10 to 18.

It was while this Knight case was pending in the Circuit Court, about a year after it was begun, and about two months after it was decided by Judge Butler in that court, that Attorney General Olney sent to Congress his first annual report of December 1, 1893.   That report devoted nearly two pages to the Sherman law; and those pages indicated that Mr. Olney was inclined to minimize that law almost to the vanishing point.   The first paragraph of his report of 1893 relevant thereto was as follows:

"There has been, and probably still is, a widespread impression that the aim and effect of this statute are to prohibit and prevent those aggregations of capital which are so common at the present day, and which are sometimes on so large a scale as to control practically all the branches of an extensive industry.   It would not be useful, even if it were possible, to ascertain the precise purposes of the framers of the statute.   It is sufficient to point out what small basis there is for the popular impression referred to."

In the next paragraph of his report he stated that it had been held that railroad companies engaged in interstate transportation were not within the purview of the statute.   This was an allusion to the decision which Judge Riner had made in November, 1892, in the Trans-Missouri case, but which the Circuit Court of Appeals for the Eighth Circuit in October, 1893, had expressly declined to affirm, and which, as we shall hereafter see, was afterward reversed by the United States Supreme Court.

The next paragraph of Attorney General Olney's report stated with approval what he understood to be five points adjudicated by Judge Jackson in the habeas corpus case of in re Greene, reported in 52 Fed. Rep. 104. Speaking of Judge Jackson's opinion in that case, Attorney General Olney proceeded as follows:

"His conclusions, as briefly summarized, are: (1) That Congress cannot limit the right of state corporations or of citizens in the acquisition, accumulation and control of property; (2) that Congress cannot prescribe the prices at which such property shall be sold by the owner, whether a corporation or individual; (3) that Congress cannot make criminal the intents and purposes of persons in the acquisition and control of property which the states of their residence or creation sanction; (4) that "monopoly," as prohibited by the statute, means an exclusive right in one party, coupled with a legal restriction or restraint upon some other party which prevents the latter from exercising or enjoying the same right; (5) and that contracts in restraint of trade and commerce as prohibited are contracts in general restraint thereof, and such as would be void at common law independently of any statute."

Attorney General Olney concluded his report of 1893 upon this subject by severely criticising, without mentioning by name, the decision which had lately been rendered by Judge Billings in the case of the United States vs. Workingmen's Amalgamated Council of New Orleans and others, saying that that decision illustrated the perversion of a law from the real purpose of its authors.

In these ways Attorney General Olney, in his annual report of December 1, 1893, to Congress, administered to the Sherman law all the blows that anybody could have thought of at that stage of its history; and that report to Congress, as Attorney General, does not indicate any diminution of that unfriendly attitude toward that statute, which Mr. Olney had taken the year before, when he was successfully defending the "Whiskey Trust" against that statute in the United States District Court for the District of Massachusetts, in the case of the United States vs. Greenhut and others.

3. United States vs. Elliott and others, 62 Fed. Rep. 801. This was a case in equity, begun in July, 1894, by the United States against certain members of the American Railway Union, including Eugene V. Debs, then president of that union.

The bill of complaint stated that the defendants had combined to prevent several railroad companies, specified in the bill, whose lines radiated from St. Louis, and which were engaged in interstate commerce, from conducting their customary business of transporting freight and passengers between points in Missouri and points in adjoining states, to which their several lines extended. The bill stated that in pursuance of that combination, the defendants had induced persons in the employ of said railroad companies to quit work, and to prevent those companies from securing other operatives to run their railroad trains.

On the basis of this bill of complaint, the United States presented to Judge Thayer, who was then United States District Judge for the Eastern District of Missouri, a motion for a preliminary injunction, restraining the defendants until final hearing of the case, from continuing to promote the railroad "strike" described in the bill of complaint. That strike was a part of that so-called "Debs" railroad strike, which occurred on many of the railroads in the United States in the summer of 1894, and which was a "sympathetic" strike, instituted in aid of the strike which had been begun earlier in the summer by the employees of the Pullman Palace Car Company, in the car shops of that corporation near Chicago, Illinois.

Judge Thayer, in passing upon the motion for the injunction, said: "A combination whose professed object is to arrest the operation of railroads, whose lines extend from a great city into adjoining states, until such roads accede to certain demands made upon them, whether such demands are in themselves reasonable or unreasonable, just or unjust, is certainly an unlawful conspiracy in restraint of commerce among the states."

For this reason Judge Thayer granted the injunction prayed for in this case.

4. United States vs. Agler, 62 Fed. Rep. 824. This was a proceeding begun in July, 1894, in the United States Circuit Court for the District of Indiana, to punish the defendant for contempt of court, said to reside in his disobedience of an injunction which had been issued by that court against certain members of the American Railway Union, to restrain them from promoting in Indiana, or elsewhere, another part of the "Debs" railroad strike. This proceeding failed, because Judge Baker, before whom it was brought for adjudication, found that the affidavit upon which it was based was defective in many respects, and particularly in that it did not allege that the defendant had done anything in combination with anybody else toward promoting any part of the "Debs" strike.

5. United States vs. Debs and others, 64 Fed. Rep. 724. This was a proceeding in the United States Circuit Court for the Northern District of Illinois in July, 1894, which was brought by the United States to punish Eugene V. Debs and other officers of the American Railway Union, for violation of an injunction which had been issued by that court, to restrain those defendants from promoting those parts of the Debs strike which had occurred within the jurisdiction of that court, and particularly that portion of that strike which had occurred on the Atchison, Topeka and Santa Fé Railroad.

The attorneys for the United States in this proceeding were T. E. Milchrist, the United States District Attorney for the Northern District of Illinois, and Edwin Walker; while the interests of that railroad company were represented by E. A. Bancroft and John S. Miller; and while the defendants were represented by Clarence S. Darrow, W. W. Erwin and S. S. Gregory.

The injunction which was claimed to have been violated by the defendants had been issued without notice to the defendants, in pursuance of a bill in equity which was based upon Section 1 of the Sherman law. After that injunction was issued, knowledge of its existence and character was conveyed to the defendants, but they continued to do what the injunction prohibited. Their answer and defense to the proceeding to punish them for contempt of court in disobeying the injunction, consisted in saying that the court had no jurisdiction to issue that injunction. In support of that contention, the defendants claimed that the Sherman law applied only to combinations of corporations and capitalists in restraint of interstate and international commerce, and did not confer any jurisdiction upon any court to interfere with any labor strike, which might operate to restrain interstate or international commerce. That was the precise defense which had been made and had been overruled in 1893, in the United States Circuit Court for the Eastern District of Louisiana, in the case of United States vs. Workingmen's Amalgamated Council of New Orleans, 54, Fed. Rep. 994. But Attorney General Olney in his annual report of December 1, 1893, had expressed the opinion that that decision was an instance of "the perversion of a law from the real purpose of its authors."

Though this Debs case was prosecuted by the United States District Attorney for the Northern District of

Illinois, it was prosecuted under the direction of Attorney General Olney; for according to Section 4 of the Sherman law, no United States District Attorney had any authority to prosecute any action in equity under that law, except under the direction of the Attorney General. It therefore appears that in directing Debs and the other officers of the American Railway Association to be prosecuted by an action in equity under the Sherman law, Attorney General Olney was doing something which in his annual report of December 1, 1893, he had pronounced to be a perversion of that law. When the attorneys for Debs and his associates took the same ground in this Debs case, they contended that the Sherman law was exclusively aimed at evils of a contractual character, resulting from combinations between corporations and capitalists, and that that statute was not aimed at torts which might be committed by laborers in the course of labor strikes. Those gentlemen supported that contention with all the ability which could have been employed in that support. But Judge Woods, who was then one of the Circuit Judges for the Seventh Circuit, overruled that defense in the following terms:

"I have not failed, I think, to appreciate the just force of the argument contrary to my opinion; but my conclusion is clear, that under the act of 1890, the court had jurisdiction of the case presented in the application, and that the injunction granted was not without authority of law nor for any reason invalid."

In pursuance of this opinion the court found Debs and all the other defendants, except one, guilty of contempt as charged by the United States; and those defendants were thereupon sentenced to imprisonment in the county jail for terms varying from three months to six months. Having been committed to jail in pursuance of that order, Debs and the other prisoners on January 14, 1895, applied to the Supreme Court of the United

States for a writ of habeas corpus, for the purpose of obtaining from the Supreme Court an order to discharge them from imprisonment, on the ground that that imprisonment was illegal.

That application for a writ of habeas corpus was original suit No. 11 on the docket of the Supreme Court of the United States for that term; and that case was argued in that court on March 25 and 26, 1895, by Attorney General Olney and Assistant Attorney General Whitney, and Mr. Edwin Walker for the United States; and by Lyman Trumbull, S. S. Gregory and C. S. Darrow for the petitioners.

In asking and recommending the Supreme Court to discharge the petitioners in this Debs case from imprisonment, Trumbull took the ground that the injunction which they had disobeyed was void, because the court had no jurisdiction in the case in which that injunction was issued. This denial of jurisdiction was based by him upon the proposition that Section 4 of the Sherman law did not authorize actions in equity to restrain crimes; or alternatively, if that section did authorize such an action, then it was unconstitutional, in that it would deny the right of trial by jury to persons accused of a particular class of crimes.

The Supreme Court having heard argument on this subject during two days, in March, 1895, rendered its decision on May 27 of that year. But that court in that decision expressly refrained from deciding anything relevant to the Sherman law; though on other grounds that court denied the petition for the writ of habeas corpus. All that the Supreme Court said or did relevant to the Sherman law in the Debs case was expressed in the following paragraph at the end of its opinion in that case.

"We enter into no examination of the act of July 2, 1890, c. 647, 26 Stat. 209, upon which the Circuit Court relied mainly to sustain its jurisdiction. It must not be

understood from this that we dissent from the conclusions of that court in reference to the scope of the act,
but simply that we prefer to rest our judgment on the
broader ground which has been discussed in this opinion,
believing it of importance that the principles underlying
it should be fully stated and affirmed."

The written opinion of the Supreme Court in this case
was delivered by Justice Brewer, and is printed on pages
577 to 600, inclusive, of Volume 158 of the reports of
that court.

6. United States vs. Cassidy and others, 67 Fed. Rep.
698. This was a trial by jury of John Cassidy and another man, who had been indicted in the United States
District Court for the Eastern District of California, for
violating Section 1 of the Sherman law, in being parties to a combination in restraint of interstate commerce
by means of their participation in that part of the "Debs"
strike of the American Railway Union, which occurred in
California and elsewhere on the Pacific Coast of the
United States. That trial began on November 12, 1894,
and continued until it ended on April 6, 1895, with a disagreement and discharge of the jury. That final disagreement followed the deliberation by the jury during
four days and nights, at the end of which eight jurors
voted for conviction and four for acquittal.

The trial was conducted by Judge Morrow, who was
then the United States District Judge for the Northern
District of California. The charge of the jury was delivered on April 1 and 2, 1895, and was based upon six
thousand pages of transcripts of testimony and other
evidence, and was probably the longest charge delivered
to any jury in the United States, and was probably never
exceeded by any charge delivered to any jury in any
country, with the single exception of the charge of Lord

Chief Justice Cockburn in the Tichborne case in England.

That charge of Judge Morrow is printed on pages 701 to 783, inclusive, of Volume 67 of the Federal Reporter. The last seventy-five pages were devoted to a review and analysis of the evidence in the case; but page 705 was devoted to a construction and explanation of Section 1 of the Sherman law. That statement began by saying that the word "trade" in that section means "the exchange of commodities for other commodities or for money, whereas the word 'commerce' in that section has a broader meaning than the word 'trade' and includes in that broader meaning the transportation of persons and property, as well as the purchase, sale and exchange of commodities." Thereupon Judge Morrow proceeded to tell the jury "that the primary object of the suit was, undoubtedly, to prevent the destruction of legitimate and healthy competition in interstate commerce by individuals, corporations and trusts, grasping, engrossing and monopolizing the market for commodities. But its provisions are broad enough to reach a combination or conspiracy that would interrupt the transportation of such commodities and persons from one state to another." The only other point of construction which Judge Morrow placed upon the Sherman law in his charge to the jury, was where he stated that according to that statute, "the doing of some act in pursuance of a conspiracy, is an ingredient of the crime and must be established as a necessary element of the offense, although the act need not be in itself criminal or amount to a crime."

7.   United States vs. Joint Traffic Association, 76 Fed. Rep. 895.   This was a bill in equity filed by the United States in the United States Circuit Court for the Southern District of New York, in January, 1896, against thirty-two railroad companies which composed the Joint

Traffic Association, and which included the Pennsylvania Railroad Company and many others which were engaged in interstate transportation between the Atlantic Ocean and the Alleghany Mountains. The attorney for the United States in this case was Wallace Macfarlane, the United States District Attorney for the Southern District of New York, while the arguments for the defendants were made by James C. Carter and Edward J. Phelps. The case was heard soon after it was brought, by Judge Wheeler, who was then the United States District Judge for the District of Vermont, and was temporarily holding the United States Circuit Court for the Southern District of New York. The bill was filed at the request of the Interstate Commerce Commission, under the direction of the Attorney General, by the District Attorney for the Southern District of New York, for the purpose of securing an injunction to prevent any further doings, by the defendants or any of them, in pursuance of a certain contract in writing which they had made for the purpose of fixing and regulating the rates to be charged by the members of the association, for transporting freight and passengers. The bill did not state what statute or statutes had been violated by this agreement, or in pursuance thereof, but on the hearing the United States claimed that the contract violated Section 5 of the Interstate Commerce law of 1887, and also violated Section 1 of the Sherman law of 1890. Judge Wheeler decided that the Interstate Commerce law did not contain any provision for enforcing its provisions by actions in equity, except to carry out orders of the Commission and that decision disposed of the bill so far as the bill was based upon Section 5 of the Interstate Commerce Act.

In respect of the Sherman law, Judge Wheeler decided that though railroads are not expressly named in that act, they are covered thereby and that the act authorized actions in equity to prevent its violation. Nevertheless, he held that the contract of the Joint Traffic Association, upon which the bill was based, did not violate the Sherman law because, as he construed that contract, it did not provide for any restraint of interstate commerce by way of restraining interstate transportation. For these reasons Judge Wheeler dismissed the bill of complaint in this case.

An appeal was taken by the United States from Judge Wheeler's decision to the United States Circuit Court of Appeals for the Second Circuit and was argued in that tribunal on behalf of the United States by Wallace Macfarlane, the United States District Attorney, and was argued on behalf of the Joint Traffic Association by several distinguished lawyers, not including those who had argued it before Judge Wheeler. The Circuit Court of Appeals, near the close of President Cleveland's administration, affirmed the decision of Judge Wheeler without writing or filing any opinion in support of that affirmance, 89 Fed. Rep. 1020.

8. United States vs. Addyston Pipe & Steel Co. and others, 78 Fed. Rep. 712. This was a bill in equity, instituted December 10, 1896, in the United States Circuit Court for the Eastern District of Tennessee by the United States, to enjoin the operations of the defendants, who were practically the only manufacturers of cast-iron pipe anywhere within thirty-six states and territories of the Union and who comprised an association which they had formed for the purpose of mutually regulating their business, and which association was known as the "Associated Pipe Works." The case was argued shortly before the close of President Cleveland's administration before Judge Clark, who was then the United States District Judge for the Eastern District of Tennessee, and it was argued by James H. Bible on behalf of the United

States, and by Brown & Spurlock and W. E. Spears on behalf of the defendants.

The bill of complaint was based upon Sections 1 and 2 of the Sherman law, and upon the statement that the purpose of the "Associated Pipe Works" was to destroy all competition in the cast-iron pipe business throughout the thirty-six states and territories, and to force the public to pay unreasonable prices for the cast-iron pipe made and sold by the corporations which constituted that combination.

The defendants made two defenses to the suit, namely, (1) that the association was not one subject to the provisions of the Sherman law; and (2) that the association did not cause any restraint of trade or constitute any monopoly such as would be unlawful at common law.

Judge Clark decided that the second of these defenses was inapplicable to the case, because he was of opinion that the Sherman law did not, and could not constitutionally, deal with any contract in restraint of trade or any monopoly which conformed precisely to the common law definition of those terms. But Judge Clark held the first defense to be sound and sufficient because, in his opinion of the evidence, the combination complained of did not relate to interstate commerce any more than any ordinary manufacturing establishment would do where the products of that establishment must find a market in other states as well as in the state wherein it was located. For these reasons Judge Clark held the decision of the United States Supreme Court in the Knight case to be applicable to the case before him and to necessitate a decision of that case in favor of the defendants. He therefore ordered the bill to be dismissed on February 5, 1897, which was less than a month before the end of President Cleveland's administration.

9. Moore vs. United States, 85 Fed. Rep. 465. This case originated with an indictment which was returned November 4, 1895, in the District Court of the Third Judicial District of the Territory of Utah. The indictment was based upon Section 3 of the Sherman law and upon the fact that the defendant Moore, as agent of the Union Pacific Coal Company, did on October 23, 1895, refuse to sell to T. P. Lewis, a carload of "Rock Springs coal" for less than $5.00 per ton, though as such agent, he was selling such coal to other parties at $3.75 per ton, and upon the fact that Moore had also refused to sell such coal at any price except to certain coal dealers who were members of an association named the "Salt Lake Coal Exchange."

The theory of the indictment was that the conduct of Moore constituted a restraint of commerce in the Territory of Utah, and therefore violated Section 3 of the Sherman law.

On December 14, 1895, Moore was arraigned in the Territorial Court in which he had been indicted, whereupon he pleaded not guilty to that indictment.

On January 4, 1896, Utah was admitted into the Union as a state. Therefore and thereafter the Moore case was transferred to the United States Court for the District of Utah.

On November 11, 1896, the defendant obtained leave of that court to withdraw his plea of not guilty and to file a demurrer to the indictment, based upon several grounds, including the claim that the admission of Utah into the Union as a state has caused the case to abate. The demurrer on that point was overruled, and thereupon the defendant entered a plea of not guilty, whereupon November 12, 1896, he was tried and found guilty, and on November 19, 1896, he was fined $200, together with one-half of the costs of the case, which were taxed at $88.60.

Thereupon, Moore sought to secure a reversal of that judgment from the United States Circuit Court of Appeals for the Eighth Circuit; and that judgment was reversed by that tribunal on the technical ground that the United States Court for the District of Utah had no jurisdiction to try the defendant after the admission of Utah into the Union as a state, in pursuance of an indictment which had been found against him when Utah was a territory, in the District Court for one of the judicial districts of that territory; where that indictment was based upon conduct of a kind which was not a misdemeanor in the state of Utah, at the time of the trial, though it was a misdemeanor in the territory of Utah at the time of the indictment.

10. United States vs. Trans-Missouri Freight Association, 166 U. S., 290. This Supreme Court case resulted from an appeal to that tribunal, by the United States, from the adverse decision which had been made by the United States Circuit Court of Appeals for the Eighth Circuit in 1893. Though that appeal was not decided until after the end of President Cleveland's administration it was argued in the Supreme Court nearly three months before that time. The argument was conducted for the United States by Judson Harmon, who had then succeeded Richard Olney as Attorney General in the cabinet of President Cleveland, and who is now Governor of Ohio. And that argument was conducted on behalf of the defendants by John F. Dillon, James C. Carter, Edward J. Phelps, W. F. Guthrie and Lloyd W. Bowers.

The Supreme Court on March 22, 1897, reversed the decision of the Circuit Court of Appeals for the Eighth Circuit, and decided the case in favor of the United States, in pursuance of the opinion of five justices of the Supreme Court, and against the dissenting opinion of the other four justices of that tribunal. The five justices were Chief Justice Fuller and Justices Harlan, Brewer, Brown and Peckham; while the four justices were Justices Field, Gray, Shiras and White. The opinions of the respective groups of justices were delivered by Justices Peckham and White, both of whom had been appointed by President Cleveland during his second administration.

The decision of the court in favor of the United States was based upon the following points of law, which were established by that decision:

1. Section 1 of the Sherman law applies to railroad companies engaged in interstate transportation, and is violated where a plurality of such companies combine to restrain interstate transportation of freight or passengers, which restraint may consist in mutual regulation of rates for such transportation.

2. Section 1 of the Sherman law applies to all combinations in restraint of interstate or foreign trade or commerce, without exception or limitation; and the prohibitions of that section are not confined to unreasonable restraints of such trade or commerce.

3. Section 1 of the Sherman law may be violated by a contract which necessarily restrained interstate or international commerce, even where that contract was not made for that purpose.

4. An agreement in restraint of interstate commerce which was made prior to the approval of the Sherman law on July 2, 1890, was automatically subjected to the operation of that law, in respect of whatever was done in performance of that agreement after that time.

5. Section 4 of the Sherman law properly authorizes the United States, through the Attorney General and the several United States District Attorneys, to bring and prosecute actions in equity for the enforcement of that law, though the United States may have no pecuniary interest in such suits, and prosecutes them for the benefit

of those who have been or may be injured by violators of Sections 1, 2 or 3 of the Sherman law.

The opinion of the Supreme Court, which was delivered by Justice Peckham on the five points above defined, is printed on pages 307 to 343 of volume 166 of the United States Reports, and is a very clear and able judicial exposition of those parts of the Sherman law to which it refers.

The opinion of the minority of the Supreme Court, which dissented from the decision of that tribunal in the Trans-Missouri case, is printed on pages 343 to 374 of volume 166 of the United States Reports. That opinion dissented from those points in the decision of the court which are defined in the above paragraphs numbered 1 and 2; but did not dissent from those paragraphs which are thus numbered 3, 4 and 5. The dissent from the proposition defined in the paragraph number 2 was direct and complete, but the dissent from what is stated in paragraph number 1 did not amount to contending that Section 1 of the Sherman law has no application to railroad companies engaged in interstate transportation. Somewhat otherwise than this, that dissent was confined to contending that Section 1 of the Sherman law does not apply to the particular kind of mutual restraint between railroad companies which may consist in mutual regulation of rates for transportation.

The dissenting opinion of the minority of the Supreme Court in this case was not any judicial decision, and has never been binding upon anybody, and not even upon the four justices who concurred in it. Justice White is the only one of the four who now remains upon the Supreme bench. If the same questions which were decided in the Trans-Missouri case were to arise in that tribunal again, those questions would have to be decided in the same way that they were decided in that case, even though the justices who might decide the new case would have decided

the Trans-Missouri case against the United States if they
had been the occupants of the Supreme bench at the time
of that decision. For that decision has now been, for
more than half of a quarter of a century, genrally recognized as representative of the law of the United States
on all the points adjudicated therein, and it would be contrary to custom and contrary to justice for the Supreme
Court to repudiate that decision now or hereafter.

The ten cases which have been explained in this chapter were all the cases which were brought or prosecuted
anywhere on behalf of the United States for violation of
the Sherman law during President Cleveland's administration; except one other case, which was brought near
the end of that administration, but was not adjudicated
until after the beginning of the administration of President McKinley, and which case will be explained under
that head in the next chapter.

Five of the ten cases which were adjudicated during
the administration of President Cleveland were brought
against men as alleged participants in labor strikes. Four
of those cases were successful, but the fifth case failed as
the result of a disagreement of the jury with which it
was tried.

Two of those ten cases were brought against "trusts,"
namely, the Sugar Trust and the Cast Iron Pipe Trust,
but both of those cases failed to accomplish anything during the administration of President Cleveland toward
any enforcement of the Sherman law.

One of those cases was brought against a man in Utah
for restraining commerce in coal in Salt Lake City, when
Utah was a territory. That case also failed, because the
trial of the defendant did not occur until after Utah became a state, and because for technical reasons he could
not be punished after the admission of Utah into the

Union, for restraining commerce in coal in Salt Lake City when Utah was a territory.

The remaining two of the ten cases were prosecuted against associations of railroad companies. The one against the Trans-Missouri Freight Association resulted in the Supreme Court in complete success, having been very ably presented to that tribunal by Attorney General Harmon against the combined resistance of three very great senior counsel, assisted by such able junior counsel as W. F. Guthrie and Lloyd W. Bowers. The other railroad association case was a failure in the United States Circuit Court for the Southern District of New York in May, 1896, and also in the Circuit Court of Appeals for the Second Circuit early in 1897. But an appeal from those adverse decisions was prosecuted to a successful result during the administration of President McKinley, as will be set forth in the next chapter of this book. That chapter will also set forth how the United States, during that administration, also prosecuted a successful appeal to the Circuit Court of Appeals for the Sixth Circuit, from the adverse decision of the Circuit Court for the Eastern District of Tennessee, in the case against the Cast Iron Pipe Trust, and also how that favorable decision of that Circuit Court of Appeals was afterward affirmed by the Supreme Court of the United States.

Eight cases of litigation between private parties, relevant to the Sherman law, occurred during President Cleveland's administration. Those litigations were the following:

1. Waterhouse and others vs. Comer, 55 Fed. Rep. 150. This was a petition presented to the United States Circuit Court for the Western District of Georgia in its Southern Division, in April, 1893, by the complainants, who styled themselves the "Committee of Adjustment of the Brotherhood of Locomotive Engineers," against H. M. Comer, as receiver of the Central Railroad and Banking Company of Georgia, asking that the receiver be directed by the court, whose officer he was, to make a contract with the locomotive engineers. The receiver presented to the court many different reasons why he thought the petition should be denied. One reason consisted in the fact that the Brotherhood of Locomotive Engineers included in their code of rules for the government of their members one rule which was claimed to be unlawful under Section 1 of the Sherman law. That was rule 12 of the code, and was as follows:

"That hereafter when an issue has been sustained by the Grand Chief and carried into effect by the Brotherhood of Locomotive Engineers it shall be recognized as a violation of the obligations if a member of the Brotherhood of Locomotive Engineers, who may be employed on a railroad, run in connection with or adjacent to said road, to handle the property belonging to said railroad or system in any way that may benefit said company with which the Brotherhood of Locomotive Engineers are at issue, until the grievances or issues of difference of any nature or kind have been amicably settled."

The Brotherhood of Locomotive Engineers frankly admitted that the effect of this rule, if applied to the railroad in the hands of the receiver, and to the engineers in his employ, would be as follows: If it should be necessary for the receiver to haul over that railroad a car belonging to another railroad company, on whose railroad there is a strike of the engineers, the rule would command the Brotherhood engineers in the employ of the receiver to refuse to haul that car or any train containing that car. It was also proved in the case that one engineer in the employ of the receiver had obeyed that rule by refusing to haul a car belonging to another railroad when an engineers' strike was pending on that other railroad.

This case was decided by Judge Speer, who was then United States District Judge for the Western District of Georgia. He decided that rule 12 of the Brotherhood of Locomotive Engineers was a direct and positive violation of Section 1 of the Sherman law.

2. Dueber Watch Case Mfg. Co. vs. Howard Watch & Clock Co. and others, 55 Fed. Rep. 851. This was an action at law begun in the United States Circuit Court for the Southern District of New York about May 1, 1893, to recover damages under Section 7 of the Sherman law for alleged violation of Sections 1 and 2 of that statute. Such alleged violation was claimed by the plaintiff to consist in the facts that the defendants had agreed among themselves to maintain an arbitrary fixed price for their goods and not to sell any of their goods to any of the plaintiff's customers, and that they had notified the plaintiff's customers of that agreement. The agreement was made before July 2, 1890, but was renewed after the enactment of the Sherman law on that day. The case was decided by Judge Coxe, who was then a United States District Judge of great ability and long experience, and who is now one of the United States Circuit Judges for the Second Circuit. He decided that the agreement complained of did not violate the Sherman law in either of its parts, it not being even alleged by the plaintiff that the prices complained of related to sales in interstate commerce, or that any sales which the defendants had agreed not to make to the plaintiff's customers would have been transactions in interstate commerce if they had been made.

After pointing out these fatal defects in the plaintiff's case Judge Coxe mentioned that no decision previously

5

rendered had gone to the extent of holding that it would constitute a violation of the Sherman law for two or more parties to fix an arbitrary price for their goods; but he did not say that the Sherman law would not be violated by a combination of parties engaged in interstate commerce, agreeing to avoid all mutual competition by means of fixing and maintaining uniform prices for commodities sold by them in such commerce. He did, however, express the opinion that the Sherman law would not be violated by an agreement between parties engaged in interstate commerce to refrain from selling their goods to parties who might be objectionable to them, for legitimate business reasons.

The decision of Judge Coxe in this case was affirmed by the Circuit Court of Appeals for the Second Circuit on March 5, 1895; though Judge Wallace, the chief judge of that court, dissented from the decision of the majority of the court, which majority consisted of Judges Lacombe and Shipman. Each of those three judges wrote a separate opinion; Judge Shipman not concurring in all the reasons which Judge Lacombe stated for affirming the decision of Judge Coxe. The only point that was really decided by the court as the result of a partial agreement in opinion between Judges Lacombe and Shipman, was that the facts stated and proved by the plaintiff were not stated or proved to relate to interstate commerce and may all have related to acts or omissions to act in particular states respectively, without having any relevancy to anything done or not done across any state line.

The separate opinions of Judges Lacombe, Shipman and Wallace in this case are printed on pages 638 to 652 inclusive, of volume 66 of the Federal Reporter; and those writings are well worthy to be read in full as containing expression of the views of three very able men, no two of whom agreed at all points, upon the subject.

3. Thomas vs. Cincinnati, New Orleans & Texas Pacific Railway Company, in re Phelan, 62 Fed. Rep. 803. In this case the United States Circuit Court, for the Southern District of Ohio, had appointed Samuel M. Felton receiver of the railway company, and that receiver filed a petition to the court to punish F. W. Phelan for contempt of court, which contempt the receiver claimed to reside in the conduct of Phelan, wherein he had combined with Eugene V. Debs and others to constrain or induce the employees of the receiver to start and maintain a labor strike on the railroad, which the receiver was running as an officer of the court.

This case was decided by Judge Taft, who was then the senior Circuit Judge of the United States for the Sixth Circuit, and who is now President of the United States. The written opinion of Judge Taft is printed on pages 804 to 823 of volume 62 of the Federal Reporter and is in every respect an admirable judicial decision.

Among the points decided by Judge Taft relevant to the combination between Phelan, Debs and others to induce a labor strike on the railroad in question, was his emphatic conclusion that that combination constituted a violation of Section 1 of the Sherman law.

The last paragraph of Judge Taft's decision in this case was as follows:

"After much consideration I do not think I should be doing my duty as a judicial officer of the United States without imposing upon the contemner the penalty of imprisonment. The sentence of the court is that Frank W. Phelan be confined in the county jail of Warren County, Ohio, for a term of six months. The marshal will take the prisoner into custody and safely convey him to the place of imprisonment."

118 HISTORY OF THE SHERMAN LAW.

4. Pidcock vs. Harrington and others, 64 Fed. Rep. 821. This was an action in equity begun in 1894 in the United States Circuit Court for the Southern District of New York. The bill stated that the defendants had conspired to ruin the complainant's business as a commission merchant and dealer in live stock, and that the defendants had ceased dealing with the complainant, and had threatened to cease dealing with anybody who might be dealing with him. The case was decided by Judge Coxe, by holding that nobody except the United States has a right to bring and prosecute an action in equity under the Sherman law; that being the only foundation which was asserted by the complainant for his suit. On this point Judge Coxe called attention to the fact that the only section of the Sherman law which provides a private remedy is Section 7, and that section provides only an action at law and not any action in equity, for an injunction or other remedy obtainable only by an action in equity.

5. Lowenstein vs. Evans and others, 69 Fed. Rep. 908. This was an action at law, brought in the United States Circuit Court for the District of South Carolina under Section 7 of the Sherman law. The defendants were all officials of the state of South Carolina, who were charged by the laws of the state with the management of the monopoly which those law had established in the business of dealing in alcoholic liquors in South Carolina. The plaintiff was a citizen of North Carolina who was engaged in the business of making alcoholic liquors in that state and selling those liquors in that state and in other states. His complaint in the case stated that on May 27, 1895, he had delivered one barrel of whiskey to the Southern Railway Company at Statesville, in North Carolina, to be transported by that company and other common carriers, to Charleston, South Carolina, and there delivered to Thomas Hartigan. The complaint also stated that on May 29, 1895, while that barrel of whiskey was passing through Columbia, South Carolina, it was seized under the authority of the South Carolina liquor law. On the basis of these facts the complaint demanded a judgment against the defendants for three times the value of the barrel of whiskey, and for costs and for a reasonable attorney's fee, in accordance with Section 7 of the Sherman law.

The theory upon which this suit was brought was that the defendants, though acting as agents of the state of South Carolina, had combined to restrain interstate commerce in that barrel of whiskey, and that in seizing and detaining it they had injured the business or property of the plaintiff to the extent of its value.

The defendants demurred to this complaint and, after an argument, that demurrer was sustained by Judge Simonton, who was then one of . the United States Circuit Judges for the Fourth Circuit. He based that decision against the plaintiff upon the ground that it was the state of South Carolina and not the defendant that had restrained interstate commerce in that barrel of whiskey, and that the suit could not be maintained against the agents of the state, because they were not responsible for the doings complained of, and that the suit could not be maintained against the state because the eleventh amendment to the Constitution of the United States provides that the judicial power of the United States does not extend to any suit at law or in equity commenced against one of the United States by any citizen of another state. He also held that even if the state of South Carolina could have been sued in the United States Circuit Court for restraining interstate commerce in that barrel of whiskey it could not have been found chargeable with any violation of Section 1 of the Sherman law because it had restrained that item of interstate com-

merce alone and not in combination with any other
organization or with any person. And he also held that
the state could not have been found chargeable with violation of Section 2 of the Sherman law because that section is aimed only at monopolization by persons, corporations or associations, whereas the state of South Carolina is neither of those, but is a sovereign exercising its
own inherent sovereignty.

6. Prescott and Arizona Central Railroad Company
vs. Atchison, Topeka and Santa Fé Railroad Company
and other railroad corporations and some persons, 73
Fed. Rep. 438. This was an action at law, begun in
1895, in the United States Circuit Court for the Southern District of New York. The action was based on the
fact that the defendants had refused to accept freight
from the plaintiff on through bills of lading, while accepting such freight on such bills from other railroad
companies. The case was heard upon a motion by all the
defendants except one, to direct a verdict in their favor,
while the remaining defendant asked judgment in his
favor on demurrer. That motion was decided in favor
of the defendants who made it, and that demurrer was
sustained on behalf of the defendant who filed it. The
judge who rendered this decision was Judge Lacombe,
one of the United States Circuit Judges for the Second
Circuit. He held that when the defendant railroad companies combined to favor certain railroad companies and
to discriminate against the plaintiff railroad company in
respect of accepting freight for transportation on through
bills of lading, those defendant companies did not violate
Section 1 of the Sherman law, as the plaintiff claimed
they had done. This conclusion was based upon the opinion of Judge Lacombe that such a discrimination as that
was did not constitute any restraint of trade such as
would have been unlawful at common law, and did not,

therefore, constitute such a restraint of interstate commerce as is prohibited by Section 1 of the Sherman law.

7. The Charles E. Wisewall, 74 Fed. Rep. 802. This was a libel in rem in admiralty, by certain tug owners against the steam dredge Charles E. Wisewall to recover the value of certain services rendered by their tugs in towing that dredge. The owner of the dredge defended upon the ground that the owners of the tugs were members of an association which was illegal under the Sherman law. The case was decided by Judge Coxe against that contention, on the ground that the existence of an illegal contract between the tug owners in mutual restraint of interstate commerce did not deprive those individuals of their right to enforce their legal contracts with the owner of the dredge. On this point Judge Coxe said: "An agreement by the owner of the tug 'Mayflower' to tow the dredge 'Wisewall' from Albany to Troy is not void because the 'Mayflower' is associated with other tugs to regulate the price of towing at Albany."

8. Greer, Mills & Co. vs. Stroller and others, 77 Fed. Rep. 1. This was a bill in equity filed in 1896 in the United States Circuit Court for the Western District of Missouri in its Western Division. The complainant was located outside of Missouri. The defendants were the members of the Board of Directors of the Kansas City Live Stock Exchange, a voluntary business association, doing business in Kansas City, Missouri. The case was decided against the complainant by Judge Philips, the United States District Judge for that district, without deciding or even discussing the question whether the Kansas City Live Stock Exchange was violating or had violated the Sherman law, as the complainants claimed. That decision was fully justified by the fact that the

Sherman law does not confer any right of action in equity for its violation, upon anybody except the United States; the remedies provided by that law for the benefit of persons, partnerships, corporations or associations, being such judgments for threefold damages and costs of suit and attorney's fees as are obtainable by an action of law under Section 7 of the Sherman act.

The foregoing explanation of the eight cases of litigations between private parties relevant to the Sherman law, which occurred during President Cleveland's administration, shows that only two of them produced any affirmative result in pursuance of any provisions of that law. Those two were the railroad labor strike cases which were decided by Judge Spear and Judge Taft respectively.

When the ten cases which were prosecuted on behalf of the United States for violation of the Sherman law during President Cleveland's administration, and the eight cases which, during that administration, were prosecuted under that law by private parties, are considered collectively, it will be seen that seven of the eighteen were labor strike cases and that six of those seven were successful in applying the Sherman law to combinations of laborers in restraint of interstate commerce. It will also be seen that ten of the other eleven cases failed to accomplish anything during the administration of President Cleveland toward any enforcement of the Sherman law, and that the only one of those eleven cases which even nominally produced any such result during that administration was the Trans-Missouri Freight Association case, wherein the Supreme Court, by a vote of five justices to four, reversed the decision of the Circuit Court of Appeals for the Eighth Circuit, which had been rendered against the United States by a vote of two judges to one in that tribunal.

The practical effect of prosecutions under the Sherman law during President Cleveland's administration was, however, reduced even below its nominal effect by the fact that the Trans-Missouri Freight Association was dissolved, by a vote of its members, after it was held by the Circuit Court of Appeals in 1893 to be legal, and before it was held by the Supreme Court in 1897 to have been illegal, as violative of the Sherman law.   166 U. S. Reports, 307.

CHAPTER VI.

The administration of President McKinley extended from March 4, 1897, to September 14, 1901. The first Attorney General during that administration was Joseph McKenna, of California, who had previously been one of the United States Circuit Judges for the Ninth Circuit, and who, during the last twelve years, has been one of the associate justices of the United States Supreme Court. His occupancy of the office of Attorney General extended from March 5, 1897, to January 25, 1898. His successor in that office was John W. Griggs, of New Jersey, who had previously been Governor of that state, and whose occupancy of the office of Attorney General continued more than three years and until March 29, 1901. The next Attorney General was Philander C. Knox, of Pennsylvania, who had previously been a distinguished lawyer in Pittsburg and who was afterward United States Senator from Pennsylvania, and is now occupying the office of Secretary of State of the United States. His incumbency of the office of Attorney General continued from April 5, 1901, through the then remaining five months and nine days of the administration of President McKinley, and continued still longer during nearly three years, and until June 30, 1904, in the administration of President Roosevelt.

During the administration of President McKinley, the number of cases which were prosecuted by the United States under the Sherman law was six, including two

which had been brought under the administration of
President Cleveland, and including one which was not
ended until after the beginning of the administration of
President Roosevelt. Those six cases were the following:

1. United States vs. Addyston Pipe & Steel Co. and
others, 85 Fed. Rep. 271 and 175 U. S. 211. The beginning and the history of this case during the administration of President Cleveland were explained in Chapter V of this book, wherein it is stated that this case was
decided against the United States by Judge Clark when
holding the United States Circuit Court for the Eastern
District of Tennessee in February, 1897. Attorney General McKenna caused an appeal to be taken from that
decision to the United States Circuit Court of Appeals
for the Sixth Circuit. And that appeal, on February 8,
1898, was decided in favor of the United States by
that court, when that court was held by Associate Justice
Harlan of the United States Supreme Court, and by Circuit Judges Taft and Lurton. The unanimous opinion of
that court was written by Judge Taft, and is printed on
pages 278 to 302, inclusive, of volume 85 of the Federal
Reporter. That opinion begins by showing that the suit
was based upon Section 1 of the Sherman law, and that
it involved two questions for decision, and that the first
of those questions was whether the association of the
defendants constituted a contract, combination or conspiracy in restraint of trade as those terms are properly
to be understood in the Sherman law; while the second
of those questions was whether the trade thus restrained
was interstate trade.

On the first of these questions the defendants contended that whatever mutual restraints they exercised
upon each other did not embrace all the states and were
not unlimited in space, and that such partial restraints

were proper at common law wherever they were reasonable, and that the partial restraints which the defendants had exercised upon each other were reasonable, because without them each of the defendants would be subjected to ruinous competition by some or all of the other members, and because those restraints did not exceed, either in scope or stringency, what was necessary to enable the defendants to obtain prices for their cast-iron pipe which were fair and reasonable to themselves and to the public, and because those restraints did not operate upon those cast-iron pipe companies which were not members of the defendants' association and which possessed more than double the capacity of all the defendants put together, to manufacture and sell cast-iron pipe in competition with the defendants.

On this first question the court decided that the association of the defendants, "however reasonable the prices they fixed, however great the competition they had to encounter and however great the necessity for curbing themselves by joint agreement from committing financial suicide by ill-advised competition, was void at common law, because in restraint of trade and in tending to a monopoly." 85 Fed. Rep. 291, line 16 from the bottom. And the court also said that "it is certain that if the contract of association which bound the defendants was void and unenforceable at the common law because in restraint of trade, it is within the inhibition of the statute if the trade it restrained was interstate." 85 Fed. Rep. 278, last three lines and first two lines of page 279.

These two adjudicated points in this formulation by Judge Taft of the decision of the Circuit Court of Appeals for the Sixth Circuit, in the Addyston case, constituted a construction of the word "restraint" in Section 1 of the Sherman law and that construction constituted a decision that that word in that law covers mutual restraint between the members of a combination.

There was no evidence in the Addyston case that the defendants' combination, as a whole or any of its members, had ever exercised any extraneous restraint upon any competitor or other outside party in respect of any making or selling of any cast-iron pipe, and therefore the court had no occasion to decide and did not decide whether the word "restraint" in addition to being indicative of mutual restraint between the members of a combination, is also indicative of extraneous restraint exercised by that combination against one or more other parties.

On the second question which was involved in the Addyston case the defendants mainly relied upon the decision of the Supreme Court in the Knight case as applicable to the facts in the Addyston case and as showing that those facts did not constitute transactions in interstate commerce. But Judge Taft explained that the defendants and the defendants' counsel misunderstood the decision of the Supreme Court in the Knight case.

On that point Judge Taft said: "It seems to us clear that from the beginning to the end of the opinion the Chief Justice draws the distinction between a restraint upon the business of manufacturing and a restraint upon the trade or commerce between the states in the articles after manufacture, with the manifest purpose of showing that the regulating power of Congress under the Constitution could only affect the latter, while the former was not under Federal control and rested wholly with the states." 85 Fed. Rep. 297, line 14 from the bottom.

On this point Judge Taft also said: "The obstacle in the way of granting the relief asked for in the Knight case was (to use the language of the Chief Justice) that 'the contracts and acts of the defendants related exclusively to the acquisition of the Philadelphia refineries and the business of sugar refining in Pennsylvania, and bore no direct relation to commerce between the states or with foreign nations."

Thereupon Judge Taft also said: "That the defendants in the present case combined and contracted with each other for the purpose of restraining trade and commerce among the states covered by their agreement, in the articles manufactured by them, is too clear to admit of dispute." Accordingly, he announced the decision of the Circuit Court of Appeals to be, that the decree of the Circuit Court must be reversed, with instructions to enter a new decree for the United States, perpetually enjoining the defendants from maintaining the combination in the cast-iron pipe business, which was described in the bill and substantially admitted in the answer, and from doing any business under that combination.

It was in this case and in this court nearly eight years after the enactment of the Sherman law that the United States first took the judgment of a court upon Section 6 of the Sherman law, which is the section that provides that any property owned under any contract or combination and being the subject of any such restraint of trade or commerce as that forbidden in Setcion 1, and being in course of transportation from one state to another, or to a foreign country, shall be forfeited to the United States. But the judgment of this Circuit Court of Appeals in this case on that point, was announced by Judge Taft to be that that section of the Sherman law could not be enforced in an action in equity and could be enforced only by special proceedings, like those provided by law for the forfeiture of property imported into the United States contrary to law and which proceedings must include a trial by jury.

The defendants in this Addyston case appealed from the decision of the Circuit Court of Appeals to the Supreme Court of the United States, and that appeal was argued in that tribunal in April, 1899, by Frank Spurlock and John W. Warrington, for the appellants, and by John K. Richards, who was then Solicitor General of the United States, for the appellee. In December, 1899, the Supreme Court unanimously affirmed the decision of the Circuit Court of Appeals in an opinion delivered by Justice Peckham and printed on pages 226 to 248 of volume 175 of the United States Reports. It appears in that opinion that the attorneys for the appellants made in the Supreme Court a different argument from that which they had presented to the Circuit Court of Appeals. That new argument was based upon the contention that by the true construction of the Constitution the power of Congress to regulate interstate commerce is limited to protecting such commerce from interference by state legislation or by some political subdivision of a state, including also power over common carriers, elevator companies, gas companies and water companies, for reasons peculiar to such common carriers and such companies. Accordingly, the appellants contended that the power of Congress to regulate interstate commerce does not include the general power to prohibit or even to interfere with private contracts between citizens, even though such contracts have interstate commerce for their object, and result in a direct and substantial restraint thereof. Justice Peckham devoted eight pages of the opinion which he delivered to this new argument, beginning as follows:

"This argument is founded upon the assertion that the reason for vesting in Congress the power to regulate commerce was to insure uniformity of regulation against conflicting and discriminating state legislation, and the further assertion that the constitution guarantees liberty of private contracts to the citizen, at least upon commercial subjects, and to that extent the guaranty operates as a limitation on the power of Congress to regulate commerce."

Thereupon Justice Peckham proceeded to review this

argument and made an admirable reply thereto, which reply ended as follows:

"We conclude that the plain language of the grant to Congress of power to regulate commerce among the several States includes power to legislate upon the subject of those contracts in respect to interstate or foreign commerce, which directly affect and regulate that commerce, and we can find no reasonable ground for asserting that the constitutional provision as to the liberty of the individual limits the extent of that power as claimed by the appellants. We therefore think the appellants have failed in their contention upon this branch of the subject."

The next defense which the appellants asked the Supreme Court to approve was to the effect that their combination was only a reasonable restraint among themselves, which had been made to prevent ruinous mutual competition among the members of the combination, and to secure from the public prices for their cast-iron pipes which were fair to the purchasers as well as to the sellers.

In respect of this defense Justice Peckham said: "Even if the objection thus set up would, if well founded in fact, constitute a defense, we agree with the Circuit Court of Appeals in its statement of the special facts upon this branch of the case and with its opinion thereon, as set forth by Circuit Judge Taft. The facts thus set forth show conclusively that the effect of the combination was to enhance prices beyond a sum which was reasonable."

The third defense which the appellants presented to the judgment of the Supreme Court was to the effect that the mutual combination of the appellants had no direct bearing upon interstate commerce, but related only to transactions conducted locally, within particular states, and that therefore the case ought to be decided in favor of the appellants in accordance with the decision of the Supreme Court in the Knight case.

Justice Peckham met and answered this third defense by saying that the direct effect of the cast-iron pipe agreement or combination was to regulate interstate commerce and that therefore the case was not covered by the Knight case, because the only combination proved in that case related to manufacture in the state of Pennsylvania and did not relate to commerce among the states or with foreign nations. Further speaking of the Knight case, Justice Peckham said that it "was decided upon the principle that a combination simply to control manufacture was not a violation of the act of Congress, because such a contract or combination did not directly control or affect interstate commerce, but that contracts for the sale and transportation to other states of specific articles were proper subjects for regulation, because they did form part of such commerce."

Thereupon Justice Peckham, in order to distinguish this Addyston case from the Knight case, proceeded to define exactly what was the character of the Addyston combination in the following sentence:

"While no particular contract regarding the furnishing of pipe and the price for which it should be furnished was in contemplation of the parties to the combination at the time of its formation, yet it was their intention, as it was the purpose of the combination, to directly and by means of such combination increase the price for which all contracts for the delivery of pipe within the territory above described should be made and the latter result was to be achieved by abolishing all competition between the parties to the combination."

Thereupon Justice Peckham said that "The direct and immediate result of the combination was therefore necessarily a restraint upon interstate commerce, in respect of articles manufactured by any of the parties to it, to be transported beyond the state in which they were made."

For these reasons, Justice Peckham expressed the conclusion of the Supreme Court to the effect that the contract of combination between the appellants constituted a mutual restraint of interstate commerce in cast-iron pipes, and in so doing violated the Sherman law.

The nine justices of the Supreme Court, when this Addyston case was decided by that tribunal in December, 1899, were the same men who had been the justices of that court when the Trans-Missouri case was decided there in March, 1897, except that Justice McKenna had taken the place in 1898 of the seat which had been occupied by Justice Field in 1897. Three of the four justices who dissented from the decision in the Trans-Missouri case still remained upon the bench, but they now concurred with Justice Peckham and all the other justices of the Supreme Court in the decision in the Addyston case. This concurrence in that decision by Justices White, Gray and Shiras indicates that their dissent in the Trans-Missouri case did not imply any assertion that the word "restraint" in Section 1 of the Sherman law is confined to extraneous restraint by a combination as a whole against other parties. For those three justices in the Addyston case, concurred in the opinion of all the other justices of the Supreme Court, that the purely mutual restraint of interstate commerce, which had been exercised by the cast-iron pipe combination upon its own members, constituted a violation of Section 1 of the Sherman law.

2. United States vs. Hopkins and others, 82 Fed. Rep. 529. This case was an action in equity, begun by the United States on December 31, 1896, in the United States Circuit Court for the District of Kansas, against the members of a voluntary association of three hundred persons, named the "Kansas City Live Stock Exchange." The members of this association were tenants of the Kansas City Stock Yards Company, which corporation owned the Kansas City Stock Yards, and which stock yards were located on both sides of the line between Missouri and Kansas, and partly in Kansas City, Missouri, and partly in Kansas City, Kansas.

The business of the members of the defendant association consisted in receiving, buying, selling and handling, as commission merchants, live stock received at the Kansas City Stock Yards from various states and territories and sold there for shipment to various other states. One rule of the association prohibited all dealings between members of the association and non-members thereof. Another rule fixed a minimum rate of commission to be charged by members of the association and prohibited the employment by any commission firm or corporation of more than three persons to travel and solicit business.

The bill of complaint was filed and prosecuted by W. C. Perry, United States District Attorney for the District of Kansas, on the theory that the articles of the association and the doing of its members in pursuance of those articles constituted a violation of the Sherman law. The answer of the defendants denied that their combination constituted either a restraint of interstate commerce or an attempt to monopolize interstate commerce, and denied that the business of the members of the Exchange constituted interstate commerce at all.

The case was decided in favor of the United States on September 20, 1897, by Judge Foster, who was then the United States District Judge for the District of Kansas. He held that the fact that the place of business of the defendants was located on both sides of a state line was immaterial. But he also held that the business of the defendant association thus located did include interstate commerce and that their conduct of that business constituted a restraint of interstate commerce.

An appeal was taken by the defendants from this decision to the United States Circuit Court of Appeals for the Eighth Circuit, which court certified on December 8, 1897, certain questions of law to the Supreme Court in pursuance of Section 6 of the judiciary act of Congress of March 3, 1891. And thereupon a writ of certiorari was issued by the Supreme Court to the Circuit Court of Appeals and operated to carry the whole case into that higher tribunal for final decision, without any intermediate decision by the Circuit Court of Appeals.

This Hopkins case was reached for argument in the Supreme Court in February, 1898, and was argued there orally and in print by several lawyers for the defendants and by Solicitor General Richards and one other lawyer for the United States. The Supreme Court, on October 24, 1898, reversed the decision of the Circuit Court, with directions to that tribunal to dismiss the bill, but Justice Harlan dissented from this decision and Justice McKenna took no part therein. 171 U. S. 579.

The decision of the Supreme Court in this case was delivered by Justice Peckham. That decision was to the effect that the doings of the defendants were all done in Kansas City and that the services they there rendered as commission merchants, acting between the sellers and owners of live stock, were local to that city and did not constitute interstate commerce, and that an agreement among the members of the association relating to the terms upon which they would render such local services, was not an agreement in restraint of interstate commerce.

3. United States vs. Anderson and others. This was an action in equity, which was begun in the United States Circuit Court for the Western District of Missouri in its western division, on June 7, 1897, against a considerable number of men, who were citizens of that district and were members of a voluntary association named the "Traders' Live Stock Exchange." The facts in this case were substantially like the facts in the Hopkins case, except that in this Anderson case the defendants were themselves purchasers of cattle in the Kansas City Stock Yards, while the defendants in the Hopkins case were only commission merchants who sold cattle upon commission as a compensation for their services.

The Circuit Court decided this case against the defendents without rendering a written opinion therein.

An appeal was taken by the defendants from this decision to the United States Circuit Court of Appeals for the Eighth Circuit from which tribunal the case was transferred without any decision to the Supreme Court of the United States by means of a certificate made in pursuance of Section 6 of the Judiciary act of March 3, 1891.

This Anderson case was reached for argument in the Supreme Court in February, 1898, and was argued there orally and in print on behalf of the appellants and defendants by another set of lawyers than those who, at about the same time, argued the Hopkins case for the defendants therein. The oral argument for the United States was made by John R. Walker, but the accompanying brief was also signed by Solicitor General Richards.

On October 24, 1898, the Supreme Court decided this case and reversed the decision of the Circuit Court, with direction to that tribunal to dismiss the bill; but Justice Harlan dissented from this decision and Justice McKenna took no part therein. 171 U. S. 604.

The decision of the Supreme Court in this case was also delivered by Justice Peckham. That opinion did not take any ground which required a decision of the question whether the defendants were engaged in interstate commerce, for that opinion found that the defendants were not engaged in restraining any commerce or in attempting to monopolize any within the meaning of the Sherman law, upon which the bill was based. The defendants' doings, which were complained of in the bill, consisted of their refusal to have any dealings relevant to live stock with any yard trader who was not a member of the Traders' Live Stock Exchange, or with anybody else who had dealt or were dealing with yard traders who were not members of the Traders' Live Stock Exchange.

The defendant association did no business itself and did not meddle with prices at which its members might buy or sell live stock. All yard traders had opportunities to become members of the Exchange and thus obtain all its advantages. The defendant association did not restrain such yard traders as declined to join that association, but only ignored them, and restrained its own members from not ignoring them. The Supreme Court recognized the possibility that, though such ignoring by the defendants of the outside yard traders might somewhat reduce the cattle trading business done by those men, it still left them free to deal with each other and with other parties who did not deal nor care to deal with the defendants. For these reasons it is to be gathered from the decision of the Supreme Court in this case that the meaning of the word "restraint" in Section 1 of the Sherman law is confined to such restraint as is extensive enough to be materially injurious to public or private welfare, and that the Sherman law, like other great statutes, is non-applicable to trifles.

4. United States vs. Coal Dealers' Association and others, 85 Fed. Rep. 252. This was an action in equity which was begun by the United States to obtain a dissolution of the Coal Dealers' Association of California, and to set aside an agreement between that association and the other defendants, relating to the sale of coal in San Francisco and violative of the Sherman law. The bill was filed in the United States Circuit Court for the Northern District of California on December 16, 1897, and the case was decided in favor of the United States on January 28, 1898, by Judge Morrow, one of the United States Circuit Judges for the Ninth Circuit. The case having been argued for the United States by H. S. Foote, United States District Attorney, and by Alfred L. Black, Special Assistant United States Attorney, and by eight lawyers for the defendants; Judge Morrow held that a preliminary restraining order which he had made without notice to the defendants on December 16, 1897, was justified by Section 4 of the Sherman law, under the circumstances sanctioned by the established usages of equity practice; and that the suit had been properly brought against the association and all its members by the service which had occurred of a proper subpœna upon the president of the association, and upon seventeen other members as representative of them all.

These two preliminary points being disposed of, Judge Morrow proceeded to decide the pivotal points in the case, which points are here summarized as follows:

The Sherman law is not limited to contracts and agreements such as were unlawful at common law.

The Sherman law prohibits all restraints on international or interstate commerce, and is not limited to such as are unfair and unreasonable in themselves and regardless of that law.

The clear and positive purpose of the Sherman law is that trade and commerce within the jurisdiction of the Federal Government shall be absolutely free, and no contract or combination will be tolerated that impedes or restricts their natural flow and volume.

The facts of the case against this coal dealers' association included the undeniable point that it was charge-

able with restraint of the coal trade, and with an attempt
to monopolize that trade in San Francisco; and with the
also undeniable point that the coal traded in by the association came from outside of California and was brought
into California by dealers and importers who had entered
into an agreement with the Coal Dealers' Association,
whereby the business of dealing in coal and its retail
prices in San Francisco were arbitrarily fixed. For these
reasons Judge Morrow held that the case before him
was substantially identical with the case of the United
States vs. Jellico Mountain Coal and Coke Company,
46 Fed. Rep. 432, which case is explained in Chapter IV
of this book. For this reason, and also as the result of
his own judicial judgment, Judge Morrow decided this
California case against the defendants. And for some
reason, which was perhaps the undeniable righteousness
of that decision, no appeal was ever taken therefrom.

5. United States vs. Chesapeake & Ohio Fuel Co.
and others, 105 Fed. Red. 93, and 115 Fed. Rep. 610.
This was an action in equity which was begun May 8,
1899, by the United States against the Chesapeake &
Ohio Fuel Company and fourteen other defendants, in
the Circuit Court of the United States for the Southern
District of Ohio, in its western division. The bill alleged that on December 15, 1897, the Chesapeake &
Ohio Fuel Company had made a contract with the other
defendants, who together constituted the Chesapeake &
Ohio Coal Association, and all of whom were miners
and shippers of coal, on the line of the Chesapeake &
Ohio Railway in West Virginia; and which contract went
into effect January 1, 1898, and which contract gave exclusive control of the output of the mines of the members of the coal association to the Fuel Company, and
also prohibited competition between the members of the
association; and also prohibited the Fuel Company from

handling any other coal than that of the association, and which contract fixed a minimum price, below which the Fuel Company was prohibited from selling coal in the Western market, and also fixed the settlement price between the Fuel Company and the association by a method of monthly averages. The fourteen coal mining defendants were not so numerous as other coal mining companies in the same part of West Virginia, and did not produce more than about half of the coal mined in that region; and what they did produce had to be sold in competition with much larger and more numerous coal mines in other regions.

Under these circumstances the defendants claimed that their contract and their doings thereunder, while it restrained competition among themselves, operated to enlarge competition as between themselves and other coal companies in the Western market; and that that enlargement of competition was much greater in amount than the partial restraint of competition among themselves, and that its resulting benefit to the public was much greater than any burden which could result to anybody.

This case was decided by Judge Thompson, who was then United States District Judge for the Southern District of Ohio, in the following terms:

"The policy of the law looks to competition as the best and safest method of securing these benefits, and not to combinations which restrain trade. It is opposed to the methods of combinations, and will not suffer competition to be destroyed under the pretense that the public will be better served by combination. In the exercise of the power of regulation conferred upon it by the Constitution, Congress has chosen competition, in preference to combination, as the best factor for the maintenance of the life and the promotion of the ends of interstate commerce, and has prohibited every contract, combination in the form of trust or otherwise, or conspiracy in restraint of trade or commerce among the several states or with foreign nations. The contract in question here and the combination of the defendants thereunder are in restraint of trade and commerce among the several states, and such trade has in fact been restrained in the performance of the contract; and the defendants and each of them, therefore, will be enjoined from selling or shipping under this contract coal into any other state than the state in which they reside, and the contract in so far as it affects interstate trade and commerce, is declared to be void and illegal, and the combination of the defendants thereunder will be dissolved."

An appeal to the Circuit Court of Appeals for the Sixth Circuit was taken from Judge Thompson's decision by the defendants in this case; and that appeal was heard by that court soon enough to be decided on April 8, 1902. At that time that court consisted of Judges Lurton, Day and Severens, who were then the Circuit Judges for the Sixth Circuit, but the first two of whom are now Associate Justices of the Supreme Court of the United States. The unanimous opinion of the three judges was delivered by Judge Day and ended in an affirmance of the decision of Judge Thompson, from which the appeal had been taken. The crucial points in the opinion which Judge Day delivered in this case were as follows:

"As we understand the decisions of the Supreme Court of the United States, the construction of the statute is no longer an open question."

"By the Constitution of the United States, Congress is given plenary power to regulate commerce between the states and with foreign nations. In the exercise of this power, Congress may prevent interference by the states with the freedom of interstate commerce, and may likewise prohibit individuals, by contract or otherwise, from impeding the free and untrammeled flow of such trade.

In the exercise of this right, Congress has seen fit to prohibit all contracts in restraint of trade. It has not left to the courts the consideration of the question whether such restraint is reasonable or unreasonable, or whether the contract would have been illegal at the common law or not. The act leaves for consideration by judicial authority no question of this character, but all contracts and combinations are declared illegal if in restraint of trade or commerce among the states."

"A contract or combination which interferes with the freedom of interstate commerce and hinders or prevents its free enjoyment, to the extent that it does so, restrains that commerce and is illegal. It was the policy of the common law to discourage monopolies, and to refuse to enforce contracts which had the effect to suppress competition. It was believed and declared by those who built up that system of jurisprudence that the public interests were best subserved when commerce and trade were left unfettered by combinations and agreements which had the effect to destroy competition in whole or in part. It was in the same spirit, and with the same end in view, that Congress passed the act under consideration, which is aimed to maintain interstate commerce upon the basis of free competition, and contracts which have the necessary tendency to restrain that freedom are within the condemnation of the law. The courts are not concerned with the policy of such a law. It is not for them to inquire whether it be true, as is often alleged, that this is a mistaken public policy, and combinations, in the reduction of the cost of production, cheapened transportation, and lowered cost to the consumer, have been productive of more good than evil to the public. The Constitution has delegated to Congress the right to control and regulate commerce between the states. In the exercise of this right, it has declared for that policy which shall keep competition free, and leave interstate commerce open to all, without the right to any to fetter it by contracts or combinations which shall put it under restraint."

"The statute is not limited to contracts or combinations which monopolize interstate commerce in any given commodity, but seeks to reach those which directly restrain or impair the freedom of interstate trade. The law reaches combinations which may fall short of complete control of a trade or business, and does not await the consolidation of many small combinations into the huge trust which shall control the production and sale of a commodity."

Having thus made the foregoing luminous exposition of the Sherman law, Judge Day applied that law to the facts of this Chesapeake Fuel case by saying: "We think this contract, within the meaning of the statute, is in restraint of interstate commerce and tends to create a monopoly." And thereupon Judge Day announced the affirmance by the Circuit Court of Appeals of Judge Thompson's decision, and that affirmance has long been final because, though it was ordered more than eight years ago, no appeal has ever been taken therefrom.

6. United States vs. Joint Traffic Association, 171 U. S. 505. This was an appeal to the Supreme Court from the adverse decisions which had been rendered by the Circuit Court for the Southern District of New York, and by the Circuit Court of Appeals for the Second Circuit, near the close of President Cleveland's administration, and which decisions are explained in Chapter V of this book. This appeal was argued in the Supreme Court in February, 1898, by Solicitor General Richards for the United States, and by James C. Carter, Edward J. Phelps and George F. Edmunds for the opposite side. And those three most eminent lawyers were also supported by printed arguments, presented by Lewis C. Ledyard, John G. Johnson, James A. Logan, Robert W. de Forrest and David Wilcox. At that time Solicitor General Richards was a young lawyer, only about forty years old, while his opponents included four most distinguished men among the older members of the Bar of the Supreme Court, and four other lawyers of high standing at that bar. The arguments of counsel on both sides were summarized by the reporter of the Supreme Court and printed on pages 511 to 558, inclusive, of Volume 171 of the United States Reports. It is not necessary to state the details of those arguments in this book; for the decision of the Supreme Court upon their respective characters was written by Justice Peckham, and conclusively sets forth the views of that tribunal upon the points discussed in those arguments. Those were not the unanimous views of all the justices of the time, but they were concurred in by the same five justices who had concurred in the decision of the Supreme Court in 1897 in the Trans-Missouri case, namely: Chief Justice Fuller, and Associate Justices Harlan, Brewer, Brown and Peckham. The dissenting justices in this Joint Traffic Association case were Justices Gray, Shiras and White; while Justice McKenna, who had succeeded to Justice Field since the Trans-Missouri case was decided, took no part in the decision of the Joint Traffic Association case.

In the first paragraph of the opinion of the court in this Joint Traffic Association case, Justice Peckham stated that the agreement upon which it was based was so similar to that in the Trans-Missouri case, as to suggest that a similar result should be reached in the two cases; but that the respondent's counsel had stated several reasons why they thought the decision in the Trans-Missouri case should not control the decision to be rendered in the Joint Traffic Association case. Those

reasons were four in number. The first two of those
reasons were based upon differences between the facts of
the two cases; which differences the Supreme Court
found to be immaterial by saying that "The natural and
direct effect of the two agreements is the same, viz., to
maintain prices at a higher level than would otherwise
prevail, and the differences between them are not sufficiently important or material to call for different judgments in the two cases on any such ground."

The third reason stated by respondents' counsel for
an opposite decision in the Joint Traffic Association case
from that which had been rendered in the Trans-
Missouri case, was to the effect that the Sherman law,
as construed in the Trans-Missouri case, was unconstitutional, as being in conflict with the Fifth Amendment to
the Constitution. And the fourth reason was to the
effect that the decision in the Trans-Missouri case was
quite plainly wrong, and that the consequences of that
error, if repeated, would be far reaching and disastrous
and clearly at war with justice and sound policy.

To support their third contention, the responednts'
counsel claimed that the Sherman law, as construed in
the Trans-Missouri case, is unconstitutional as being
contrary to the Fifth Amendment, which provides that
no person shall be deprived of liberty without due process of law, and also provides that private property shall
not be taken for public use without just compensation.

Justice Peckham stated that the last mentioned constitutional limitation was plainly irrelevant to the case.
Thereupon he said that as to the other limitation invoked by the respondents' counsel, they claimed that a
citizen is deprived of his liberty without due process of
law when, by a general statute, he is arbitrarily deprived of the right to make such contracts, as that involved in the Joint Traffic Association case.

In response to this contention, Justice Peckham wrote

an argument which is printed on pages 572 and 573 of Volume 171 of the United States Reports, and which concludes with the following paragraph:

"Notwithstanding the general liberty of contract which is possessed by the citizen under the Constitution, we find that there are many kinds of contracts which, while not in themselves immoral or *mala in se,* may yet be prohibited by the legislation of the states or, in certain cases, by Congress. The question comes back whether the statute under review is a legitimate exercise of the power of Congress over interstate commerce and a valid regulation thereof. The question is, for us, one of power only, and not of policy. We think the power exists in Congress, and that the statute is therefore valid."

To support their fourth contention, the respondents' counsel appealed to the Supreme Court to reverse its own decision in the Trans-Missouri case, because that decision was plainly erroneous, and had already created widespread alarm, and would, unless reversed, produce disasters to many combinations of parties engaged in interstate commerce.

In response to this entreaty, Justice Peckham said:

"There have heretofore been in effect two arguments of precisely the same questions now before the court, and the same arguments were addressed to us on both those occasions. The report of the Trans-Missouri case shows a dissenting opinion delivered in that case, and that opinion was concurred in by three other members of the court. That opinion, it will be seen, gives with great force and ability the arguments against the decision which were finally arrived at by the court. It was after a full discussion of the questions involved and with the knowledge of the views entertained by the minority, as expressed in the dissenting opinion, that the majority of the court came to the conclusion it did. Soon after the decision, a petition for a rehearing of the case was made, supported by a printed argument in its favor, and pressed with an earnestness and vigor and at a length which was certainly commensurate with the importance of the case. This court, with care and deliberation, and also with a full appreciation of their importance, again considered the questions involved in its former decision. A majority of the court once more arrived at the conclusion it had first announced. And now for the third time the same arguments are employed and the court is again asked to recant its former opinion, and to decide the same question in direct opposition to the conclusion arrived at in the Trans-Missouri case."

"While an erroneous decision might be in some cases properly reconsidered and overruled, yet it is clear that the first necessity is to convince the court that the decision was erroneous. It is scarcely to be assumed that such a result could be secured by the presentation for a third time of the same arguments, which had twice before been unsuccessfully urged upon the attention of the court. It is not a matter for surprise that we still are unable to see the error alleged to exist in our former decision, or to change our opinion regarding the questions therein involved."

At the end of his patient and elaborate review of what he called the most able arguments of the numerous counsel for the respondents, Justice Peckham announced the decision of the Supreme Court in the following sentence:

"An agreement of the nature of this one which directly and effectually stifles competition must be regarded under the statute as one in restraint of trade, notwithstanding there are possibilities that a restraint of trade may also follow competition that may be indulged in until the weaker roads are completely destroyed and the survivor thereafter raises his rates and maintains them."

The six cases which have thus far been explained in this chapter were all the cases which were brought or prosecuted by the United States for violation of the Sherman law during President McKinley's administration. Two of those cases were the Kansas City Stock Yards cases, and though both of them succeeded in the Circuit Courts in which they were brought, both of them failed in the Supreme Court of the United States. Two more of those cases were brought against coal combinations, and both of them were so emphatically sustained by the lower court, that neither of them was appealed to the Supreme Court. The other two cases were decided in favor of the United States by the Supreme Court, and the first of them had already been decided in favor of the United States by the Circuit Court of Appeals for the Sixth Circuit in an elaborate opinion delivered by Judge Taft. These two cases, against the industrial combination in the cast-iron pipe case and the railroad combination in the Joint Traffic Association case, respectively, embody the principal achievements of the McKinley administration toward enforcing the Sherman law.

Cases of litigation between private parties, relevant to the Sherman law, which occurred during McKinley's administration were eleven in number. And those litigations may now be explained in their order:

1. Gulf, Colorado & Santa Fé Railway Co. and others vs. Miami Steamship Co., 86 Fed. Rep. 407. This was an action in equity which was originally brought on February 12, 1898, in the United States Circuit Court for the Eastern District of Texas, by the Miami Steamship Company against three railway companies. The bill stated that the Miami Steamship Company and the Mallory Line of steamships were competitors, and the only

6

competitors in the business of water transportation between Galveston, Texas, and the port of New York
City; and that the defendant railroad companies had
been favoring the Mallory Line against the Miami Steamship Company, in respect of contracts and customs for
transporting freight over the land and over the water
in opposite directions from Galveston. The complainant contended that this conduct was contrary to the common law and to certain statutes of Texas, and to the
United States Interstate Commerce Law of February 4,
1887, as amended March 2, 1889, and was also contrary
to the Sherman law. The judge of the Circuit Court,
March 2, 1898, made a decree in favor of the complainant, which decree ordered a preliminary injunction to
stop the said doings of the railroad companies until the
final hearing of the case; but that decree was not accompanied by an opinion, stating on which law it was based.

Thereupon the defendant railroad companies appealed
from that decree to the Circuit Court of Appeals for the
Fifth Circuit, and on March 29, 1898, that court, when
held by Circuit Judges Pardee and McCormick, and District Judge Swayne, reversed the decree of the Circuit
Court and dissolved the injunction. This reversal, so
for as it related to the Sherman law, was based upon the
plain proposition that that law does not authorize any
other party than the United States to maintain a bill in
equity for an injunction against any party claimed to
have violated that law.

2. Southern Indiana Express Co. vs. United States
Express Co. and others, 88 Fed. Rep. 659. This was a
bill in equity, which was filed in the United States Circuit Court for the District of Indiana, by one express
company against three others, alleging that the defendants had been guilty of combined conduct, which was
contrary to the common law, and to the Interstate Com-

merce law, and to the Sherman law, and to one of the statutes of Indiana. The case was heard on demurrer on August 4, 1898, by Judge Baker, who was then District Judge for the District of Indiana. He decided that the question whether the contract complained of violated the Sherman law, could not be investigated in the case, because that law does not authorize any party except the United States to bring an action in equity for its enforcement.

3. Cravens vs. Carter-Crume Company, 92 Fed. Rep. 479. This was originally an action at law, begun in the Circuit Court of the United States for the Southern District of Ohio. The object of the action was to enforce a certain contract. Upon the trial of the case, the judge of the circuit court directed the jury to find a verdict for the defendant, and that being done, that judge entered a judgment for the defendant. Thereupon the plaintiff took the case to the Circuit Court of Appeals for the Sixth Circuit by means of a writ of error, and in pursuance of the proper practice in such cases, the whole case was thereby opened to the judgment of that court, which court at that time consisted of Judges Lurton, Severens and Clark. Judge Severens delivered the opinion of the court, affirming the judgment of the circuit court, on the ground that the contract sought to be enforced was contrary to the common law and also to the Sherman law, and on the further ground that no court of justice will enforce such a contract.

The significance of this case therefore resides in the character of the contract which was found to be illegal. That illegality resulted from the fact that that contract was made in pursuance of a combination of manufacturers of woodenware, which was formed for the purpose of restricting the production of wooden dishes and keeping up the price thereof, and which contract provided that the plaintiff should participate in the doings of the combination in the matter of restricting the production and maintaining the prices of wooden dishes throughout the country.

4. Block and others vs. Standard Distilling and Distributing Company, 95 Fed. Rep. 979. This was an action in equity which was decided on demurrer on July 31, 1899, by Judge Thompson in the United States Circuit Court for the Southern District of Ohio. It was an attempt to enforce Section 7 of the Sherman law by an action in equity, and moreover in the same action, with an attempt to enforce a trademark right. But Judge Thompson decided that Section 7 of the Sherman law authorizes only a recovery of threefold damages with costs and attorney's fee, and that such a recovery cannot be had in any action in equity, but only in an action at law.

5. Lowry and others vs. Tile, Mantel and Grate Association of California and others, 98 Fed. Rep. 817. This was an action at law, based on Section 7 of the Sherman law, and brought to recover damages for injuries inflicted by the defendant association upon the complainants. The defendants demurred to the complaint on the alleged ground that it did not state such facts as amounted to a violation of the Sherman law. That question was argued on that demurrer before Circuit Judge Morrow, and he decided on November 13, 1899, that the facts stated in the complaint did constitute a violation of the Sherman law. Those facts were as follows: The Tile, Mantel and Grate Association of California was an unincorporated organization composed of wholesale dealers in tiles, mantels and grates, which wholesale dealers were the other defendants in the case, and were conducting their tile, mantel and grate business in the different states wherein they were located. The defendants, with intent to form a contract, trust and conspiracy in restraint of trade and commerce between six different states, to the extent of the tiles, grates and mantels that could be used in California in the erection of buildings, did conspire to confine that business to the members of the defendant association, by refusing to sell or deliver tiles, grates or mantles to any other party in California, and did conspire to raise the prices of those articles in the California market. Previous to this combination, the plaintiffs were making an annual profit of about five thousand dollars from their established business of selling tiles, mantels and grates; but after that organization, the plaintiffs were unable to purchase tiles, mantels or grates from any of the defendants. This conduct and combination of the defendants had damaged the plaintiffs to the claimed extent of $10,000.

Judge Morrow decided that the complaint in making these statements stated a cause of action under the Sherman law, and he supported that decision by citing the Jellico Mountain Coal case in 46 Fed. Rep. 432, and the Coal Dealers' Association case in 85 Fed. Rep. 252, and the Addyston case, in 85 Fed. Rep. 279.

This Lowry case was tried by Judge Morrow with a jury in December, 1900, and that trial resulted in a verdict in favor of the plaintiffs, which fixed their damages at $500, 106 Fed. Rep. 38. The charge which Judge Morrow gave to the jury at that trial included an instruction, that the stated and proved conduct of the defendants constituted a contract and combination in restraint of trade and commerce, and an attempt to monopolize a part of the trade and commerce between dealers in tiles in San Francisco and manufacturers of such tiles in Eastern states, and thus constituted a violation of the Sherman law.

That charge left nothing to the jury to consider except

the question of damages, and on that question the judge told the jury that its verdict must be limited to the actual damages which the evidence showed the plaintiffs had sustained by reason of the defendant's violation of the Sherman law; and that it would be the duty of the court to render a judgment for three times the amount of those actual damages. The judge also charged the jury that "The plaintiffs in an action of this kind are not permitted to claim damage to their business by reason of an association contrary to the statute, where it was within their own power, in the exercise of reasonable diligence to avert any such damage."

6. Union Sewer Pipe Co. vs. Connolly, 99 Fed. Rep. 354, and 184 U. S. 540. This was an action at law which was decided in the United States Circuit Court for the Northern District of Illinois, in its northern division, of January 29, 1900, by Judge Kohlsaat, who was then United States District Judge for that district. The object of the action was to recover payment on certain promissory notes which had been given by the defendant for sewer pipe sold to him by the plaintiff. The defendant interposed three defenses, which were based upon the theory that the plaintiff was a trust or combination, organized for the express purpose of restraining state and interstate trade, contrary to the common law, and also contrary to the Sherman law, and also violative of an Illinois statute of July 1, 1893.

Judge Kohlsaat overruled the first defense on the ground that "The fact that one party to a contract is engaged in illegal acts will not, at common law, avail the other party as a defense to the enforcement of a contract, in itself legal." And he held that the Sherman law was no defense to the action, because the action was based upon a contract which was not contrary to that law. And he held that though the Illinois statute of

July 1, 1893, did provide in terms for such a defense in such a case; that statute was unconstitutional, because it expressly exempted from its operation all agricultural products and all live stock while in the hands of the producer or raiser. Judge Kohlsaat held that this exemption of those who produce or raise agricultural products or live stock from the provisions of a statute, which by its terms was binding on every other person in Illinois, was violative of the Fourteenth Amendment to the Constitution of the United States, in that it denied the equal protection of the laws to many persons within the jurisdiction of Illinois. And he held that the statute of Illinois was in contravention of Section 22 of Article 4 of the Constitution of Illinois, in that it was a case of special legislation, where a general law could have been made applicable.

This case was taken to the Supreme Court of the United States by means of a writ of error; and on March 10, 1902, Justice Harlan delivered the opinion of that court, holding that the decision of Judge Kohlsaat was right in all respects, including that part which held that the fact that one party to a contract is engaged in an illegal business, does not deprive him of the right to enforce in court a legal contract which he may make independent of that illegal business or even collateral thereto.

7. City of Atlanta vs. Chattanooga Foundry & Pipe Co., 101 Fed. Rep. 900. This case, and its companion case of Manion & Co. vs. the same defendant, were actions at law brought to recover damages under Section 7 of the Sherman law. The defendant corporation had been one of the defendants in the Addyston case, which case had resulted, in December, 1899, in a decision of the Supreme Court of the United States to the effect that those defendants comprised a combination engaged

in restraint of interstate commerce in cast-iron pipes.
These two cases against the Chattanooga Foundry &
Pipe Company were thereupon brought in the United
States Court for the Eastern District of Tennessee, and
were decided in that tribunal on May 5, 1900, by Judge
Clark, who was then the United States District Judge
for that district. The declarations in the two cases
stated that the plaintiffs therein had purchased large
quantities of cast-iron pipe from the defendant at unfair
and exorbitant prices, which the defendant had been
enabled by the Addyston combination to extort. Those
declarations therefore prayed judgments for triple damages and costs and attorneys' fees, and claimed that the
specific damages which should thus be multiplied by
three should be ascertained by deducting what would
have been a just and fair price for purchased cast-
iron pipe, from the exorbitant and unfair price which
had been extorted by the defendant and paid by the
plaintiffs, respectively.

The defendants defended by interposing a Tennessee
statute of limitations, which provided that no action at
law for injuries to real or personal property could be
brought in the courts of that state more than three years
after the injuries occurred. The plaintiffs demurred to
this defense on the ground that the Tennessee Statute of
Limitations was not applicable to an action based on the
Sherman law and brought in a United States court. This
demurrer raised a very interesting combination of questions of law, the statements and arguments on the two
sides of which logically ran as follows:

The defendant claimed that the Tennessee Statute of
Limitations was applicable to the case, in pursuance of
Section 721 of the Revised Statutes of the United States,
which section provides that "The laws of the several
states, except where the Constitution, treaties, or stat-

utes of the United States otherwise require or provide, shall be regarded as rules of decision in trials at common law, in the courts of the United States in cases where they apply."

The plaintiffs responded that Section 721 of the United States Revised Statutes did not operate to make the Tennessee Statute of Limitations a rule of decision in any case based upon Section 7 of the Sherman law; because there was a statute of the United States that did otherwise require or provide for all such actions. That statute was Section 1047 of the Revised Statutes of the United States, which section provides that no suit or prosecution for any penalty or forfeiture accruing under the laws of the United States shall be maintained, unless it is commenced within five years from the time when the penalty or forfeiture accrues.

The defendant rejoined that Section 1047 of the Revised Statutes did not contain any provision or requirement relevant to Section 7 of the Sherman law, or to any suit thereunder, because that section did not provide for any penalty or forfeiture, but only for recovery of exemplary damages. Judge Clark decided that the defendant's argument on this issue was the true argument, and that the Tennessee Statute of Limitations was applicable to the suit under Section 7 of the Sherman law.

The corresponding Statutes of Limitations in many of the states allow more than three years, and in some states as many as six years in which to begin suits for injuries to property committed without violence. But until Congress enacts a special statute of limitations for application to suits brought under Section 7 of the Sherman law, every such suit will be subject to whatever statute of limitations relevant to such suits is in force in the state wherein the district is located in which such a suit is brought.

8. Gibbs vs. McNeeley and others, 102 Fed. Rep. 594. This was an action at law to recover damages under Section 7 of the Sherman law. The case was decided in the United States Circuit Court for the District of Washington in its Western division, on June 8, 1900, by Judge Hanford, the United States District Judge for that district. The complaint stated that the plaintiff was formerly engaged in business at Tacoma, as a buyer and exporter of red cedar shingles, and that the defendants and other persons, firms and corporations mentioned in the complaint, were manufacturers of such shingles, and had formed and constituted an unincorporated association to suppress competition in the business of furnishing such shingles to dealers therein, and that that combination was violative of the Sherman law.

Judge Hanford decided that those facts did not constitute a cause of action, because they did not include the point that damage had resulted to the plaintiff therefrom.

For a second cause of action the complaint stated that the defendant combination had advanced the prices of red cedar shingles, and had restrained all its members from selling such shingles below that advanced price; and that thereupon the plaintiff's customers had refused to buy shingles from him at the advanced prices, which refusal had caused him damage in the loss of trade to the amount of $1,200. For a third cause of action the complaint stated that the defendant combination had caused all its shingle mills to suspend work for sixty days for the purpose of preventing an oversupply of shingles, and that this reduction in quantity caused the plaintiff to sustain damages by loss of trade to the amount of $1,000.

Judge Hanford decided that this second and this third cause of action were both unfounded in the Sherman law, because they both related to transactions confined to the

State of Washington, and had no direct relation to interstate commerce, and he based that decision upon the decision of the Supreme Court in the Knight case, which is reported in Volume 156 of the United States Reports. Judge Hanford also took occasion to commend that portion of the defendants' conduct upon which these two alleged causes of action were based; because that conduct tended to conserve the cedar forests in the State of Washington.

The fourth and last cause of action stated by the plaintiff in his complaint was that the defendants and the other members of the association, with intent to injure the plaintiff and destroy his business, at a meeting of the central committee of the association, had adopted certain resolutions which were false and defamatory, concerning the plaintiff and the plaintiff's business as a dealer in shingles, which resolutions had been printed and distributed through the United States mails by the association to all the manufacturers of shingles in the State of Washington, and to various retail and wholesale dealers in the United States and in Canada, including customers of the plaintiff, and had been sent to a number of newspapers and trade journals having a circulation among the plaintiff's customers; and the complaint stated that this combined conduct of the defendants had cast odium and discredit upon the plaintiff, and had operated to totally destroy his business, and had thus damaged him to the amount of $15,000.

Judge Hanford decided that this fourth cause of action was well founded, because the actions of the defendants in adopting and circulating the resolution constituted an agreement on their part to assail the character of a man engaged in interstate commerce, for the purpose of crippling him as a competitor in that business. On that point Judge Hanford said: "By annihilating a man of experience and skill in a particular branch of commerce, the restraint upon commerce is quite as effectual as would be any contract binding him to abstain from competition."

This Gibbs case, nearly a year after Judge Hanford's decision, and in March, 1901, was tried by Judge Bellinger and a jury, the circuit court at that time being temporarily held by that judge, though he was the United States District Judge for the District of Oregon, and not for the District of Washington. He directed the jury to find a verdict for the defendants on that fourth cause of action which Judge Hanford had sustained. 107 Fed. Rep. 210. This direction was partly based upon the fact that the evidence did not fully sustain the statements of the complaint on that subject, and partly upon the opinion of Judge Bellinger that the decision of Judge Hanford had been wrong in holding that the complaint in respect of that fourth cause of action, if true in point of fact, would have been sound in point of law. For Judge Bellinger held that even if it had been true in point of fact, it would not have been sound in point of law, inasmuch as what it alleged was a libel upon a man, and not an attempt to restrain or monopolize interstate trade or commerce.

9. Otis Elevator Co. vs. Griger and others, 107 Fed. Rep. 131. This was an action in equity in the United States Circuit Court for the District of Kentucky, based on alleged infringement of certain letters patent for inventions. The defendants' answer stated that the plaintiff was a corporation organized for the purpose of holding the legal title to those patents, and to other elevator patents, for the purpose of controlling the sales and enhancing the prices of the apparatus covered thereby, without itself engaging in the manufacture and sale of such apparatus; and that those facts constituted a violation of the Sherman law, and thereby disentitled the complainant corporation to maintain any action for any infringement of those patents.

Judge Evans, then the United States District Judge for the District of Kentucky, on March 30, 1901, rendered the opinion of the court on this point, which opinion was to the effect that the Sherman law does not authorize a mere infringer of letters patent of the United States to escape the consequences of his infringement, on the ground that the complainant may have violated that law, in acquiring and managing the patents infringed.

10.   Metcalf vs. American School Furniture Co. and others, 108 Fed. Rep. 909.   This was an action in equity in the United States Circuit Court for the Western District of New York.   It was a multifarious attempt to enforce Section 7 of the Sherman law by means of an action in equity, which was also devoted to an attempt to seek equitable relief in respect of certain complicated corporation affairs and doings, which were disconnected with the Sherman law.   The case was argued before Judge Hazel, United States District Judge for the Western District of New York, upon a motion for a temporary injunction, and upon demurrers to the bill of complaint.   On May 13, 1901, he decided that Section 7 of the Sherman law cannot be enforced by an action in equity, but only by an action at law; and that the damages recoverable under that section cannot be recovered in an action in equity, which is mainly devoted to some subject within equity jurisdiction, on any such ground as that such damages are incidental to the demand for equitable relief.

11.   Delaware, Lackawanna & Western Railroad Co. vs. Frank and others, 110 Fed. Rep. 689.   This was an action in equity, brought in 1901, in the United States Circuit Court for the Western District of New York, and was decided in that tribunal by Judge Hazel on August 26, 1901. The bill of complaint stated that in pursuance of a request which had been presented to the railroad company by the officers of the Pan-American Exposition, that complainant and other railroad companies connecting with it, had caused to be sold at its various stations special tickets for round trips and excursions from other places to Buffalo, New York, at greatly reduced prices; and that such tickets were limited on their faces to the particular persons purchasing them from the railroad company, and were also limited to a specified number of days wherein they could be used; and the bill also stated that the defendants were ticket brokers in Buffalo, and had in many instances purchased the return portions of such excursion tickets from the original purchasers and had sold the same to other persons, who by falsely impersonating the original purchasers and forging the names of such purchasers upon such tickets, were enabled to use them for transportation over the complainant railroad. The bill also stated that the defendants in promoting this fraudulent scheme. instructed purchasers of return tickets from them how to impersonate the original purchasers so as to escape detection.

Judge Hazel decided that the bill of complaint stated a proper case for equitable relief. But he also decided that the complainant was proved in the evidence to be a party to a combination of nine railroad corporations which were engaged in pooling railroad rates, and in fixing fares for railroad transportation in order to avoid mutual competition between those nine railroad companies, and that the special Pan-American tickets referred to in the bill of complaint had been issued in pursuance of that combination, and which combination was known as the Trunk Line Association. In view of these facts, Judge Hazel stated that the complainant appeared to be guilty of violating Section 1 of the Sherman law, in what it had done with those Pan-American excursion tickets, and that that evil practice was the very practice which the bill asked the court to protect from the doings of the defendant. The case presented was that of one law breaker praying a court of equity to prevent other law breakers from fraudulently interfering with the law-breaking business of the complainant. For these reasons, Judge Hazel held that the complainant was out of place in a court of equity, having presumed to enter with unclean hands.

The eleven litigations relevant to the Sherman law, between private parties which occurred during McKinley's administration, included eight cases in which that law was invoked in vain, and two cases in which it was successfully invoked by the defendants, and only one case in which it was successfully invoked by a plaintiff or complainant as a means of remedying a wrong which had been inflicted by the defendants in violation of that law.

CHAPTER VII.

Chapters IV, V and VI of this book are devoted to stating concise and substantially complete accounts of all the litigations relevant to the Sherman law, which were adjudicated in the United States during the eleven years, two months and twelve days which passed between the approval of that law by President Harrison on July 2, 1890, and the end of the administration of President McKinley, on September 14, 1901. This chapter is devoted to a classified review of those litigations, and to an investigation of the question what practical results followed therefrom, prior to Roosevelt's administration.

Those litigations occurred in precisely forty different cases, eighteen of which were brought and prosecuted by the United States, and eighteen of which were brought and prosecuted by private parties, for alleged violations of the Sherman law by other private parties, and four of which were defended by private parties on the ground that the Sherman law disentitled the plaintiffs in those four cases to recover judgments therein.

Among those four cases the Sherman law defense was successful in three, and was unsuccessful in only one. In the three cases, that defense succeeded on the ground that the complainants or petitioners in those cases were asking the courts to help them to gather the fruits of their violations of the Sherman law, which those courts refused to do. The one unsuccessful defense was made in a case in which the defendant sought to avoid paying a promissory note, which had been given by the defendant to the plaintiff for sewer pipe sold to him. That defense was overruled on the ground that the sale of the sewer pipe was legal, although the plaintiff may have been a party to a combination of sewer pipe manufacturers and interstate dealers, and though that combination may have been violative of the Sherman law.

Among the eighteen cases which were brought and prosecuted by private parties for alleged violations of the Sherman law, only two succeeded, while sixteen failed. One of those which succeeded was the Phelan case, wherein the success consisted in an order made by Judge Taft in the United States Circuit Court for the Southern District of Ohio, that Frank W. Phelan be confined in the County Jail of Warren County, Ohio, for six months, for contempt of court, which had consisted in his violation of an injunction which had been issued by Judge Taft in the Thomas case, and which commanded those to whom it was directed to abstain from participating in a railroad strike, which strike Judge Taft held to be a violation of the Sherman law. The other successful case among these eighteen was the Lowry case in the United States Circuit Court for the Northern District of California. The success in that case consisted in a recovery of a verdict for $500 damages, and a judgment for three times this amount, plus an attorney's fee of $750, in pursuance of Section 7 of the Sherman law.

The sixteen unsuccessful cases which were brought by private parties for alleged violations of the Sherman law by other private parties failed for a considerable variety of reasons, which are stated in detail in those of the foregoing chapters which explain those sixteen cases respectively. Most of those failures resulted from errors committed by the attorneys who prosecuted those cases, respectively, while none of them resulted from any weakness or ambiguity in the Sherman law.

Among the eighteen cases which were brought and prosecuted by the United States for alleged violation of the Sherman law prior to Roosevelt's administration, ten were successful and eight were defeated. Two of the eight cases which failed were the Kansas City Stock Yard cases; and they ought to have failed, for the defendants were not shown therein to have violated the Sherman law in any way. Another of the eight cases was decided adversely to the United States, because the judge who decided it held the opinion that the word "restraint," in Section 1 of the Sherman law, should be construed to signify extraneous restraint; whereas the only "restraint" of interstate commerce with which the defendants in that case were chargeable was purely mutual restraint. This case was decided in 1892, and long before any of those Supreme Court decisions were rendered which construed the word "restraint" to include mutual restraint among the members of a combination engaged in interstate commerce. Another of the eighteen cases failed because the jury with whom it was tried could not agree what verdict to render. And another one failed because it was brought in Utah when Utah was a territory, and for a technical reason, quite disconnected with the Sherman law, could not be maintained after Utah became a state.

The remaining three cases which failed were the cases against the "Whiskey Trust," and the Cash Register Company, and the "Sugar Trust," respectively, and which cases are designated in the reports as United States vs. Greenhut and others; United States vs. Patterson and others, and United States vs. E. C. Knight Company and others, respectively. Whenever those three cases are thoroughly examined and adequately understood by able and disinterested lawyers, with a view to ascertain why they were decided against the United States, those lawyers will necessarily decide in their own minds that each and all of them were lost because they were not brought and prosecuted with adequate professional ability by the respective district attorneys who brought them and prosecuted them. No escape from this conclusion can be found, except on the theory that those district attorneys did not wish to win those cases, and therefore did not bring them and did not prosecute them in good faith. Therefore their failure must be ascribed to want of exercise of adequate professional ability. This view does not imply any criticism of any of the courts which decided any of those three cases; for those courts necessarily decided those cases upon the records of pleadings and evidence therein, and not upon the basis of any fact or facts which might have been pleaded and proved, but were not pleaded, nor otherwise embodied in the respective records.

The ten successful cases which were brought and prosecuted by the United States for alleged violation of the Sherman law, prior to Roosevelt's administration, were of four classes. The most numerous class comprised four labor strike cases, in each of which an injunction was prayed for and was granted, to restrain combinations of laborers from interfering with interstate commerce. Another class comprised three combinations of coal miners and coal dealers, which had been restraining interstate commerce in pursuance of certain contracts made between them for that purpose. Another class comprised the two railroad association cases, namely, the Trans-Missouri case and the Joint Traffic Association case. The remaining one of the ten cases was the Addyston case against the cast-iron pipe combination, which had been restraining interstate commerce in pursuance of a special contract made bteween them, which had that operation.

The practical effect of the four successful labor strike cases was very great and very important, in that the decisions of the courts in those cases were so clear and so comprehensive, and so evidently just, that they have long been generally acquiesced in by labor organizations.

The practical effect of the three coal combination cases was to suppress those three combinations; and they may have had some deterring effect to prevent other coal combinations from being formed or maintained. But it is not generally known that the decisions in those cases ever had any effect to prevent any of the railroad companies who are engaged in transporting anthracite coal from Pennsylvania into other states, or any of the coal companies which are managed by any of those railroad companies, from organizing and maintaining combinations in restraint of interstate commerce in anthracite coal.

The practical effect of the decisions of the Supreme Court in the two railroad association cases was unimportant to the public. For the members of those railroad associations, and all other railroad companies, who attempted so to do, were soon able to make new arrangements for accomplishing the same results which those railroad associations had been organized to accomplish.

The practical effect of the decision of the Supreme Court in the Addyston case was to suppress the combination of cast-iron pipe manufacturers and sellers which was condemned in that case. But other industrial corporations who wished to combine for purposes similar to those of that combination were soon guided by their lawyers into other forms of combination, which were still more efficient methods of suppressing competition between them.

This review of the history of the Sherman law litigation prior to Roosevelt's administration shows that during
the eleven years two months and twelve days in which
that law had then been upon the statute books, it was
not used, or even efficiently attempted to be used, to
suppress any of those combinations in restraint of interstate or international commerce, at which it was primarily and particularly aimed by the Congress which
enacted it. Those were the great "trusts" or other plans
of placing the power and property of many corporations
under the government of a few men for the primary
purpose of suppressing all mutual competition between
those corporations, and for the secondary purpose of
restraining all extraneous competition of other parties
with the corporations thus combined.

It was about midway of that period of eleven years
two months and twelve days that the House of Representatives, on January 7, 1896, passed a resolution re-
questing the Attorney General to report what steps, if
any, had been taken by the Department of Justice to
enforce the Sherman law. The passage of that resolution indicates that the House of Representatives was
under the impression that the Sherman law had been
neglected by the Department of Justice during the nearly
six years which had then passed since its enactment.

In response to this resolution, and on February 8,
1896, Judson Harmon, who was then Attorney General,
sent a report to the House of Representatives, in which
all that he said, in response to the above inquiry, was in
the two following sentences, namely: "Two actions are
now pending, based partly or wholly on alleged violations of what is known as the Sherman act. They both
relate to agreements among interstate carriers."

The two actions to which Attorney General Harmon
referred must have been the Trans-Missouri case and the

Joint Traffic Association case, neither of which had yet been argued in the Supreme Court.

The House resolution of Janury 7, 1896, also asked the Attorney General what further legislation, if any, was needed, in his opinion, to protect the people against trusts, combinations and conspiracies in restraint of trade and commerce. In response to this request, Attorney General Harmon suggested that "Congress may make it unlawful to ship from one state to another, in carrying out or attempting to carry out, the designs of such organizations, articles produced, owned or controlled by them or any of their members or agents," and that "The law should contain a provision, like that of the interstate commerce law, to prevent the refusal of witnesses to answer on the ground of self-incrimination," and that "The purchase or combination, in any form, of enterprises in different states, which were competitive before such purchase or combination, should be prima facie evidence of an attempt to monopolize," and that "If the Department of Justice is to conduct investigations of alleged violations of the present law, or of the law as it may be amended, it must be provided with a liberal appropriation and a force properly selected and organized."

Congress never has enacted into law any of the four suggestions thus made by Attorney General Harmon. The first and third of those suggestions were perhaps too drastic to be enacted in 1896, when so little had been attempted in the direction of enforcing the Sherman law, without such assistances. The second suggestion was quite unnecessary in respect of any prosecutions of the great trusts and combinations, because the facts in those cases are mainly provable by documentary evidence; and so far as they are not thus provable, they are provable by the testimony of witnesses without any self-incrimination of those witnesses. The fourth suggestion relates to the degree with which the Department of Justice can enforce the Sherman law; and the absence of a special organization of lawyers and investigators in that department, devoted to the sole purpose of enforcing the Sherman law, was not a good reason for the Attorney General in February, 1896, being engaged in doing nothing whatever in that direction, except waiting for two cases which had already been decided by the circuit courts and the circuit courts of appeals to be reached for argument in the Supreme Court. The fact undoubtedly is, that the lawyers and investigators who are subordinate to the Attorney General in the Department of Justice, while they have always included a few earnest men, have also included a number of men whose work was much less efficient, and much less continuous than it should have been.

Attorney General McKenna was in charge of the Department of Justice less than one year, and therefore rendered but one annual report to Congress of the doings of that department. That report was made November 30, 1897; and what it said on the subject of the Sherman law was said in the following paragraph:

"The Supreme Court rendered on the 22d of March last a very important decision under the act of Congress of July 2, 1890, United States vs. Trans-Missouri Freight Association (166 U. S., 290). The decisions of the lower courts were reversed, and it was held that that act applies to railroad companies as well as others; that it applies to all contracts in restraint of trade, and not merely to contracts making unreasonable restraints; that the effect in restraining trade, rather than the purpose of the contract is to be inquired into; and that a contract, legal when made, became illegal upon the passage of that act, so that acts done thereafter were done in violation of it. An injunction prohibiting the continuance of the association, or of any similar arrangement was upheld.

The combination was of eighteen railways west of the Missouri River and was for the purpose of maintaining rates of freight. The case was argued in person by Attorney General Harmon."

This luminous report of the character of the decision of the Supreme Court in the Trans-Missouri case was not accompanied by any criticism of the Sherman law, nor by any complaint of want of means in the Department of Justice for its enforcement; and it plainly shows that Attorney General McKenna was satisfied that the Sherman law was a strong enactment, which required only to be earnestly used to be made comprehensively effective.

The next report from the Department of Justice relevant to the Sherman law was the annual report of Attorney General Griggs, of November 30, 1898. That report said nothing about that law except to give to Congress a clear account of the Joint Traffic Association case, which had then lately been decided by the Supreme Court. Attorney General Griggs ended that account of that case by saying that it holds "That Congress in dealing with interstate commerce, and in the course of regulating it in the case of railroad corporations, has the power to say that no contract or combination shall be legal which shall restrain trade and commerce by shutting out the operation of the general law of competition." This interpretation by Attorney General Griggs of the decision of the Supreme Court in the Joint Traffic Association case shows that he also, like Attorney General McKenna, understood the Sherman law to be a strong and comprehensive statute.

The annual report from the Department of Justice, which was made November 30, 1899, was also made by Attorney General Griggs. The pages of that report which related to the Sherman law were confined to summaries of the Trans-Missouri case and the Joint Traffic Association case, and the two Kansas City Stock Yards cases. The only noteworthy portions of those summaries now are the sentences in which Attorney General Griggs informed Congress that the Supreme Court held in the Trans-Missouri case, that the Sherman law applies to railroads, and that it prohibits all agreements in restraint of interstate trade or commerce, whether the restraint be reasonable or unreasonable; and that that court affirmed both those propositions in the Joint Traffic Association case, and additionally held that the Sherman law is valid and constitutional, and that Congress has the power to enact that a contract or combination is illegal, which restrains commerce among the several states by shutting out the operation of the general law of competition.

Thus again in his second annual report Attorney General Griggs indicated his opinion that the Sherman law required no amendment; for while explaining how constitutional, valid and effective the Supreme Court had held that law to be, he did not suggest that it required any amendment, or could be improved by any change.

The third and last annual report of Attorney General Griggs was made near the end of the nineteenth century, on November 30, 1900. What that report contained relevant to the Sherman law was an account of the Addyston case, which had been decided by the Supreme Court nearly a year before. The most noteworthy part of that account consisted in saying that the Supreme Court in that case held that Congress may prohibit the performance of any agreement between individuals or corporations where the natural and direct effect of it is to regulate or restrain interstate commerce; and that the court also held that any agreement or combination which directly restrains not only the manufacture, but also the sale of a commodity within the several states comes within the anti-trust law.

Thus a third time in his third annual report, Attorney General Griggs represented the Sherman law as good and strong, and did not say or intimate that he knew of any deficiency or error therein.

Nine months and a half after that last annual report of Attorney General Griggs, the administration of President McKinley ended on September 14, 1901. Before proceeding to trace the history of the Sherman law through the long administration of the strenuous President, who succeeded McKinley, it seems suitable to ascertain and state what was being done by the Department of Justice toward enforcing that law during the last months of McKinley's administration.

Such an ascertainment has been made in the course of the extensive researches relevant to the whole history of the Sherman law, which had to be made in order to render possible such a book as this. But the result of that ascertainment was remarkably small, because it disclosed the fact that when McKinley died, the Department of Justice had not begun any suit to enforce the Sherman law at any time since May 8, 1899, when the bill was filed in the United States Circuit Court for the Southern District of Ohio, in the Chesapeake and Ohio Fuel case; and that that was the only case of the kind which was pending in any court during the last year before the end of McKinley's administration; and that nothing was done during that year in that case, except to wait for it to be reached for argument in the Circuit Court of Appeals for the Sixth Circuit, in pursuance of an appeal which was taken by the defendants in the year 1900, from the adverse decision of the United States Circuit Court for the Southern District of Ohio.

It was during the last part of McKinley's administration that hundreds of "holding" companies were organized as state corporations, the purpose of each of which organizations was to place the property and power of a number of theretofore competing corporations under the control of a few men, or of one man, in order to suppress all mutual future competition between those corporations, and also to restrain all future extraneous competition by other parties with any of the combined corporations. More of those holding companies were incorporated in New Jersey than in any other state; but some such companies were then or afterward incorporated in each state and territory of the Union, except possibly Idaho, Nevada, Oregon, Utah and Washington. The greatest of all the holding companies which were organized during the latter part of McKinley's administration, and indeed the greatest holding company which was ever organized, is the United States Steel Corporation, which was organized in New Jersey in February, 1901, with a capital of $1,100,000,000, for the purpose of acquiring and holding the stock and subjecting the business of many previously competing corporations, to the management of a few men who were to be officers or directors of the United States Steel Corporation. The general plan of this organization consisted in the purchase by the United States Steel Corporation, of more than half of the stock of each of the many corporations to be combined, and the payment for those stocks thus purchased by issuing to the sellers such numbers of shares of the stock of the United States Steel Corporation as might be agreed upon between those sellers and those promoters of the United States Steel Corporation who contrived and executed that particular holding company scheme. The organization having been thus completed, the business of the corporations thus combined was thereafter managed by their respective directors and officers; but those respective groups of men performed their managerial functions under the general direction of the officers and directors of the United States Steel Corporation, all of whom were practically governed by a very few men acting together, which few men included Mr. J. P. Morgan, the original promoter of the combination, and Mr. E. H. Gary, the chairman of the Board of Directors of the United States Steel Corporation, and whatever man was president of that corporation, whether Mr. Schwab or Mr. Corey.

The hundreds of holding companies which were organized in different states of the Union during the latter part of McKinley's administration, and the much smaller number of such companies which have been organized since that time were all organized on the same general plan as that of the United States Steel Corporation, though with some variations in many cases. The most important of those variations has consisted in so organizing the holding company as to make it incidentally an operating company. In such cases the holding company performs two independent functions. In so far as it is an operating company its business is conducted harmoniously with the business of the other operating companies, which it dominates in its capacity as a holding company. But in such a case as this the whole business of the combination is controlled by one man or by a few men, as truly as such control is exercised by one man or by a few men who are the officers or the directors of a corporation which is a holding company only.

The holding company scheme was originally contrived nearly twenty years ago, by or on behalf of John D. Rockefeller and his associates, to take the place of the

"Standard Oil Trust," which those gentleman had organized in 1882, and had operated until March, 1892, when the Supreme Court of Ohio decided that it was illegal according to the common law and according to the laws of Ohio, and thereupon enjoined it from continuing to do business.   Thereupon Mr. Rockefeller, or some of his associates or some of their attorneys, contrived the holding company scheme, to take the place of the illegal Standard Oil Trust. At that time the trustees, who controlled that trust, held stock in eighty-four corporations, all of which they had been managing in unitary and monopolistic methods, which were contrary to the common law, and had been condemned as such by the Supreme Court of Ohio. Those trustees were nine in number, and they had issued trust certificates amounting to $97,250,000 to those persons who had conveyed to them, as trustees, the stock in the eighty-four corporations. The trust scheme provided that the nine trustees were to elect all the directors and officers of the eighty-four corporations, and were to control all the business of those corporations through those directors and officers and were to distribute among the owners of the trust certificates all the dividends which they would receive from the officers of the eighty-four corporations, on the stocks thereof, which they held for the benefit of the owners of the trust certificates.

This "Standard Oil Trust" was created by an elaborate written agreement on January 2, 1882, from which time until the trust was dissolved, in pursuance of a decision of the Supreme Court of Ohio, rendered ten years later, the business of all the corporations which had established or which had joined that organization, was controlled absolutely by the nine trustees, of whom John D. Rockefeller was the chief.

The fact that this Standard Oil Trust and other similar organizations were the prevailing form of combination in restraint of trade and commerce in the United States in 1890, was the reason why the Sherman law mentioned "combination in the form of trust," as being the typical form of combination which that law was framed and enacted to prohibit; and has always been the reason why the Sherman law has been often called the "Anti-Trust Law." But the name of that law which was affixed to it by Congress was "An act to protect trade and commerce against unlawful restraints and monopolies," which name being too long for general use, the statute has always been generally designated as the Sherman law, because it was the initiative and energy of Senator Sherman which caused it to be enacted.

But the "trusts" which existed and were illegally flourishing in 1890 were all dissolved before the end of the nineteenth century, and their respective places were taken by such holding companies as the Standard Oil Company of New Jersey, and the United States Steel Corporation, and the American Tobacco Company, and the Amalgamated Copper Company, and the American Smelting and Refining Company, and the American Sugar Refining Company of that state, and hundreds of other holding companies organized as corporations in one or another of nearly every state of the Union. Nevertheless, these holding companies which are corporations and are not trusts, are often called trusts in conversation and in print, because they have the same purpose and substantially the same mode of operation which characterized the Standard Oil Trust prior to its dissolution in 1892.

Not even one "trust," accurately so called, was ever prosecuted prior to the end of McKinley's administration, for violation of the Sherman law; and only two such prosecutions were begun prior to that time against any holding company, as if they were trusts. Those two prosecutions were the Greenhut case and the Knight case, but the combinations at which those cases were aimed were two holding companies, namely, the Distilling and Cattle Feeding Company, and the American Sugar Refining Company, respectively; which corporations were often designated among the people as the Whiskey Trust and the Sugar Trust, respectively. Both those prosecutions failed, because neither of them was prosecuted skilfully. But neither of those failures was based upon any distinction between a holding company and a trust; and the decision in neither of them expressed or implied anything unfavorable to the view that a combination in restraint of interstate commerce by means of a holding company, is violative of Section 1 of the Sherman law. Nevertheless that point had not been adjudicated in any court prior to the end of McKinley's administration. And inasmuch as during the last few years of that administration the Department of Justice was making hardly any attempt to enforce the Sherman law against anybody, or to apply it in any way to any combination whatever; thousands of men who wanted to evade that law, and even to disobey it if necessary, for their monopolistic purposes, took part in hundreds of organizations of holding companies, during a few years, about the end of the nineteenth century, and particularly about the year 1900.

At the end of McKinley's administration the Sherman law still stood with its original completeness and clearness unchanged by any amendment; and during the eleven years, two months and twelve days through which it had been thus standing, it had been supported with strength and expounded with favor in several invulnerable judicial decisions, including four which had been rendered by the United States Supreme Court. And although it suited the purpose of some lawyers who wished to weaken the Sherman law, to claim that the decision of the Supreme Court in the Knight case must have that effect, that claim was always invalid, because that decision was not a decision against the Sherman law, or in derrogation of its strengtn, but was only a decision to the effect that the record in the Knight case was confined to showing that the defendants had made a combination to restrain, or at least to regulate, the manufacture of sugar in one city of one state, and did not show that they had combined to restrain interstate commerce, in sugar, or to do anything about sugar elsewhere than in a particular state.

CHAPTER VIII.

The administration of President Roosevelt covered nearly seven years and a half, and extended from September 15, 1901, to March 4, 1909. The first Attorney General who served during that administration was Philander C. Knox of Pennsylvania, who continued at the head of the Department of Justice until June 30, 1904, and who is now Secretary of State in the administration of President Taft. The second Attorney General under President Roosevelt was William H. Moody of Massachusetts, who served from July 1, 1904, to December 16, 1906; and the third and last Attorney General in that administration was Charles J. Bonaparte of Maryland, who conducted the Department of Justice from December 16, 1906, to March 4, 1909.

The Sherman law does not require any President of the United States to enforce that statute; that duty being put by that law upon the Attorney General of the United States, and upon his subordinates, the District Attorneys of the United States, in the several Judicial Districts, which are about ninety in number.

The first annual report of Attorney General Knox was made to Congress November 30, 1901; but he did not mention the Sherman law therein, nor any past or prospective litigation thereunder. Nevertheless, during the years of his occupancy of the office of Attorney General, ending on June 30, 1904, he did begin five of the forty-four prosecutions under the Sherman law which

7

were commenced and carried forward on behalf of the United States during the administration of President Roosevelt. Nineteen of those forty-four cases were begun under the direction of Attorney General Moody, and the remaining twenty were begun under the direction of Attorney General Bonaparte.

Those chapters of this book which record the history of the Sherman law during the administrations of Presidents Harrison, Cleveland and McKinley, respectively, contain accounts of all of the cases which were brought and prosecuted under that law, at any time during those three administrations. But the public cases which were prosecuted under that law during the administration of President Roosevelt, and the private cases, which during that administration were litigated between private parties, relevant to that law, were so numerous, that this chapter will give accounts of only those of them which resulted in the adjudication of important points, which were not adjudicated prior to the beginning of the administration of President Roosevelt. Those public cases which are thus noteworthy were the following:

1. United States vs. Northern Securities Co. and others, 120 Fed. Rep. 721, and 193 U. S. 197. This was an action in equity which was begun March 10, 1902, by the United States, in the Circuit Court of the United States for the District of Minnesota, to enjoin the Northern Securities Company from holding any of the shares of the capital stock of the Northern Pacific Railway Company, or of the Great Northern Railway Company, and from exercising any control over either of those railway companies.

The facts which were established in the case were essentially as follows: The Northern Pacific Railway Company and the Great Northern Railway Company were the owners respectively of two theretofore com-

peting railways, which extended from the shores of the
Mississippi River and of Lake Superior to the shores of
Puget Sound. In the summer of 1901 certain large stockholders in the Northern Pacific Company, and certain
large stockholders in the Great Northern Company, who
had practical control of those two companies respectively, combined to make a plan to organize a holding
company in New Jersey, with a capital stock of $400,-
000,000, and to transfer most of that stock to the holders
of the majority of the stock of the Northern Pacific
Company and to the holders of the majority of the
stock of the Great Northern Company, in exchange for
a majority of the stock of each of those railway companies.   This plan was executed by the organization of
such a holding company in New Jersey, in November,
1901, which holding company was named the Northern
Securities Company.   When the Securities Company was
organized it assented to the plan which it was organized
to promote ; and that plan was thereupon executed to the
extent of the acquirement by the Northern Securities
Company of about 96 per cent. of all the stock of the
Northern Pacific Railway Company, and about 76 per
cent. of all the stock of the Great Northern Railway
Company.

The bill of complaint stated that these facts constituted
a contract combination or conspiracy in restraint of interstate commerce in violation of the Sherman law, and
prayed for a decree to judicially establish that proposition.

On February 11, 1903, Congress enacted, and President Roosevelt approved, an Act to expedite the hearing and determination of suits in equity brought under
the Sherman law, or brought under the interstate commerce law. That act provided that any such suit in equity
brought by the United States should, at the request of the
Attorney General, be assigned for hearing at the earliest

practical day in the Circuit Court in which it was brought, before not less than three judges; and that whatever appeal might be taken from the decision of the Circuit Court, thus held by not less than three judges, must be taken directly to the Supreme Court of the United States.

In pursuance of this expediting statute, the Northern Securities case was argued in March, 1903, in the United States Circuit Court for the District of Minnesota, with all the four Circuit Judges of the Eighth Judicial Circuit sitting as that Circuit Court. These were Judges Caldwell, Sanborn, Thayer and Van Devanter.

The arguments for the United States were made by Attorney General Knox himself, assisted by four other counsel. The arguments for the defendant were made by John W. Griggs, assisted by five other counsel; Mr. Griggs having been the predecessor of Mr. Knox as Attorney General of the United States.

The opinion of the court was delivered by Judge Thayer, without any dissent from any other judge among the four who heard the arguments and participated in the decision of the court. That opinion was among the last of the writings of its distinguished author, for Judge Thayer died in 1905. After stating the facts of the case, somewhat more elaborately than they have been stated in this chapter, Judge Thayer proceeded as follows:

"The scheme which was thus devised and consummated led inevitably to the following results: First, it placed the control of the two roads in the hands of a single person, to wit, the Securities Company, by virtue of its ownership of a large majority of the stock of both companies; second, it destroyed every motive for competition between two roads engaged in interstate traffic, which were natural competitors for business, by pooling

the earnings of the two roads for the common benefit of
the stockholders of both companies; and, according to
the familiar rule that every one is presumed to intend
what is the necessary consequence of his own acts when
done wilfully and deliberately, we must conclude that
those who conceived and executed the plan aforesaid
intended, among other things, to accomplish these ob-
jects."

"It will not do to say that, so long as each railroad
company has its own board of directors, they operate
independently, and are not controlled by the owner of
the majority of their stock.   It is the common experience of mankind that the acts of corporations are dic-
tated, and that their policy is controlled by those who
own the majority of their stock."

"The general question of law arising upon this state
of facts is whether such a combination of interests as
that above described falls within the inhibition of the
anti-trust act or is beyond its reach.   The act brands as
illegal, 'every contract, combination in the form of
trust or otherwise, or conspiracy in restraint of trade or
commerce among the several states or with foreign nations.'   Learned counsel on both sides have commented
on the general language of the act, and the generality of
the language employed is, in our judgment, of great
significance.   It indicates, we think, that Congress, being
unable to foresee and describe all the plans that might
be formed and all the expedients that might be resorted
to to place restraints on interstate trade or commerce, deliberately employed words of such general import as, in
its opinion, would comprehend every scheme that might
be devised to accomplish that end."

"If the same indivaduals who promoted the Securities
Company had transferred their stock in the two railroad
companies to a third party, and had agreed to induce
other shareholders to do likewise, until a majority of the

stock of both companies had been vested in a single individual or association of individuals, and had empowered
the holder or holders to vote the stock as their own,
receive all the dividends thereon, and divide them among
those shareholders of the two companies who had transferred their stock, the result would have been a combination in direct restraint of interstate commerce, because it would have placed in the hands of a small coterie
of men the power to suppress competition between two
competing interstate carriers, whose lines are practically
parallel."

"It is manifest, therefore, that the New Jersey charter
of the Northern Securities Company is about the only
shield which the defendants can interpose between themselves and the law. The reasoning which led to the acquisition of that charter would seem to have been that
while, as individuals, the promoters could not, by agreement among themselves, place the majority of the stock of
the two competing and parallel railroads in the hands of
a single person, or a few persons, giving him or them the
power to operate the roads in harmony and stifle competition, yet that the same persons might create a purely
fictitious person termed a corporation, which could neither
think nor act except as they directed, and, by placing
the same stock in the name of that artificial being, could
accomplish the same purpose. The manifest unreason-
ableness of such a proposition, and the grave consequences
sure to follow from its approval, compel us to assume
that it must be unsound; especially when we reflect that
the law, as administered by courts of equity, always
looks at the object accomplished, rather than upon the
particular devices or means by which it has been accomplished."

"If the State of New Jersey had undertaken to invest
the incorporators of the Securities Company with power
to do acts in the corporate name, which would operate

to restrain interstate commerce, we have no doubt that such a grant would have been void, under the provisions of the anti-trust act, or at least that the charter could not be permitted to stand in the way of the enforcement of that act."

After Judge Thayer had thus discussed and settled that one of the arguments of the defendant which was based upon the New Jersey charter of the Securities Company, he proceeded to state and upset several other arguments, the original equilibrium of which was quite unstable, and all of which are quite obsolete now. Having disposed of those minor matters, Judge Thayer reached the final contention of the defendant, which was that the Northern Securities combination was not formed to restrain commerce, but to promote commerce and to enlarge the volume of interstate traffic, and thus to benefit the public.

After stating the defendant's argument in support of this defense, and of the propositions upon which it was based, in terms extremely favorable to that argument and to those propositions, Judge Thayer concluded his discussion of the whole case with the following paragraph:

"We shall neither affirm nor deny either of these propositions, because they present issues which we are not called upon to determine, and some of them are issues which no court is empowered to hear or decide, involving, as they do, questions of public policy which Congress must determine. It is our duty to ascertain whether the proof discloses a combination in direct restraint of interstate commerce; that is to say, a combination whereby the power has been acquired to suppress competition between two or more competing and parallel lines of railroads engaged in interstate commerce. If it does disclose such a combination—and we have little hesitation in answering this question in the affirmative—

then the anti-trust act, as it has been heretofore interpreted by the court of last resort, has been violated, and
the government is entitled to a decree."

The decree which was accordingly made, was entered
on April 9, 1903. That decree adjudged in substance,
that the defendants had theretofore entered into a combination or conspiracy in restraint of trade and commerce
among the several states, in violation of the Sherman
law; and that all the stocks of the Northern Pacific
Railway Company, and all the stocks of the Great Northern Railway Company, then claimed to be owned and held
by the Northern Securities Company, were acquired and
were being held in virtue of said combination or conspiracy; and that the Northern Securities Company was
thereby enjoined from acquiring, or attempting to acquire,
any more stock of either of those railway companies, and
from voting any of the stock which it then held, at any
meeting of the stockholders of either of the said railway
companies, and from exercising, or attempting to exercise, any control, direction, supervision or influence over
any of the acts or doings of either of said railway companies, by virtue of holding said stock therein; and that
the Northern Pacific Railway Company and the Great
Northern Railway Company be likewise enjoined from
paying any dividends to the Northern Securities Company on account of any stock in either of said railway
companies, claimed to be owned or held by the Northern
Securities Company.

This decree expressly omitted to provide what was to
be done with the stocks of the Northern Pacific Railway
Company and the Great Northern Railway Company,
respectively, which the decree prohibited the Northern
Securities Company from using any more, either as
means of controlling the Northern Pacific Railway Company and the Great Northern Railway Company, or as

means of collecting dividends from those railway companies, respectively.

An appeal to the Supreme Court of the United States was taken by the defendants from the adverse decree of the Circuit Court for the District of Minnesota, and that appeal in December, 1903, was argued in the Supreme Court by Mr. Griggs and other counsel for the appellants, and by Attorney General Knox for the United States. Condensations of those arguments are printed on pages 257 to 317 of Volume 193 of the United States Reports, where they can be read by those who wish to ascertain in detail what views of the Sherman law were held, or at least were stated in 1903 by those distinguished lawyers, respectively.

The decision of the Supreme Court, in pursuance of that appeal and those arguments, was announced by Justice Harlan on March 14, 1904, in the following sentence:

"The judgment of the court is that the decree below be and hereby is affirmed, with liberty to the Circuit Court to proceed in the execution of its decree, as the circumstances may require."

Justice Harlan also delivered a written opinion, stating the reasons which caused him to favor that judgment of the court which he announced; and Justices Brown, McKenna and Day concurred in that written opinion of Justice Harlan.

Justice Brewer also delivered a written opinion in which he stated that he concurred in the judgment of the court, which Justice Harlan had announced, but that he did not concur with every part of the opinion which Justice Harlan had delivered.

Justice White delivered a written opinion in which Chief Justice Fuller, Justice Peckham and Justice Holmes concurred, and which opinion dissented from the judgment of the court; and set forth one particular line of argument, in support of that dissent.

Justice Holmes also delivered a written opinion in which Chief Justice Fuller, Justice White and Justice Peckham concurred, and which opinion also dissented from the judgment of the court; and set forth another particular line of argument in support of that dissent.

These four written opinions comprised about forty thousand words, and are printed on pages 317 to 411 of Volume 193 of the United States Reports. They are all very learned and very able writings which require careful analysis, followed by careful comparison, in order to be fully understood.

Such an analysis of the opinions of Justice Harlan and Justice Brewer, respectively, when followed by such a comparison of those opinions, will show that the points which both of those opinions agreed in adjudicating, can be accurately stated as follows:

The Northern Securities Company was organized as a holding company to acquire a majority of the stock of the Northern Pacific Railway Company, and also a majority of the stock of the Great Northern Railway Company, in exchange for its own stock, which was issued to those stockholders of the two railway companies, respectively, from which the Northern Securities Company acquired such stock in the two railway companies.

The purpose of the parties to this transaction was to stop forever all competition between the two railway companies, relevant to transporting freight or passengers over the theretofore competing railroads, which were owned by those two railway companies, respectively, and used by them in very extensive interstate commerce.

The foregoing purpose, followed by the foregoing transaction, constituted a violation of Section 1 of the Sherman law; because it amounted to a "combination or conspiracy in restraint of trade and commerce among the several states."

Section 1 of the Sherman law is violated wherever a holding company is organized and used to acquire a majority of the corporate stock of two or more theretofore competing operating companies, for the purpose of stopping their competition, and thereafter managing those operating companies, without any mutual competition, in some business which includes some form of interstate or international commerce.

An analysis and comparison of the dissenting opinions which were written by Justices White and Holmes, respectively, will show that those two opinions comprise two independent but harmonious arguments, both of which were concurred in by both of their authors, respectively, and also by Chief Justice Fuller and Justice Peckham.

Justices White and Holmes simply divided between themselves the work of setting forth in writing all the grounds upon which the dissents of the four minority justices were based: Justice White formulating one argument, which was thought by all four justices to be fatal to the case of the United States; and Justice Holmes formulating another argument, which all four of the minority justices likewise thought to be fatal to that construction to the Sherman law, which the majority of the court held to be its true construction.

The pivotal point in the argument which Justice White made in the dissenting opinion which he wrote, was to the effect that the constitutional power of Congress to regulate interstate commerce does not include any power to regulate the acquirement of instrumentalities suitable for use in interstate commerce; though it does include the power to regulate the use of those instrumentalities,

after they have been acquired. Holding this view of
constitutional law, Justice White quite logically concluded
that the decree of the Circuit Court ought to be reversed,
because none of the defendants were shown in the record
to have taken part in any overt act in restraint of interstate commerce, in pursuance of any combination or conspiracy to that end, which may have been comprised in
the organization and business of the Northern Securities
Company.

The written opinion of Justice White comprises an
elaborate and animated argument in support of his view,
that the Sherman law is not violated by any combination
or conspiracy to restrain interstate commerce, unless that
combination or conspiracy is followed by some actual
restraint of interstate commerce. One of the places
wherein Justice White stated that view is near the middle
of page 393 of Volume 193 of the United States Reports,
where he inserted the following two sentences:

"True, the instrumentalities of interstate commerce are
subject to the power to regulate commerce, and therefore
such instrumentalities, when employed in interstate commerce may be regulated by Congress as to their use in
said commerce. But this is entirely distinct from the
power to regulate the acquisition and ownership of such
instrumentalities, and the many forms of contracts from
which such ownership may arise."

The pivotal point in the argument which Justice
Holmes made in the dissenting opinion which he wrote,
was to the effect that the word restraint in Section 1 of
the Sherman law should be construed as confined to extraneous restraint, exercised against strangers to the contract, combination or conspiracy which is used to produce
that restraint.

The written opinion of Justice Holmes covers only
eleven pages, and is characterized by the charming and

luminous literary style of its accomplished author.   Its argument is that the words "contract, combination, or conspiracy in restraint of trade or commerce," should be construed in the light of the common law, rather than in the light of the dictionary; and that when those words are thus construed, it will be found that "contracts in restraint of trade" occur only when a contract is made between two strangers, which provides that one of them shall not compete with the other in a particular business, or which at least restricts his previously existing freedom to engage in such competition; and that it will likewise be found that the words "combination or conspiracy in restraint of trade" occur only when two or more otherwise independent parties make a combination or conspiracy for the purpose of keeping strangers to the agreement from competing with the parties to the agreement.

These views are vividly set forth in those two paragraphs of the written opinion of Justice Holmes, the first of which begins with line 12 from the bottom of page 403, and the second of which ends with line 19 from the top of page 405 of Volume 193 of the United States Reports.

Holding this view of the proper construction of the Sherman law, Justice Holmes concluded that the decree of the Circuit Court ought to be reversed, because the Northern Securities combination first established a permanent community of interest between the Northern Pacific Railway Company and the Great Northern Railway Company, after which it would be impossible for either of those railway companies to make a "contract" with the other to restrict the freedom of competition of either with the other; for that community of interest being established, the two railway companies were no longer strangers; and because the combination of the two railway companies, by means of the Northern Securities Company, did not include any purpose of extraneous restraint upon strangers to that combination.

Justice Holmes recognized the probability that some readers of his written opinion might find that opinion inconsistent with the decisions of the Supreme Court in the Trans-Missouri case and in the Joint Traffic Association case. He therefore distinguished the decisions of the court in those two cases from the decision which he thought ought to be made by the court in the Northern Securities case, by pointing out that the combination which was made in each of those two cases was confined to regulating interstate commerce, and left the parties to that combination quite independent in other respects; whereas the combination which was made in the Northern Securities case practically operated to unite the parties thereto, not only in respect of their interstate commerce business, but also in all respects whatever.

On this point, Justice Holmes, in speaking of the Trans-Missouri case and the Joint Traffic Association case, said: "I accept those decisions absolutely, not only as binding upon me, but as decisions which I have no desire to criticise or abridge."

This analysis of the dissenting opinion of Justice Holmes reduces the ground of his dissent to the proposition that where two railroad companies combine to mutually restrain their interstate commerce, but do not combine in any other respect, they thereby violate the Sherman law; but that where two railroad companies combine to mutually restrain all their businesses, including their interstate commerce, they do not violate the Sherman law.

It was not necessary to the argument of Justice Holmes for him to say that he accepted absolutely, as binding upon him, the prior decisions of the Supreme Court in the Trans-Missouri case and in the Joint Traffic Association case. But he did insert that proper and loyal statement in his dissenting opinion in the Northern

Securities case, though he knew that the decision of the Supreme Court in each of the cases to which he referred was concurred in by only five of the nine justices, who constituted the Supreme Court, when that decision was rendered. In like manner it is to be expected that hereafter Justice Holmes will accept the decision of the Supreme Court in the Northern Securities case as binding upon him, though that decision was concurred in by only five of the nine justices who constituted the Supreme Court when that decision was rendered.

Three of the five justices who constituted the majority of the Supreme Court when the Northern Securities case was decided, are still members of that tribunal, while only two of the four justices who dissented from that decision are now members of that court. It is not to be expected that hereafter any of those three justices will dissent from the proposition of law which they helped to establish in the Northern Securities case; whereas it is to be expected that both of the justices who dissented from that decision, and who still remain upon the bench, will hereafter acquiesce in that proposition of law, on the ground that though they were originally unable to agree thereto, it was established by a majority vote of the court, and has now stood so long unreversed and unmodified by any other decision, that it would be unjust to the people to modify it or reverse it now.

After the decision of the Supreme Court of March 14, 1904, was rendered in this Northern Securities case, it became necessary for the Northern Securities Company to dispose, in some way or another, of the shares which it had been holding of the capital stock of the Northern Pacific Railway Company, and also the shares which it had been holding of the capital stock of the Great Northern Railway Company, and thereupon to distribute the proceeds among its own stockholders. In pursuance of this duty, the Board of Directors of the Northern Securities Company, on March 22, 1904, adopted certain preambles and resolutions, reciting that the company had acquired and then held 1,537,594 shares in the capital stock of the Northern Pacific Railway Company, and 1,181,242 shares in the capital stock of the Great Northern Railway Company, and that there was then outstanding 3,954,000 shares of its own capital stock, and that it was going to distribute those shares of Northern Pacific stock pro rata among its own stockholders, and was also going to distribute those shares of Great Northern stock pro rata among its own stockholders, in exchange for outstanding shares of its own stock, which when thus recovered was going to be retired.

This plan would not operate to return the Northern Pacific stock to the Northern Pacific stockholders, nor the Great Northern stock to the Great Northern stockholders, who had respectively transferred those stocks to the Northern Securities Company at the time of its organization. Quite otherwise, this plan would operate to give to the original Northern Pacific Stockholders, and also to the original Great Northern stockholders about one-third more Northern Pacific stock than Great Northern stock. That method of distribution resulted in giving the men who controlled the Great Northern Company, prior to the organization of the Northern Securities Company, control of both railway companies. But this arrangement was not admired by Mr. E. H. Harriman, for it left him the leader of only a minority interest in the two railway companies, instead of being, as he had formerly been, the leader of the majority interest in the Northern Pacific Company. But Mr. James J. Hill liked the scheme immensely, because it gave the interests of which he was the leader control of both railway companies, whereas before the organization of the

Northern Securities Company, the Hill interests controlled only the Great Northern Railway Company.

Under these circumstances, Mr. Harriman and his associates promptly filed a bill in equity in the United States Circuit Court for the District of New Jersey, stating the facts and praying that his party should somehow be enabled to get back its original Northern Pacific stock, leaving the original Great Northern stock to go to those who had contributed it to the Northern Securities combination. The defendants to this bill in equity were the Northern Securities Company and others, the president of the Northern Securities Company being James J. Hill, who was also president of the Great Northern Railway Company. This case was decided in favor of Harriman and his associates on July 15, 1904, by Judge Bradford, then holding the United States Circuit Court for the District of New Jersey, 132 Fed. Rep. 464. But the Circuit Court of Appeals for the Third Circuit in pursuance of an opinion of Judge Dallas, concurred in by Judge Acheson, but dissented from by Judge Gray, reversed the decision of Judge Bradford on Janury 5, 1905, 134 Fed. Rep. 331. And the Supreme Court of the United States on April 3, 1905, delivered an opinion through its Chief Justice, affirming the decision of the Circuit Court of Appeals, and directing the Circuit Court to dismiss the bill of complaint, 197 U. S. 244.

The pivotal point in this opinion of the Supreme Court was its decision that when the stocks of the Great Northern Railway Company and the Northern Pacific Railway Company were assigned to the Northern Securities Company at the time of its organization, the Northern Securities Company took the unconditional ownership of those stocks, and did not take them as trustee for the parties who assigned them to the Northern Securities Company in exchange for shares of Northern Securities stock.

That decision was therefore to the effect that the Northern Securities Company was a holding company which
owned the stocks which it held, and was not a trustee
or a "trust."

The result of the entire Northern Securities scheme
was to confer upon the interests of which James J. Hill
was the leader the control of both the Great Northern
Railway Company and the Northern Pacific Railway
Company; and while he lives to lead those interests, and
while a majority of the stock of each of those railroad
companies is owned or controlled by various combinations
of men or corporations, who will follow his leadership,
he will constitute a confederating bond of the two railway companies, perhaps nearly as effective as the Northern Securities Company would have constituted, if it had
been permitted to continue to act as such a bond. But
the charter of the Northern Securities Company provided
that that corporation was to live forever; whereas, Mr.
James J. Hill is an old man whose extraordinary powers
of leadership cannot long continue.

For this reason the practical difference between the
government of two naturally competing corporations by
one immortal holding corporation, on the one hand, and
the government of those two competing corporations by
one man on the other hand, is the difference between the
continuance of such an arrangement for a short time
and its continuance forever.

Whether the Sherman law words "combination in the
form of trust or otherwise," constitutionally can, or con-
structively do, cover the present combination of the Great
Northern Railway Company and the Northern Pacific
Railway Company in the form of James J. Hill, is a
question, the answer to which cannot be positively
deduced from the decision of the Supreme Court in the

Northern Securities case, for such a question was not involved in that case.

2.   United States vs. Swift & Co. and others, 122 Fed. Rep. 529, and 196 U. S. 375. This was an action in equity, brought by the United States in the Circuit Court for the Northern District of Illinois, in its northern division, in May, 1902, against seven corporations, one partnership and twenty-three individuals.   The petition stated that the defendants, in violation of the Sherman law, and in order to restrain competition among themselves in the purchase of live stock necessary to the production of the meats produced by them, had made a combination and conspiracy between themselves to refrain from bidding against each other when buying live stock from owners who sent such stock from different states to the Chicago Stock Yards for competitive sale; and had also combined to execute other schemes in restraint of interstate commerce in live stock and also in meat.

The defendants filed a demurrer to this petition, and that demurrer having been argued before Judge Grosscup, one of the Circuit Judges for the Seventh Circuit, he overruled it on April 18, 1903, and immediately granted a preliminary injunction against the defendants, in pursuance of Section 4 of the Sherman law.

The written opinion of Judge Grosscup in deciding this case against the defendants, contained several strong paragraphs such as are characteristic of much of Judge Grosscup's judicial writing.   Among those paragraphs were the following:

"Commerce, briefly stated, is the sale or exchange of commodities.   But that which the law looks upon as the body of commerce is not restricted to specific acts of sale or exchange.   It includes the intercourse—all the initiatory and intervening acts, instrumentalities and dealings

—that directly bring about the sale or exchange. Thus, though sale or exchange is a commercial act, so also is the solicitation of the drummer, whose occupation it is to bring about the sale or exchange. The whole transaction from initiation to culmination is commerce."

"When commerce, thus broadly defined, is between parties dealing from different states—to be effected so far as the immediate act of exchange goes by transportation from state to state—it is commerce between the states, within the meaning of the Constitution and the statute known as the Sherman Act."

"The statute has no concern with prices, but looks solely to competition, and to the giving of competition full play, by making illegal any effort at restriction upon competition. Whatever combination has the direct and necessary effect of restricting competition, is, within the meaning of the Sherman Act as now interpreted, restraint of trade."

"Thus defined, there can be no doubt that the agreement of the defendants to refrain from bidding against each other in the purchase of cattle, is combination in restraint of trade; so also their agreement to bid up prices to stimulate shipments, intending to cease from bidding when the shipments have arrived. The same result follows when we turn to the combination of defendants to fix prices upon, and restrict the qualities of meat shipped to their agents or their customers. Such agreements can be nothing less than restriction upon competition, and, therefore, combination in restraint of trade; and thus viewed, the petition, as an entirety, makes out a case under the Sherman Act."

"The Sherman Act, as interpreted by the Supreme Court, is the law of the land, and to the law as it stands, both court and people must yield obedience."

An appeal from Judge Grosscup's decision was promptly taken by the defendants to the Supreme Court of the United States, and was argued and decided in that tribunal in January, 1905. The Supreme Court opinion was written by Justice Holmes, and was concurred in by all the other justices of the Supreme Court. The writ of injunction which had been issued in pursuance of the decision of Judge Grosscup, prohibited the defendants from doing a considerable number of illegal things therein specified; and also prohibited the defendants from restricting competition by "any other method or device." The Supreme Court decided that the injunction ought to be modified by striking out that non-specific provision and that being thus modified, it was right and should be affirmed. This modification was ordered on the ground that the writ of injunction was complete enough without those words, and that it is improper, in a writ of injunction, to command a defendant to obey the law without telling him wherein disobedience would consist.

3. United States vs. MacAndrews & Forbes Co. and others, 149 Fed. Rep. 823. This was a decision rendered by Judge Hough in December, 1906, in the United States District Court for the Southern District of New York, overruling a demurrer to an indictment, which was based on alleged violations of Sections 1 and 2 of the Sherman law. The first eight pages of Judge Hough's decision were devoted to stating his reasons for overruling five objections to the form of the indictment; and which objections, though elaborately explained in those pages, were too technical to be suitable for explanation here. The last three pages of Judge Hough's decision were devoted to overruling five objections to the substance of the indictment; and his decisions on those five objections were respectively as follows:

"The defendants' doing did directly affect interstate commerce. Commerce among the states is not a technical legal conception, but a practical one drawn from the course of business. The criterion as to whether any given business scheme falls within the prohibition of the statute, is its effect upon interstate commerce, which need not be a total suppression of trade, nor a complete monopoly; it is enough if its necessary operation tends to restrain interstate commerce, and to deprive the public of the advantages flowing from free competition. Applying these general considerations to the case in hand, I have no doubt that the arrangement alleged in the indictment immediately, directly, and of intention, restrained interstate commerce."

"A corporate act may also be an act of whatever officer or officers actively performed that act, for the corporation chargeable therewith."

"Those officers of a corporation which is engaged in interstate commerce, who conduct that business as officers of that corporation, are themselves engaged in interstate commerce."

"A corporation can conspire; and the old notion has long since vanished, that a corporation is not responsible for doing anything which is not authorized by its charter."

"The monopolization or attempt to monopolize which is prohibited by Section 2 of the Sherman law, can be committed by one person alone; whereas a contract, combination or conspiracy to violate the Sherman law cannot be made by one person only."

The trial of the defendants in this case was begun by Judge Hough with a jury on December 19, 1906; and on January 10, 1907, two corporations defendant were found guilty, while a verdict of acquittal of the individual defendants was rendered. Thereupon the two corporations defendant made motions in arrest of judgment, and also to set aside the verdict on the ground that that verdict found them guilty of violating Section 1 and also of violating Section 2 of the Sherman law, and thus subjected them to double punishment for what was really only one offense; although that offense was not only a contract, combination or conspiracy in restraint of interstate commerce, contrary to Section 1, but was also an attempt to monopolize some interstate commerce contrary to Section 2 of the Sherman law. Judge Hough overruled those motions on January 17, 1907, on the ground that the offenses prohibited by Sections 1 and 2 of the Sherman law, respectively, are different in substance and effect, and are different in law.

Thereupon Judge Hough rendered a judgment fining one of the corporations defendant $5,000 for its violation of each of Sections 1 and 2 of the Sherman law, making $10,000 in all; and fining the other corporation defendant $4,000 for its violation of Section 1 of the Sherman law and $4,000 for its violation of Section 2 of that law, making $8,000 in all. 149 Fed. Rep. 836. Those two corporations defendant thereupon sought to avoid their punishment by taking their cases to the Supreme Court of the United States by means of writs of error; but on October 13, 1908, they themselves asked and secured from that court dismissals of their own cases from that tribunal. 212 U. S. 585.

4. Judge Speer's charge to a Grand Jury in the United States District Court for the Eastern District of Georgia, of February 7, 1907, printed on pages 834 to 846, inclusive, of Volume 151 of the Federal Reporter, was a valuable contribution to the history of the Sherman law, in that it delineated much of the history of the law of England, relevant to restraints of business by means of combinations and monopolies; and in that it set forth

some account of the efforts which during many years had
been made by the people of the United States to protect
themselves from trusts and combinations; and in that it
quoted important statements from the writings of great
thinkers in England and America relevant to the same
subject; and in that it commented instructively upon
some of the decisions which had been rendered by the
Supreme Court relevant to the Sherman law. Some of
the additions of Judge Speer to the judicial literature of
the subject were the following:

"The anti-trust laws of the United States are but the
evolution of the ancient laws of our law-loving race
against the monopolies which oppressed the people.
Monopolies are equally obnoxious to the philosophy of
Thomas Jefferson and of Sir Edward Coke; the shib-
boleth of the former—equal rights to all and special privileges to none—is often heard. The latter, three hundred
and fifty years ago denounced them."

"The efforts of the people of this country to protect
themselves against the injurious results of trusts and
combinations have lasted now for many years. This is
true of constitutional as of statutory law. Modern state
Constitutions of Illinois, Arkansas, Califorina, Colorado,
Georgia, Massachusetts, Nebraska, Pennsylvania, Texas
and West Virginia have provisions on the general subject."

"Monopolies first began in a large way to betray their
injustice to the masses of the people in the reign of
Queen Elizabeth. She granted her courtiers and ser-
vants the privileges of certain monopolies. These they
sold to others, who were thereby enabled to raise commodities to what prices they pleased and to put invin-
cible restraints upon commerce and industry. Currants,
salt, iron, powder, leather, oil, potash, vinegar, steel,
brushes, pots, bottles, saltpetre, lead, glass, paper, starch,
tin, sulphur, were some but not all of the commodities

which were monopolized in England during the reign of Queen Elizabeth."

Judge Speer thereupon set forth to the Grand Jury a sketch of the history of a bill which was introduced into Parliament before the end of the reign of Elizabeth for the purpose of checking her exercise of the royal prerogative in respect of granting monopolies to particular persons among her subjects. During the debate in the House of Commons on that bill Sir Francis Bacon delivered a speech in opposition thereto wherein he said:

"With regard to monopolies, the case hath ever been to humble ourselves unto Her Majesty and by petition desire to have our grievancs remedied, especially when the remedy touched her so nigh in point of prerogative. I say, and I say it again, that we ought not to deal, to judge or meddle with Her Majesty's prerogative. I wish, therefore, every man to be careful of this business."

Other members, who were less famous, but more brave than Sir Francis Bacon, advocated the bill, among these Mr. Montague said: "The grievances are great and I would note only unto you thus much that the last Parliament we proceeded by way of petition, which had no successful effect."

And Mr. Francis More said:

"I know the Queen's prerogative is a thing curious to be dealt withal; yet all grievances are not comparable. I cannot utter with my tongue or conceive with my heart the great grievances that the town and country for which I serve, suffereth by some of these monopolies. It bringeth the general profit into a private hand and the end of all this is beggary and bondage to the subjects. Out of the spirit of humiliation do I speak it, there is no act of hers that has been or is more derogatory to her own majesty, more odious to the subjects, more dangerous to

the commonwealth, than the granting of these monopolies."

Mr. Martin, with even higher spirit, declared:

"I do speak for a town that grieves and pines, for a
country that groaneth and languisheth, under the burden
of monstrous and unconsciencable monopolies of starch,
tin, cloth, oil, vinegar, salt and I know not what; nay,
what not! The principalest commodities, both of my
town and country, are engrossed into the hands of these
bloodsuckers of the commonwealth. Such is the state of
my own town and country; the traffic is taken away, the
inward and private commodities are taken away and dare
not be used without the license of these monopolitans. If
these bloodsuckers be still let alone to suck up the best
and principalest commodities which the earth there hath
given us, what will become of us, from whom the fruits
of our own soil and the commodities of our own labor
shall be taken by warrant of supreme authority, which
the poor subject dare not gainsay."

But the "monopolitans" of the Elizabethan age were
powerful enough to prevent the passage of the bill which
had been introduced into the House of Commons by Mr.
Lawrence Hyde, and which had been thus eloquently advocated by Mr. Montague, Mr. More and Mr. Martin,
and no such bill was enacted by Parliament prior to the
end of the reign of Queen Elizabeth.

Having traced the subject of monopolies down to this
point of time, Judge Speer imparted to the Grand Jury
the following information:

"It was not until the reign of her successor, James I,
that relief to the people was afforded. In the first Parliament of this King a Committee of Grievances was appointed, of which Sir Edward Coke was the chairman,
and it is doubtless ascribable to the labors of this great
lawyer that the English statute was enacted which to this

day stands in all its original vigor among the laws of England. Of this act against monopolies our own anti-trust law is intended to be the equivalent, as affecting all matters to which the legislative and judicial power of the United States may extend. The heart of man to-day is much the same as in the days of Elizabeth and James. The greed and avarice of the powerful sometimes take little thought of the losses they entail on others not so powerful. Not only do such combinations tend to destroy all healthy rivalry and competition among those who purchase or sell the products of the people, but they sometimes little reck the miseries and destitution inflicted on the producers themselves, the stories of whose lives are often told in the short and simple annals of the poor."

The English statute, referred to by Judge Speer in the last paragraph, was the "Statute of Monopolies," which was passed by Parliament and approved by King James I on March 24, 1624. Section 1 of that statute was as follows:

"All monopolies and all commissions, grants, licenses, charters and letters patent to any person or persons, bodies politic or corporate, whatsoever, of or for the sole buying, selling, making, working or using anything within the realm or walls, or of any other monopolies, and all proclamations, exhibitions, restraints, warrants of assistance, and all other matters whatsoever anyway tending to the instituting, strengthening, furthering or countenancing of the same or any of them, are altogether contrary to the laws of the realm, and so are and shall be utterly void, and of none effect, and in nowise to be put in execution."

Judge Speer followed his delivery to the Grand Jury of the last paragraph quoted from him by making to them the following additional statements:

"Like the Parliament of England the Congress of the

United States has enacted the present law, prohibiting modern combinations in restraint of trade. These are not the result of patents granted by a partial monarch, but they are the outgrowth of far-reaching schemes, planning combinations to seize a suitable occasion to oppress by unlawful compacts the many for the aggrandizement and enrichment of the few. The law finds its authority in the power of Congress, granted by the Constitution, to regulate commerce with foreign nations and among the several states."

"Congress passed the act, approved July 2, 1890, entitled 'An Act to protect trade and commerce against unlawful restraints and monopolies,' commonly known as the Sherman anti-trust law."

Thereupon Judge Speer read to the Grand Jury Sections 1 and 2 of the Sherman law and followed that reading by expositions of the decisions of the Supreme Court in the Trans-Missouri case and the Joint Traffic Association case, and the Addyston case, and the Swift case, and the Northern Securities case. He closed his explanation of the Northern Securities case by speaking of that Justice of the Supreme Court who delivered the judgment of that tribunal in that case as "that renowned and venerable American jurist, Mr. Justice Harlan, ever insistent to protect the rights of those who cannot help themselves."

The admirable charge of Judge Speer to the Grand Jury from which these extracts have been taken to adorn and illuminate this book, was followed by evidence which was presented to that Grand Jury by the United States. That charge and that evidence resulted in an indictment of the Atlantic Investment Company and three other corporations, and of two individuals for violating the Sherman law through restraint of interstate commerce in turpentine. Each of those defendants made a plea of guilty to that indictment and then Judge Speer announced the judgment of the court to be that each defendant must be punished by the maximum fine of $5,000. He could also have ordered each of the individual defendants to be imprisoned for a year, but he refrained from doing that on their assurance that they would never violate the Sherman law again.

5. United States vs. Virginia-Carolina Chemical Co. and others, 163 Fed. Rep. 66. This was an indictment found on May 25, 1906, by the Grand Jury of the United States Circuit Court for the Middle District of Tennessee, upon information furnished by the Department of Justice, under the direction of Attorney General Moody. The defendants were fifty-six in number, and were charged in the indictment with having violated Section 1 of the Sherman law by combining to restrain interstate commerce in agricultural fertilizers in many of the states of the Union, including Tennessee. In support of this charge the indictment stated that the defendants were all engaged in interstate commerce in fertilizers and that they had combined to fix the price of fertilizers in eight specified states of the Union, and to apportion the trade in fertilizers between those states among themselves, according to an agreed percentage.

Of course, the indictment, if true in its statements of fact, was sound in its charge that the facts thus stated constituted violation of the Sherman law and it does not appear in the case that any of the defendants denied that the indictment was true in its statements of fact.

What the defendants did under these circumstances was to employ seven lawyers to get them out of their trouble on some technical ground or other. The technical defenses which those seven lawyers combined to make were three in number, namely, first, a motion to quash the summons which had been issued against each of that class of the defendants which were corporations chartered under the laws of other states than Tennessee and which had not complied with the laws of Tennessee in relation to such corporations doing business within that state, and which had no agents and were not doing business in Tennessee; and second, a demurrer to the indictment on behalf of all the defendants, except those attempted to be protected by the motion to quash; and third, a plea in abatement, filed on behalf of the same defendants as those attempted to be protected by the demurrer.

The question of the validity of each of these various defenses was argued in the fore part of 1908 by three lawyers for the United States and seven for the defendants before Judge McCall, who was then the United States District Judge for the Western District of Tennessee, temporarily holding the United States Circuit Court for the Middle District of Tennessee.

Judge McCall decided the case on July 3, 1908. That decision denied the motion to quash the summons on the ground that Section 716 of the Revised Statutes of the United States, operated to validate each summons which had been issued for service in another state upon a corporation defendants which could not be found in Tennessee. That decision overruled the demurrer on the ground that the indictment charged the defendants with apt language and with certainty of meaning, with acts prohibited by the Sherman law. But that decision sustained the plea in abatement on the ground that the facts stated therein and admitted by the United States to be true, operated to make the indictment illegal. Those facts were that Mr. E. T. Sanford and Mr. J. H. Graves assisted the Grand Jury in their investigation which resulted in the finding of the indictment by the Grand Jury, though neither of those gentlemen was present in the Grand Jury room after the testimony had been taken

there or when the Jury was deliberating as to its find-
ings, or was voting upon the question of whether to
indict or not indict the defendants, Sanford and Graves
gave to the Grand Jury what assistance they did give in
pursuance of a written commission, which was given by
the Attorney General of the United States to each of
them and which commissions appointed Sanford and
Graves special assistants to the United States Attorney
for Middle District of Tennessee, to do what they did
do toward assisting the Grand Jury.

Judge McCall decided that when the Attorney General
issued those commissions, he was mistaken in supposing
that the law authorized him so to do; and that when
Sanford and Graves acted as assistants to the Grand
Jury in pursuance of those commissions, they were
in error in supposing that the commissions and their
acting thereunder, were authorized by law. Judge Mc-
Call recognized the fact that when the case was argued
before him, there was an existing statute which authorized such commissions as those which the Attorney
General had issued to Sanford and Graves, and which
authorized the doing, under such commissions, of the
very things which Sanford and Graves had done in the
Grand Jury room. But the judge pointed out that
though that statute was more than two years old when he
was deciding the case, it was not enacted until June 30,
1906, which was thirty-five days after the indictment
had been found by the Grand Jury in the case before
him.

Under these circumstances, Judge McCall decided
that when the Grand Jury was investigating the conduct
of the defendants, the then existing law of the United
States prohibited the presence in the Grand Jury room
of anybody and everybody, except the Grand Jurors
and the witnesses, and the United States District Attorney for the Middle District of Tennessee, and that there-

fore the presence of Sanford and Graves in the Grand
Jury room invalidated the indictment which resulted
from the investigations which they assisted the Grand
Jury to make; though that assistance was rendered in
good faith in pursuance of especial appointment by the
Attorney General of the United States, and was not
claimed to have included any false or misleading statements or suggestions to the Grand Jury. But they were
in the Grand Jury room when the law did not permit
them to be there; and their presence there was held by
Judge McCall to invalidate the indictment, which the
Grand Jury, after they had gone away, deliberated upon
and decided to return as a true bill.

And this was how the seven lawyers of the fifty-six
defendants in this case, contrived to avert punishment
from all those defendants, except the few who could
not be found in Tennessee, and therefore could not be
punished there.

6. United States vs. Standard Oil Company of New
Jersey and others, 152 Fed. Rep. 290. This was a bill
in equity, filed November 15, 1906, under the direction
of Attorney General Moody, by the United States, in
the United States Circuit Court for the Eastern District
of Missouri, against the Standard Oil Company of New
Jersey, and about seventy subsidiary corporations, and
seven individual defendants. The bill stated that the
defendants had made and were maintaining a combination and conspiracy contrary to the Sherman law, to
restrain commerce in petroleum and its products, among
the states and territories of the United States, and with
foreign nations; and the bill prayed the court to make
a decree to stop all further violation of that law by the
defendants. After the filing of the bill, the court made
an order that the non-resident defendants should be
brought before the court, in pursuance of Section 5 of

the Sherman law, by means of subpoenas to be served upon them in the districts in which they respectively existed or resided.

Thereupon seven lawyers appeared before the court, when held by all four of the Circuit Judges of the United States for the Eighth Circuit, and moved to vacate that order, and to quash the service of subpoenas which had been actually made upon the non-resident defendants, in pursuance of that order. But this dilatory motion was overruled on March 7, 1907. Thereupon, after one more dilatory defense was made and was over-ruled by the Court, the defendants filed their answers to the bill of complaint. The taking of evidence in the case thereupon occupied more than a year, and continued until nearly the end of President Roosevelt's administration.

The argument of the case before the Circuit Court, when held by the four Circuit Judges in St. Louis, Missouri, and the decision of the case by that court, and the transfer of the case from that court to the Supreme Court of the United States, and the first argument of the case in that tribunal, all occurred in the first year of the administration of President Taft, and when the case was being prosecuted under the direction of Attorney General Wickersham. Therefore, those great transactions are explained in the next chapter of this book, which chapter is devoted to that part of the history of the Sherman law which occurred during Taft's administration.

7. United States vs. American Tobacco Company and others, 164 Fed. Rep. 700. This was a bill in equity filed July 10, 1907, by the United States under the direction of Attorney General Bonaparte, in the United States Circuit Court for the Southern District of New York, for alleged violation of the Sherman law, by the Amer-

8

ican Tobacco Company, and many other corporations, including the United Cigar Stores Company, the R. P. Richardson, Jr., Company, and the Imperial Tobacco Company; the latter company being a British corporation. The bill of complaint stated that the defendants had made and were maintaining a combination in restraint of interstate and international trade in tobacco; and the bill prayed that a writ of injunction might be issued to restrain the defendants from conducting interstate or international commerce in tobacco, unless and until they should have dissolved the illegal combination between them. And the bill also prayed that receivers should be appointed by the court to conduct their respective tobacco businesses under competitive conditions.

Voluminous testimony and other evidence was taken in the case during the later months of 1907 and the early months of 1908, and the case was argued in May, 1908, in the Circuit Court, when that court was held by all four of the Circuit Judges of the Second Circuit, sitting together. Those were Judges Lacombe, Coxe, Ward and Noyes. The argument for the United States was made by J. C. McReynolds and Edwin P. Grosvenor, special assistants to the Attorney General. The argument for the Imperial Tobacco Company was made by William B. Hornblower and three other lawyers; that for the United Cigar Stores Company was made by S. M. Stroock, and that for the R. P. Richardson, Jr., Company was made by Charles R. Carruth; while the argument for all the other defendants, which were the American Tobacco Company and its constituent corporations, was made by ex-Judge William J. Wallace and three other lawyers.

The case was decided on November 7, 1908. That decision was not adverse to the United Cigar Stores

Company, nor to the R. P. Richardson, Jr., Company, nor to the Imperial Tobacco Company; but it was adverse to the American Tobacco Company and its constituent American corporations. That adverse decision resulted from the harmonious opinions of three of the judges of the court, but Judge Ward dissented from the judgment of the majority of the court.

The written opinions of all four of the judges of the court are printed on pages 701 to 728 of Volume 164 of the Federal Reporter; and the substance of the decree which was made by the court in pursuance of the opinions of its three majority judges is printed on pages 1024 and 1025 of the same volume.

The facts in the case were stated in the written opinion of Judge Coxe in the following paragraph:

"The 'Tobacco Trust,' so called, consists of over 60 corporations, which since January, 1890, have been united into a gigantic combination, which controls a greatly preponderating proportion of the tobacco business in the United States in each and all its branches; in some branches the volume being as high as 95 per cent. Prior to their absorption, many of these corporations had been active competitors in interstate and foreign commerce. They competed in purchasing raw materials, in manufacturing, in jobbing and in selling to the consumer. To-day those plants, which have not been closed, are, with one or two exceptions, under the absolute domination of the supreme central authority. Everything directly or indirectly connected with the manufacture and sale of tobacco products, including the ingredients, the packages, the bags and boxes, are largely controlled by it. Should a party with moderate capital desire to enter the field, it would be difficult to do so against the opposition of this combination. That many of the associated corporations were not coerced into joining the combination but entered of their own volition is quite true, but in many other instances it is evident that, if not actually compelled to join, they preferred to do so, rather than face an unequal trade war, in which the odds were all against them and in which success could only be achieved by a ruinous expenditure of time and money."

The evidence in the case did not convince any of the judges that the defendants had made any contract, combination or conspiracy in extraneous restraint of interstate or international trade or commerce; but Judges Lacombe, Coxe and Noyes all agreed in finding that the evidence proved that the American Tobacco Company and its constituent American corporations constituted a combination in mutual restraint of interstate commerce in tobacco. In this respect, the American Tobacco case is identical with the Northern Securities case, wherein two railway companies had made a combination in mutual restraint of interstate commerce, but had not made any combination in extraneous restraint of interstate commerce, exercised or to be exercised upon any other party.

Judges Lacombe, Coxe and Noyes also agreed in holding that the combination in mutual restraint of interstate commerce in tobacco, which the American Tobacco Company and its constituent American corporations were proved to have made and to be maintaining, was a combination contrary to Section 1 of the Sherman law. Speaking of that section, Judge Lacombe said: "This language is to be construed as prohibiting any contract or combination whose direct effect is to prevent the free play of competition." And Judge Coxe said: "The natural effect of competition is to increase commerce, and an agreement whose direct effect is to prevent this play of competition, restrains trade and commerce."

And Judge Noyes said that "Every combination restraining competition in interstate trade is a combination in restraint of interstate commerce."

The dissenting opinion of Judge Ward was primarily based upon his idea that the American Tobacco case was substantially like the Knight case, wherein no interstate or international commerce was proved to have occurred or to have been restrained. But Judge Ward overlooked the fact that the Knight case was based only upon the manufacturing part of the "Sugar Trust" business, whereas the Tobacco case was based upon the whole business of the "Tobacco Trust," but particularly upon its doings relevant to interstate commerce.

Assuming, however, that the Knight case should not be held to control the decision of the American Tobacco case, Judge Ward took the secondary and independent ground that the combination in the Tobacco case did not violate Section 1 of the Sherman law, because, in his view of the evidence, it was not organized to restrain any trade or commerce, but was organized to increase trade and commerce in tobacco throughout the United States and although that organization did incidentally prevent competition between the members of the combination, that result was unimportant. And Judge Ward held that the American Tobacco Company and its subsidiary corporations had not violated Section 2 of the Sherman law, because they had not done anything to prevent other parties from engaging in interstate or international commerce in tobacco and therefore had not monopolized or attempted to monopolize that business or any part of it, as he understood the legal meaning of the word "monopolize" as that word is used in that section.

The American Tobacco Company and its constitutent American corporations took an appeal from the decision of the Circuit Court in this case to the Supreme Court of the United States, but that appeal was not reached for argument in that tribunal until after the end of President Roosevelt's administration. An explanation of what has occurred in that case in the Supreme Court will be found in the next chapter of this book, which is devoted to the history of the Sherman law during the administration of President Taft.

The seven cases which have thus far been explained in this chapter were not all the cases which were brought or prosecuted by the United States for violation of the Sherman law during the administration of President Roosevelt. But they do comprise all of those cases which were adjudicated during that administration and which adjudications included points having enough novelty and enough importance to be noteworthy contributions to the history of the Sherman law. The United States was successful in all of the seven cases, except that against the Virginia-Carolina Chemical Company and others, and its failure in that case was not due to any defect or weakness in the Sherman law, nor to any innocence among the defendants who were indicted for violating that law; for that failure was entirely due to the harmless but then illegal presence in the Grand Jury room of two special assistants of the Attorney General of the United States when the Grand Jury was receiving the evidence upon which afterward, in the absence of those two gentlemen, the Grand Jury based its indictment of the defendants.

Cases of litigation between private parties relevant to the Sherman law which occurred during Roosevelt's administration were between twenty and thirty in number, and those of them which involved any new and important points relevant to the Sherman law were the following:

1. Foot vs. Buchanan, 113 Fed. Rep. 156. This was
a petition which was presented in January, 1902, to the
United States Circuit Court for the Northern District of
Mississippi in its Western Division, for a writ of habeas
corpus to discharge the petitioner, Lawrence Foot, from
the custody of the United States Marshal Buchanan,
Foot having been committed to that custody by the District Court for the Northern District of Mississippi for
contempt of court, claimed to have been committed by
him in refusing to answer certain questions which had
been put to him by the District Attorney before the
Grand Jury of that court when that Grand Jury was
engaged in investigating alleged violations of the Sherman law. When the witness refused to answer those
questions he stated as a reason for his refusal that "in
answering the questions he would incriminate himself
and put the Government in possession of information
which might supply the means of convicting him of the
same offense."

Judge Shelby decided that in Grand Jury investigations
based upon the Sherman law a witness could not be compelled to answer questions the answers to which would
criminate him, and therefore he ordered the petitioner to
be discharged from the custody of the United States
Marshal. But Judge Shelby also held that a witness cannot avoid answering questions upon his own mere statement that the answers to them would tend to criminate
him, it being for the judge to decide whether any answer
might probably have that tendency.

2. Montague & Co. and others vs. Lowry and others,
115 Fed. Rep. 27; 193 U. S. 38. This was the decision
in the Circuit Court of Appeals for the Ninth Circuit
of that Lowry case which is No. 5 of the litigations between private parties relevant to the Sherman law, which
are explained in Chapter VI of this book and which case

is therein shown to have been decided by the Circuit
Court for the Northern District of California in favor of
the plaintiffs. The judgment of that Circuit Court was
affirmed on February 17, 1902, by the Circuit Court of
Appeals in an opinion delivered by Judge Gilbert, the
chief judge of that court.

Thereupon the defendants took the case to the United
States Supreme Court by means of a writ of error. But
the Supreme Court, on February 23, 1904, affirmed the
judgment of the courts in California in an opinion delivered by Justice Peckham. That opinion began with
the statement that the qustion in the case was whether
the association of the defendants constituted a combination in restraint of trade within the meaning of the
Sherman law. The Supreme Court unanimously
answered that question in the affirmative and Justice Peckham said that they regarded the case as a plain one, being
analagous to the Addyston case and not analagous to the
Knight case. The Supreme Court also decided that the
judgment of the Circuit Court in awarding to the plaintiffs $750 as an attorney's fee under Section 7 of the
Sherman law was not unreasonable, the trial of the case
having taken about five days.

3. Bement vs. National Harrow Company, 186 U. S.
70. This case was brought to the Supreme Court of the
United States from the Court of Appeals of the State of
New York to settle a Federal question which was involved in a suit which the National Harrow Company
had brought against Bement to recover damages for
alleged violation of certain contracts executed between
the parties in relation to the manufacture and sale of
certain harrows under a considerable number of patents
owned by the Harrow Company. That Federal question was whether those contracts were void because violative of the Sherman law.

The Supreme Court decided on May 19, 1902, that if those contracts were violative of the Sherman law that fact would constitute a good defense to the action. But that court also decided that those contracts were not violative of the Sherman law, because that statute does not refer to that kind of restraint of interstate commerce which may result from contracts between patentees, limiting the terms upon which the articles covered by their patents may be sold and regulating the prices to be received therefor. On that point Justice Peckham said that the very object of the patent laws is monopoly and that Congress never intended or expected that the Sherman law would be construed as prohibiting the exercise by patentees of the exclusive right granted to them in pursuance of those laws.

4. Board of Trade of Chicago vs. Christie Grain & Stock Co. and others, 116 Fed. Rep. 944; 121 Fed. Rep. 608; 125 Fed. Rep. 161. This was an action in equity which was brought in 1901 in the United States Circuit Court for the Western District of Missouri in its Western Division to restrain the defendants from appropriating to its own use certain information of the prices at which, from moment to moment, grain was bought and sold between members of the Board of Trade on the floor of the exchange hall, owned and maintained by that board. That certain information was delivered from moment to moment by employees of the Board of Trade to telegraph companies with authority to send that information by telegraph to certain parties, not including the defendants. Nevertheless, the defendants had somehow been obtaining that information from the Telegraph Company and the suit was brought to enjoin the defendants from receiving such information in the future.

The defendants interposed several defenses to the suit,

all of which were overruled by Judge Hook, who was
then the United States District Judge for the District of
Kansas, temporarily holding the Circuit Court for the
Western District of Missouri. The opinion of Judge
Hook was delivered on July 5, 1902, but it does not appear therein that the Sherman law was invoked at that
time by either party to the litigation. But that decision
of 1902 was based upon a preliminary hearing and that
preliminary was followed by a final hearing in the following year. At that final hearing the defendants took
the ground that the Board of Trade, in making an arrangement with the telegraph companies for the trans-
mission and distribution of the information covered by
that agreement, had violated the Sherman law, because
that agreement provided for furnishing that information
to many parties while withholding it from other parties,
and therefore operated to restrain interstate commerce.
Judge Hook overruled this defense in the opinion which
he delivered March 19, 1903, and which is printed on
page 608 of volume 121 of the Federal Reporter.

An appeal from Judge Hook's decision was taken by
the Christie Grain & Stock Company and the other defendants to the United States Circuit Court of Appeals
for the Eighth Circuit. On October 8, 1903, that court,
when it was held by Circuit Judges Sanborn and
VanDevanter and by District Judge Shiras, reversed the
decree of Judge Hook and ordered the complainant's
bill to be dismissed. The opinion which resulted in that
reversal was delivered by Judge Shiras and is printed on
pages 161 to 169 of volume 125 of the Federal Reporter.
That opinion states that the defendants asked for a reversal of the decree on several grounds, including their
contention that the doings of the complainant constituted
a violation of the Sherman law. But the Circuit Court
of Appeals based its reversal of the decision of Judge

Hook on one of the other grounds, which were presented by the defendants without deciding anything about the Sherman law.

Thereupon the case was taken to the United States Supreme Court by means of a writ of certiorari and was decided in that tribunal on May 8, 1905, in an opinion which was delivered by Justice Holmes and is printed on pages 245 to 253 of volume 198 of the United States Reports, but which opinion was dissented from by Justices Harlan, Brewer and Day. That opinion overruled all the defenses which had been made in the Circuit Court and thereupon ordered a reversal of the decree of the Circuit Court of Appeals, which had itself reversed both the decisions of Judge Hook in the Circuit Court. In overruling that one of the defendants' defenses, which was based on the Sherman law, the Supreme Court held that the information which the Board of Trade communicated to some parties, while withholding it from the defendants, was information which the Board of Trade had a right to withhold from everybody, or to communicate to everybody, or to withhold from some people while communicating to other people; and that a contract to communicate it to some people, while withholding it from some others, was not a contract in restraint of trade, and therefore was not violative of the Sherman law.

5. Whitwell vs. Continental Tobacco Co. and others, 125 Fed. Rep., 454. This was an action at law which was originally brought by Whitwell against the Tobacco Company in the United States District Court of the District of Minnesota and having been decided against the plaintiff in that tribunal was taken by him to the Circuit Court of Appeals for the Eighth Circuit, where the judgment of the Circuit Court was affirmed on November 12,

1903. The theory of the case was that the Tobacco Company and one of its agents named McHie had combined to restrain interstate commerce by refusing to sell tobacco to the plaintiff at the same prices at which they sold tobacco to other people. The Circuit Court of Appeals decided that this conduct did not constitute any mutual restraint of interstate commerce between the Tobacco Company and its agent, for they had never been competitors, and the agent was simply an instrument of the Tobacco Company. And that court also decided that the conduct complained of did not constitute any extraneous restraint of interstate commerce because it did not impede the plaintiff in any effort he might make to buy tobacco from other parties than the Continental Tobacco Company. On this point Judge Sanborn in delivering the opinion of the court said:

"The sole cause of the damages claimed in the complaint is shown to be the refusal of the defendants to sell their goods to the plaintiff at prices which would enable him to resell them with a profit. But the defendants owed him no duty to sell their products to him at any price—much less at prices so low that he could realize a profit by selling them again to others."

6. Phillips vs. Iola Portland Cement Co., 125 Fed. Rep. 593. This was an action at law in the United States Circuit Court for the Western District of Missouri, which was brought by the Cement Company against Phillips to recover damages for breach of contract for the sale of certain cement. Phillips defended in the Circuit Court, on the ground that the contract was illegal under the Sherman law, because it provided that the purchasers should not sell the cement outside of Texas, nor ship it or allow it to be shipped thence to any other state or territory or country. That defense having been held unsound by the Circuit Court, Phillips took the case to the

Circuit Court of Appeals for the Eighth Circuit. That tribunal on November 12, 1903, in an opinion delivered by Judge Sanborn, decided that that provision of the contract of sale which prohibited export from Texas of the property sold was a mere incident of the contract of sale and imposed no direct restraint upon competition in interstate commerce and was not violative of the Sherman law.

7. City of Atlanta vs. Chattanooga Foundry and Pipe Works and others, 127 Fed. Rep., 23. This was an appeal to the Circuit Court of Appeals for the Sixth Circuit from the decision of the United States Circuit Court for the Eastern District of Tennessee in that case, which is No. 7 among those cases between private litigants under the Sherman law, which are explained in Chapter VI of this book as having occurred in the administration of President McKinley. The decision of the Circuit Court of Appeals was delivered on December 8, 1903, by Judge Lurton, who was then the chief judge of that court, and who is now one of the associate justices of the Supreme Court of the United States. That decision found that Judge Clark had erred in the court below in his selection of the particular Tennessee statute of limitation which was applicable to the case; for Judge Clark had selected a Tennessee three-year statute of limitation, whereas the Circuit Court of Appeals found that the applicable Tennessee statute of limitation was one which permitted suits to be brought within ten years after the right of action accrued. Inasmuch as the case had been brought within that ten years, this decision made it necessary for the Circuit Court of Appeals to review and decide the whole case, which it proceeded to do by reaching the following conclusions upon the following points:

A municipal corporation is a business corporation in respect of such of its functions as consist in creating and maintaining a system of water works, by means of which it collects water in reservoirs and distributes it to the people for compensation paid by the respective users of the water thus distributed. And where such a business of a municipal corporation has been injured by a combination in restraint of interstate commerce, violative of the Sherman law, that corporation may maintain an action for damages under Section 7 of that law.

Where a combination in restraint of interstate commerce results in one of the members of the combination, selling the commodities which are the subject of the combination at an excessive price, the purchaser thus cheated may maintain an action under Section 7 of the Sherman law against any one or more members of the combination, whether that defendant is, or those defendants are, found to have made the particular sale complained of.

It is no defense to an action for damages brought under Section 7 of the Sherman law against a combination engaged in restraint of interstate commerce, to show that the plaintiff was not engaged in interstate commerce.

One measure of damages recoverable in an action based on Section 7 of the Sherman law is the difference between the amount of money which was extorted from the plaintiff for commodities or services, in pursuance of a combination in restraint of interstate commerce, and the smaller amount of money which the plaintiff would have paid for the same commodities or services, under natural competitive conditions in the absence of any combination in restraint of interstate commerce.

The defeated defendants in this case took the controversy to the Supreme Court of the United States, by means of a writ of error. But on December 3, 1906, Justice Holmes delivered the opinion of that court, affirming the judgment which had been rendered by the Circuit Court of Appeals. The points which were established by the decision rendered by Justice Holmes in this case were the following:

The City of Atlanta was a person, within the meaning of Section 7 of the Sherman law, as that word is defined in Section 8 of that statute, and having been injured by the combination of the defendants, it was entitled to bring and maintain the suit.

A person whose property is diminished by a payment of money wrongfully induced is injured in his property within the meaning of Section 7 of the Sherman law.

Congress had power to enact Section 7 of the Sherman law and thus to give an action for damages to persons suffering injuries from violations of that law, even where those injuries were incurred within the boundaries of one state.

The fact that the sale was not so connected with the unlawful combination as to be itself unlawful does not contradict the proposition that the extortion involved therein was unlawful.

The applicable statute of limitation was the ten-year Tennessee statute, which was selected by the Circuit Court of Appeals in that behalf.

8. A. Booth & Co. vs. Davis and others, 127 Fed. Rep., 875. This was an action in equity in the United States Circuit Court for the Eastern District of Michigan in its Southern Division, which was decided by Judge Swan, the District Judge for that district, on January 19, 1904. The purpose of that suit was to restrain the defendants from violating a contract by which Davis was bound for ten years to the complainant to refrain from transacting the business of catching, buying or selling salt or fresh fish in or in the vicinity of a considerable number of specified cities located in Ohio, Kentucky, Tennessee, Missouri, Michigan or New York, respectively. The defendant made several defenses to the action, the first of which was that they were not bound by the contract because it was void as being contrary to the Sherman law in that it provided for a restraint of interstate commerce in fish. Judge Swan overruled this defense on the ground that the business of the complainant, though scattered over a considerable number of states, was not interstate commerce, because it consisted of separate parts conducted in separated states respectively and did not include transactions which began in one state and ended in another.

An appeal was taken by the defendants from the decision of Judge Swan in this case to the Circuit Court of Appeals for the Sixth Circuit, and on August 6, 1904, the case was decided in that tribunal, when it was held by Judges Lurton, Severens and Richards. The opinion of the court on that occasion was delivered by Judge Severens, and it resulted in an order affirming the decree of Judge Swan, with some modifications which had no relevancy to the Sherman law. So far as the decision of the Circuit Court of Appeals related to the Sherman law that reference implied an agreement with what Judge Swan had decided on that subject.

9. Loewe & Co. vs. Lawlor and others, 130 Fed. Rep., 633; 142 Fed. Rep., 216; 148 Fed. Rep., 924, and 208 U. S., 283. This was an action at law in the United States Circuit Court for the District of Connecticut, which was begun about the beginning of 1904, to recover damages under Section 7 of the Sherman law. The plaintiffs composed a partnership, which, during many years, had been manufacturing hats in Danbury, Connecticut, and selling those hats to dealers in many states of the Union. The defendants were members of the Danbury Hatters'

Union, which was a branch of the United Hatters of North America, which was a part of the American Federation of Labor.

The complaint stated that on or about July 25, 1902, the defendants, individually and collectively, and as members of the Danbury Hatters' Union and of the United Hatters of North America and of the American Federation of Labor, had entered into a combination and conspiracy to boycott the plaintiffs' hats throughout the United States by preventing the plaintiffs from selling their hats in other states than Connecticut, and by preventing purchasers of hats in other states than Connecticut from buying any hats which had been made by the plaintiffs.

The action was begun by the filing of an elaborate complaint, and in pursuance of a statute of Connecticut that complaint was accompanied by certain attachments levied upon property of the defendants to secure the payment of whatever judgment might be recovered in the action. The first motion made by the defendants consisted in filing a plea in abatement and a motion to vacate the attachments, on the ground that a suit for the same cause of action had previously been brought and was still pending in the superior court of the state. To maintain that plea the defendants had to take the ground that the state court had jurisdiction to enforce Section 7 of the Sherman law, for if such jurisdiction was absent, it was not possible that a suit for the same cause of action was pending in the state court. The plaintiffs filed a demurrer to the plea of abatement, and on June 9, 1904, Judge Platt, the United States District Judge for the District of Connecticut, sustained that demurrer and held the plea in abatement to be bad, because he held that the state court had no jurisdiction to enforce Section 7 of the Sherman law.

Another dilatory defense made by the defendants consisted in a motion to compel the plaintiffs to expunge many of the statements of the complaint, on the ground that they were immaterial to the suit. But on December 13, 1905, Judge Platt denied this motion, on the ground that the case was so complicated that it was right to state in the complaint all the facts which might be found to be relevant thereto.

The next thing done by the defendants was to file a demurrer to the complaint, which demurrer, in accordance with the law of demurrers, temporarily assumed that the complaint was true in point of fact. On that assumption the demurrer took the ground that the facts stated in the complaint did not constitute a violation of the Sherman law, for although the Supreme Court had decided in the Debs case that the Sherman law was applicable to restraint of interstate commerce by means of labor strikes, the defendants in this Danbury case took the ground that the Sherman law was not applicable to labor boycotts. On December 7, 1906, Judge Platt sustained this demurrer *pro forma,* in order that the question of law which it raised might be taken immediately by a writ of error to the Circuit Court of Appeals for the Second Circuit.

Thereupon the case was taken to the Circuit Court of Appeals; and without being decided in that tribunal, the case was transferred therefrom to the Supreme Court of the United States by means of a writ of certiorari.

The decision of the Supreme Court in this Danbury Hatters' case was delivered on February 3, 1908, by Chief Justice Fuller and was concurred in by all the associate justices of that tribunal, which were Justices Harlan, Brewer, White, Peckham, McKenna, Holmes, Day and Moody. The opinion which Chief Justice Fuller delivered in this case is printed on pages 283 to 309 of

Volume 208 of the United States Reports. That opinion concluded with the statement that the facts stated in the complaint did constitute a violation of the Sherman law and with an order that the judgment of Judge Platt in sustaining the demurrer to the complaint should be reversed and the case sent back to his court with directions to proceed to a trial of the question of the truth of the complaint and of the amount of damages recoverable by the plaintiffs.

This conclusion was said by Chief Justice Fuller to rest on many judgments of the Supreme Court to the effect that the Sherman law prohibits any combination whatever which essentially obstructs the free flow of commerce between the states or restricts in that regard the liberty of a trader to engage in business. Thereupon the Chief Justice stated that the restraint complained of belongs to the class of extraneous restraints which are aimed by combinations at other parties to compel them to not engage in interstate commerce, except on terms imposed by the combinations.

His Honor next reviewed the grounds upon which the defendants had contended in the Supreme Court that the facts stated in the complaint did not constitute a violation of the Sherman law.

The first of those contentions was to the effect that the boycott complained of was one unitary scheme which covered the restraint of the sale of the plaintiff's hats in Connecticut as truly as in other states and that inasmuch as the restraint of the sale of those hats in Connecticut was not a restraint of interstate commerce the boycott in its unitary fulness was not a violation of the Sherman law. The Chief Justice stated this contention, but he did not dignify it with any other comments than to say that it was untenable.

The next contention was that the complaint did not allege that the defendants had interposed any physical obstacle to prevent the plaintiffs from selling their hats, which contention was also simply said to be untenable.

The next position taken by the defendants was that they were not themselves engaged in interstate commerce and that therefore their boycott on the interstate commerce business of the plaintiffs did not include any restraint of interstate commerce among themselves. This contention implied that the only restraint prohibited by the Sherman law is mutual restraint of interstate commerce by the members of a combination and that that law does not prohibit the members of a combination from restraining other parties from engaging in interstate commerce. Chief Justice Fuller overruled this contention as untenable and held that it had been disposed of by previous decisions of the Supreme Court, as it certainly had been in several cases, and particularly in the Debs case in Volume 158 of the United States Reports.

The decision of the Supreme Court in this Danbury Hatters' case was a great judicial landmark, which was erected by Chief Justice Fuller, and which will long remain, though the Chief Justice himself has gone away to return no more.

10. Bobbs-Merrill Co. vs. Straus and others, 139 Fed. Rep., 155. This was an action in equity in the United States Circuit Court for the Southern District of New York, brought by an Indiana corporation engaged in the business of publishing and selling books, against a partnership engaged in selling books at retail in the City of New York. The bill of complaint stated that the complainant was the owner of a copyright on a book entitled "The Castaway" and that each copy of that book which had been published by the complainant contained a printed notice immediately below the statutory copyright notice to the effect that the retail price of the book was $1 and that no dealer was licensed to sell the book at retail

at less than $1 and that any such sale at a less price
would be treated as an infringement of the copyright.
The bill of complaint also stated that the defendants had
sold many copies of that book at retail at the uniform
price of 89 cents a copy and was still offering to sell other
copies of that book at that price without the consent of
the complainant.

The defendants set up several defenses to the action,
one of which was that the complainant belonged to the
American Publishers' Association, which included a large
number of publishers located throughout the United
States, and that the complainant's attempt to prevent
copies of "The Castaway" being sold for less than $1
each at retail was made in pursuance of an agreement
which had been entered into by the complainant and the
other members of the American Publishers' Association,
and which agreement provided that the members of the
Association would all combine to carry out the above
mentioned scheme to prevent retail sales of their books at
less than specified prices fixed by the publisher. On the
basis of these facts the defendants contended that the
notice limiting the retail price to $1, which was printed
in each of the books which they had sold at 89 cents,
was ineffective and void, because it was thus printed in
pursuance of the described combination of the members
of the American Publishers' Association, which was violative of the Sherman law as being in restraint of interstate commerce.

This case was decided by Judge Ray, the District
Judge for the Northern District of New York, then holding the Circuit Court for the Southern District of New
York, on July 11, 1905. He decided that the notice printed on the books limiting the retail price to $1 would not
be enforced by the court because it was a part of a
scheme of a combination of book publishers to restrain
interstate commerce; and that the defendants, when pur-

chasing the books which they afterward sold for 89 cents, took the absolute ownership of those books stripped from any limitation such as the notice was intended to create; and that in selling those books at retail at 89 cents each they had not infringed the copyright thereon.

11. Cincinnati Packet Co. vs. Bay, 200 U. S., 179. This was an action at law, which was brought to the Supreme Court of the United States from the Supreme Court of Ohio by means of a writ of error, because it involved a Federal question. That was the question whether the contract upon which the suit was based was void because violative of the Sherman law in providing for restraint of interstate commerce. That was a contract in writing which purported to convey from Bay and another party to the Cincinnati Packet Company two steamboats, two deck barges and two coal flat boats and which contract also provided that Bay and the party which joined in selling that property should refrain for five years from engaging in any way in operating any transportation for freight or passengers on the Ohio River between certain specified points on the Ohio shore of that river or between intermediate points. The contract also provided that the Cincinnati Packet Company would maintain the rates formerly charged by the sellers between all points above Portsmouth, Ohio, said rates, however, not to exceed the railroad rates between those points.

On January 2, 1906, Justice Holmes delivered the unanimous opinion of the Supreme Court, affirming the judgment of the Supreme Court of Ohio and holding that the contract in question did not violate the Sherman law. He explained that the agreement of the sellers of the boats to refrain during five years from competing with the purchasers of the boats was incidental to the sale of the boats and was not a contract in restraint of interstate commerce, even if the boats did cross over to the Kentucky shore when passing between Cincinnati, Ohio, and Portsmouth, Ohio. And he explained that the agreement to maintain rates above Portsmouth, Ohio, did not vitiate the contract of sale, because it was not made in consideration of the sale of the boats and also because the rates agreed to be maintained were rates charged between points in Ohio and did not include any rates charged for any interstate transportation.

12. Rubber Tire Wheel Co. vs. Milwaukee Rubber Works, 142 Fed. Rep., 531, and 154 Fed. Rep., 358. This was an action at law in the United States Circuit Court for the Eastern District of Wisconsin to recover royalties claimed to be due from the defendant to the plaintiff in pursuance of a license granted by the plaintiff to the defendant under a patent for an invention. The defendant resisted the suit on the allegation that the license contract was void and non-enforceable, because it was a result of a combination in restraint of interstate commerce, contrary to the Sherman law. To this defense the plaintiff replied by taking the ground that the alleged restraint of interstate commerce was outside of the Sherman law, because it was attended to by the patent law. To this reply the defendants responded by saying that the patent under which the license was granted was void and was believed by all the parties to the license contract to be void and had been adjudged to be void by the United States Circuit Court of Appeals for the Sixth Circuit, and that the license contract had been made to appear to exist under the authority of that patent as a mere pretext, while its real character was well known by the parties thereto to constitute a contract in restraint of interstate commerce in an article not covered by any valid patent.

On January 23, 1906, this case was decided by Judge Sanborn, the District Judge for the Eastern District of

Wisconsin. He held that though the patent had been adjudged to be void by the Circuit Court of Appeals for the Sixth Circuit, it had been held to be valid by two Circuit Courts in other circuits; and that the license contract had been executed in good faith to accomplish the proper purpose of mutual restraint among the licensees of all commerce which they were to conduct under the authority of the patent. But he also held that the entire license contract was void under the Sherman law, because it contained a particular paragraph, No. 10, which provided that thereafter, upon a written consent of a majority of the parties to the contract, an effort might be made on behalf of all the parties to crush competition by underselling competitors, which competition might otherwise be conducted in interstate commerce by outside parties without infringing the patent upon which the license contract was based. Judge Sanborn held that this paragraph 10 constituted a contract in restraint of interstate commerce and, that not being justified by the patent law, it was violative of the Sherman law; and being violative of the Sherman law, it vitiated the entire license contract, including those parts which, if they had stood alone, would have been justified by the patent law and therefore would not have been violative of the Sherman law.

The plaintiff took this case to the Circuit Court of Appeals for the Seventh Circuit, in pursuance of a writ of error, and on April 16, 1907, that court, when held by three of its Circuit Judges, reversed the judgment of the Circuit Court and sent the case back to that tribunal with directions to enter a judgment for the plaintiff.

The opinion of the majority of the Circuit Court of Appeals was delivered by Judge Baker with the entire concurrence of Judge Kohlsaat, while Judge Grosscup delivered a separate opinion concurring in the judgment of the Circuit Court of Appeals, but not concurring in that part of the opinion of the majority, which held that articles covered by patents are never articles of trade or commerce among the several states within the meaning of the Sherman law.

The opinion of Judge Baker, though it went to that extent, did not need to do so in order to furnish a foundation for a reversal of the judgment of the Circuit Court. For the reversal of that judgment resulted from the opinion of the Circuit Court of Appeals that paragraph 10 of the license contract did not vitiate any other part of that contract. That opinion was based upon the fact that that paragraph was never acted upon, and upon the view that it would not have been illegal if it had been acted upon, and upon the ground that if it had been acted upon and had been illegal it would not have vitiated any other part of the contract being separable therefrom. The most important of these three reasons was the one which held that even if paragraph 10 had been acted upon that action would not have been illegal. That holding was based upon the opinion of the court that the restraint of interstate commerce which is prohibited by the Sherman law does not result from shifting particular cases of interstate commerce from one seller of commodities of a particular kind to competitors as a consequence of reduction of prices by those competitors.

13. Indiana Mfg. Co. vs. Case Threshing Mach. Co., 148 Fed. Rep., 21, and 154 Fed. Rep., 365. This was an action in equity in the United States Circuit Court for the Eastern District of Wisconsin. The suit was brought to enforce by an injunction and otherwise certain contracts between the parties relevant to certain patents on pneumatic straw stackers, which were the property of the complainant. The defendant set up three defenses, the first of which was that the contracts were void, as being

in restraint of interstate commerce and therefore violative of the Sherman law. The case was decided on
August 22, 1906, by Judge Seaman, who was one of the
Circuit Judges for the Seventh Judicial Circuit. His
decision was in favor of that defense. But, inasmuch as
that decision was afterward reversed by the Circuit
Court of Appeals for the Seventh Circuit when that
court was held by the other three circuit judges of that
circuit, it is proper at present to pass over the argument
of Judge Seaman and proceed at once to state what
points of law are embodied in the decision of the Circuit
Court of Appeals.

That decision was expressed in the written opinion of
Judge Baker, which was fully concurred with by Judge
Kohlsaat and was concurred with in respect of its result
by Judge Grosscup. The opinion of Judge Baker in this
case took the same ground that was taken by him in the
Rubber Tire Wheel case, on the same day, which was
April 16, 1907. That ground was the proposition that
articles covered by patents are never articles of trade or
commerce within the operation of the Sherman law. The
reasons which the defendants invoked to support their request that their particular case be taken out of that general rule were two in number. One was that the complainant's license system included all the makers of
threshing machinery in the United States, and the other
was that that license covered a very large number of
patents, some of which were independent of the others.
Both those reasons were found to be invalid by the Circuit Court of Appeals, and therefore that tribunal reversed the decision of the Circuit Court with a direction
to enter a decree in favor of the complainant.

14. Continental Wall Paper Co. vs. Voight & Sons
Co., 148 Fed. Rep., 939, and 212 U. S., 227. This was
an action at law in the Circuit Court of the United States

for the Southern District of Ohio to recover $57,762 claimed to be due for wall paper which had been sold and delivered by the plaintiff to the defendant and had not been paid for. The defendant defended by stating in its answer that the plaintiff was a member of an illegal combination among wall paper manufacturers contrary to the Sherman law, and that the defendants had been compelled to become parties to that combination and that the contract of sale upon which the suit was based was one of the agreements which constituted the illegal combination. The plaintiff demurred to this defense and the Circuit Court overruled that demurrer. Thereupon the plaintiff declined to plead further and judgment was rendered for the defendant, dismissing the case. From that judgment the case was taken to the Circuit Court of Appeals for the Sixth Circuit. That court on January 5, 1906, affirmed the judgment of the Circuit Court in pursuance of an opinion delivered by Judge Lurton, who was then the senior Circuit Judge for the Sixth Circuit, but who is now one of the associate justices of the Supreme Court.

The opinion of Judge Lurton in this case is printed on pages 946 to 950 of Volume 148 of the Federal Reporter. And that opinion possesses peculiar importance, because it was afterward affirmed by the Supreme Court of the United States in an opinion delivered by Justice Harlan and concurred in by Chief Justice Fuller and by Justices McKenna, Day and Moody, while being dissented from by Justices Brewer, White, Peckham and Holmes.

Thus it appears that this Continental Wall Paper case presents to the public an instance of the application of the Sherman law to a particular set of facts, wherein five of the present justices of the Supreme Court agreed that those facts were so far violative of the Sherman law as to require a decision for the defendant corporation and wherein the other two of the present seven justices of the Supreme Court agreed to dissent from that conclusion.

The admitted facts of the case were essentially as follows:

On July 1, 1898, the National Wall Paper Company was the owner of factories for the manufacture of wall paper, which factories were located in certain cities in New York, New Jersey, Pennsylvania and Massachusetts, and at that time there were certain other wall paper factories owned by other persons and corporations in other states. All of said parties were engaged in manufacturing upward of 98 per cent. of all the wall paper manufactured and sold in the United States, and they were engaged in selling that wall paper, partly in the states where it was manufactured, respectively, but also in all the other states and territories and in some foreign nations. Thereupon the Continental Wall Paper Company was organized to be the sole selling instrumentality of the National Wall Paper Company and of all the other above mentioned manufacturers of wall paper, each of which made a separate contract with the Continental Wall Paper Company in substantially identical language. That contract provided that the particular manufacturer of wall paper executing it was to purchase and pay for some shares of the common stock of the Continental Wall Paper Company and was to sell to that company its entire product of wall paper and that the wall paper thus acquired by the Continental Wall Paper Company was to be sold to jobbers for the account of that company at particular specified prices with particular discounts.

The papers which recorded this scheme are printed on pages 941 to 946 of Volume 148 of the Federal Reporter and on pages 236 to 241 and pages 246 to 249 of Volume 212 of the United States Reports, where the entire plan can be learned in detail. A study of that plan will show that the Continental Wall Paper Company was not a holding company, organized to control through stock ownership the manufacturing wall paper corporations, but that it was a selling company, organized to control all the selling business of the manufacturing wall paper corporations, partnerships and persons who owned the stock of the Continental Wall Paper Company and made separate contracts with that corporation, giving it entire control of the selling business of the manufacturer.

The Circuit Court duly decided that the combination which was constituted by the Continental Wall Paper Company and the manufacturers of wall paper who organized that company and owned its stock was illegal under the Sherman law, and that that illegality disentitled the Continental Wall Paper Company to collect by an action at law the $57,762 claimed to be due from the Voight Sons & Company. Thereupon it became necessary for the attorney for the Continental Wall Paper Company, in the Circuit Court of Appeals, to show on what ground or grounds those conclusions of the Circuit Court should be reversed. Therefore that attorney presented to the consideration of that tribunal a contention that the Continental Wall Paper Company's scheme was not violative of the Sherman law, and alternatively, if thus violative, that fact afforded no defense to a suit to recover pay for the wall paper which had been sold by the Continental Wall Paper Company and delivered to the defendant. In disposing of these contentions Judge Lurton wrote a convincing opinion. That opinion held that the Continental Wall Paper scheme was violative of the Sherman law and so held in the following paragraph:

"Before the combination each of the combining companies was engaged in both state and interstate commerce. The freedom of each, with respect to prices and terms, was restrained by the agreement, and interstate commerce directly affected thereby, as well as by the enhancement of prices which resulted. A more complete monopoly in an article of universal use has probably never been brought about. It may be that the wit of man may yet devise a more complete scheme to accomplish the stifling of competition, but none of the shifts resorted to for suppressing freedom of commerce and securing undue prices shown by the reported cases is half so complete in its details. None of the schemes with which this may be compared is more certain in results, more widespread in its operation and more evil in its purposes. It must fall within the definition of a restraint of trade, whether we confine ourselves to the common law interpretation of that term or apply that given to the term, as used in the Federal act, by the cases we have cited above." Those cases were the Trans-Missouri case, the Joint Traffic Association case, the Chesapeake & Ohio Fuel case and the Northern Securities case.

Upon the question whether the unlawful Continental Wall Paper Company combination constituted a defense to the action to recover the $57,762, which the defendant had promised to pay for wall paper sold in pursuance of that combination, Judge Lurton said that the attorney for the plaintiff contended that the contract upon which the action was brought was entirely collateral to the contract between the plaintiff and the other members of the illegal combination and was therefore not vitiated thereby. But Judge Lurton overruled this contention on the ground that the contract to pay for the wall paper sold to the defendant was a part of the entire Continental Wall Paper scheme, and as that scheme included illegal stipulations the courts would not enforce any part of that scheme.

In announcing the judgment of the court at the end of his opinion Judge Lurton substantially said that the judgment of the Circuit Court must be affirmed because the defense thus sustained had to be sustained in order to protect the public against extortion of excessive prices by refusing all assistance toward carrying out an illegal agreement.

The opinion of the Supreme Court affirming the decision of the Circuit Court of Appeals delivered by Justice Harlan is printed on pages 254 to 267 of Volume 212 of the United States Reports. The first few paragraphs of that opinion are devoted to an emphatic expression of approval of the opinion which had been written by Judge Lurton to the effect that the Continental Wall Paper Company scheme was violative of the Sherman law. That point being thus disposed of, Justice Harlan proceeded to discuss the question whether the plaintiff was entitled to recover a judgment for the $57,762, notwithstanding the illegality of its organization. On that point Justice Harlan said:

"The plaintiff comes into court admitting that it is an illegal combination whose operations restrain and monopolize commerce and trade among the states and asks a judgment which will give effect, as far as it goes, to agreements that constituted that combination and by means of which the combination proposes to accomplish forbidden ends. We hold that such a judgment cannot be granted without departing from the statutory rule long established in the jurisprudence of both this country and England that a court will not lend its aid in any way to a party seeking to realize the fruits of an agreement that appears to be tainted with illegality. In such cases the aid of the court is denied, not for the benefit of the defendant, but because public policy demands that it should be denied, without regard to the interests of individual parties. Its interests must be put out of view altogether when it is sought to have the assistance of the court in accomplishing ends forbidden by the law."

One dissenting opinion in this case was delivered by Justice Holmes and concurred in by Justice Brewer, Justice White and Justice Peckham, and a supplemental dissenting opinion was also delivered by Justice Brewer.

The dissenting opinion which was delivered by Justice Holmes assumed the illegality of the Continental Wall Paper Company scheme, but held that the sale of the paper, to collect pay for which the suit was brought, was not affected by the general agreement between the plaintiff and the defendant, which was a part of that scheme. On the contrary, according to the view taken in the Holmes opinion, the contract of sale of that paper was an ordinary parol contract, which was made some time after the general agreement in writing was made between the plaintiff and the defendant, and therefore the courts ought to enforce such a parol contract, notwithstanding the fact that the general written contract between the parties was illegal as violative of the Sherman law.

The supplemental opinion of Justice Brewer was to the effect that the refusal of the court to compel the defendant to pay to the plaintiff the $57,762 which, aside from the Sherman law, was due to the plaintiff, amounted to inflicting upon the plaintiff a punishment for its violation of the Sherman law, which was not among the punishments or penalties prescribed in that act for that purpose. On this point Justice Brewer said that "The present case comes within the proposition that where a statute creates a new offense and denounces the penalty or gives a new right and declares the remedy the punishment or the remedy can be only that which the statute prescribes."

The question whether in a particular case a corporation, partnership or person engaged in business in a com-

bination in restraint of interstate commerce, violative of
the Sherman law, can successfully invoke the assistance of
the courts to collect pay for commodities sold in the
course of that business depends upon whether that particular case is like this Continental Wall Paper case on
the one hand, or, on the other hand, is like the case of
Connolly vs. Union Sewer Pipe Co., 184 U. S., 540, the
opinion in which was delivered by Justice Harlan on
March 10, 1902, and thus nearly seven years before he
delivered the opinion of the Supreme Court in the Continental Wall Paper case.

Justice Holmes in his dissenting opinion in the latter
case expressed his inability to detect any real difference
between the two cases in respect of their relations to the
Sherman law and expressed his opinion that they ought
to have been decided the same way, instead of contrari-
wise. But Justice Harlan, who wrote the opinion of the
Supreme Court in each of those cases, stated in the last
of them that it was entirely different from the Connolly
case. The character and extent of that difference was
precisely as follows: In the Connolly case the defendant, who purchased the commodities from the law-
breaking plaintiff, was a stranger to the plaintiff, and his
purchase of those commodities was entirely independent
of the illegal contract, which the defendant set up as a
reason why he should not be compelled to pay for those
commodities. On the other hand, in the Continental Wall
Paper case, the defendant was a party to the illegal contract, which it set up as a reason for not being compelled to pay for commodities which it purchased from
the plaintiff by means of an oral contract which resulted
from the illegal contract to which it was a party.

The two cases taken together may appear to be unreasonable in that as between two parties to an illegal combination, they refused assistance to both; whereas as be-
9

tween an illegal combination on the one hand and an innocent stranger on the other hand, the two cases extend assistance of the law to the illegal combination as against the innocent stranger. The reason for this paradox resides in the fact that illegality is absent from the contract of sale made to the innocent stranger by the illegal combination; whereas illegality is present in the contract of sale made between the members of the illegal combination.

Whatever view a particular citizen or other party may take of the respective reasonings of Justices Harlan and Holmes is immaterial to the points of law which have been established by the Supreme Court in the opinions delivered by Justice Harlan in the Connolly case and the Continental Wall Paper case, respectively. And those points of law are precisely as follows:

A stranger to a combination which is selling commodities in interstate commerce in a way violative of the Sherman law, must pay for whatever commodities he buys from that combination or from any member thereof.

A party to a combination, which is selling commodities in interstate commerce, in a way violative of the Sherman law can not be compelled to pay for any commodities which he buys from that combination or from any member thereof, in pursuance of the contract which he himself made in joining that combination.

15. Loder vs. Jayne and others, 142 Fed. Rep., 1010. This was an action at law brought in the United States Circuit Court for the Eastern District of Pennsylvania under Section 7 of the Sherman law to recover damages which had been inflicted upon Loder's retail drug business by a contract, combination and conspiracy into which the defendants had entered with other parties throughout the United States to restrain interstate commerce. The case was tried at the October term of 1905, at which trial the jury rendered a verdict for $20,738 against all the defendants except two. Thereupon the defeated defendants filed a motion for a new trial and for a judgment contrary to the verdict. Those motions were decided by Judge Holland on January 22, 1906, which decision was to the effect that a new trial would be granted unless the plaintiff would consent to a reduction of the damages to $10,880.52, in which event a judgment would be entered for three times that amount, namely $32,-641.56, plus an attorney's fee of $2,500, to be paid to the plaintiff's attorney.

The facts which Judge Holland found to justify such a judgment consisted primarily in a combination between numerous manufacturers, wholesalers and retailers of drugs and medicines, which combination was organized to fix an arbitrary minimum retail price for such articles and also restricted the sale of such articles to such retailers as conducted their retail business in accordance with that arbitrary standard of prices. Judge Holland held that this combination constituted a clear restraint of interstate commerce, in so far as it affected interstate commerce, and was therefore a violation of the Sherman law.

At the time of the trial the plaintiff claimed that the injuries which had been inflicted upon him by the combination amounted to $34,416.72. But the jury took a different view of the evidence and reduced the damages to $20,738. And the judge took a still more moderate view of the facts and computed therefrom that the injuries which the plaintiff had suffered amounted only to $10,880.52.

16. Delaware, Lackawanna & Western Railroad Company vs. Kutter and others, 147 Fed. Rep., 51. This was an action at law originally brought in the United

States Circuit Court for the Eastern District of New York by Kutter et al vs. Lackawanna Railroad Company to recover damages for the breach by the railroad company of a contract dated July 9, 1886, made with Robert E. Westcott, to remain in force for ten years and which contract was afterward extended for five years more. The contract provided that Westcott was to manage that part of the business of the railroad company which consisted in the transportation of milk and was to receive 20 per cent. of the freight money earned thereby, and that contract also provided that the company would give Westcott the exclusive privilege of transporting milk over its railroad, so far as it was permitted to do so by law. This contract was in actual operation more than thirteen years and until February 1, 1900, when Mr. Truesdale, the president of the Lackawanna Railroad Company, notified Westcott that he was going to treat the contract as no longer in force. Thereupon Truesdale prevented Westcott from doing anything under the contract. At that time the unexpired part of the time covered by the contract was about seventeen months. After the end of that time Kutter et al, on behalf of Westcott's rights, brought this action to recover the profits which Westcott would have made during that seventeen months if he had been permitted to continue to act under the contract until its appointed end.

The trial judge in the Circuit Court did not make any special finding of fact or of law when the case was tried before him without a jury, but he made a general finding that the plaintiffs were entitled to recover $137,853 with interest, and he ordered a judgment therefor.

From this judgment the railroad company took the case to the United States Circuit Court of Appeals for the Second Circuit by means of a writ of error, and on May 22, 1906, that court affirmed the judgment of the Circuit

Court in an opinion delivered by Judge Wallace, the chief judge of the Circuit Court of Appeals. That opinion is printed on pages 52 to 64 of Volume 147 of the Federal Reporter. It is set forth in that printed opinion that the railroad company asked the Circuit Court of Appeals to reverse the judgment of the Circuit Court on any one of three grounds; upon all of which it sought to excuse itself for its arbitrary repudiation of its own contract. The first of those grounds was that the contract was void as being beyond the corporate power of the railroad company to make, and the second was that the contract was void as being contrary to public policy, and the third was that the contract was void as being violative of the Sherman law and also of the interstate commerce law.

The Circuit Court of Appeals decided that the contract was not void for any reason, and in explaining that it was not violative of the Sherman law Judge Wallace said that though it operated upon interstate commerce it did not have any tendency to create a monopoly nor any operation in restraint of any commerce, and that it could only have operated in restraint of commerce by permitting Westcott to charge such extortionate rates to milk shippers as would discourage them, which was a thing the contract prohibited. In support of this conclusion of the court Judge Wallace wrote the following paragraph:

"The privileges accorded to Westcott were only those which were incident to the anomalous relations existing between him and the defendant, created by the contract. It is quite inconceivable that there were or could have been any shippers of milk who would have been willing or able to undertake his duties and responsibilities. In consideration of his assumption of peculiar obligations and hazards the defendant gave him exceptional privileges appertaining to his relations as a manager of the traffic. This was not an undue and unreasonable preference."

In concluding his analysis of the case Judge Wallace, when speaking of the conduct of Mr. Truesdale relevant to the Westcott contract, wrote the following animated sentences:

"The repudiation of the contract was without any justification. It was repudiated for sordid motives and with an arrogance born of the scorn of consequences. Although Truesdale was primarily responsible for this conduct and the directors of the defendant may not have been personally cognizant of it, they cannot escape their share of the moral responsibility which ensues from endeavoring to establish the defenses interposed in this action. It is conduct like Truesdale's, by those who manage the affairs of great corporations, that has aroused the spirit of resentment in the public mind which is so intense to-day and which is not unlikely to result in legislation and in municipal interference, which will bring serious loss upon stockholders."

17. John D. Park & Sons Co. vs. Hartman, 153 Fed. Rep., 24. This was an action in equity which was originally begun in the United States Circuit Court for the Eastern District of Kentucky by Hartman against the John D. Park & Sons Company. The bill stated that Hartman was the manufacturer and seller of "Peruna," the formula for the manufacture of which was a secret known only to him and his trusted employees, and that he was engaged in the business of selling the "Peruna" to wholesale druggists only, who in turn sold it to retail druggists, who in turn sold it to consumers; and that he had fixed uniform prices for all three classes of sales, but that the defendant corporation had been selling said Peruna to retailers at less than the prices fixed by Hartman for such sales and that those retailers had been selling Peruna to consumers at less than the retail prices fixed by Hartman. The bill prayed for an injunction to stop the defendant corporation from selling Peruna or causing it to be sold at less than the prices fixed by Hartman.

In the Circuit Court the defendant filed a demurrer to the bill of complaint. That demurrer was overruled and an interlocutory injunction was granted.

Thereupon the case was taken to the Circuit Court of Appeals for the Sixth Circuit by an appeal prosecuted by John D. Park & Sons Company. That appeal was argued in that court by Alton B. Parker and two other lawyers for the appellant, and by Frank F. Reed and two other lawyers for Hartman. Judge Lurton, then chief judge of that Circuit Court of Appeals, on March 14, 1907, delivered the elaborate opinion of that court, deciding that the decision of the Circuit Court was wrong and holding that Hartman's system of fixing prices on Peruna was not enforceable in court because violative of the Sherman law and that the injunction which had been issued to enforce it must be discharged.

This case is particularly interesting because its decision represents the contention which had been made in the court by Alton B. Parker, the famous jurist and statesman, as well as representing the opinion of the Chief Judge Lurton of the Circuit Court of Appeals for the Sixth Circuit, who is now one of the justices of the Supreme Court of the United States.

In the first paragraph of his elaborate written opinion Judge Lurton stated that the question to be decided in the case was whether that exemption from the laws against restraints of trade and against monopoly, which had been extended to contracts relevant to the sale and resale and the prices of articles covered by patents or by copyrights should be held to extend also to articles made by a secret process or compounded according to a secret formula. Thereupon, after writing an opinion which discloses very extensive learning, as printed on pages 26 to

46 of Volume 153 of the Federal Reporter, Judge Lurton announced the judgment of the court to be that that question must be decided in the negative.

In the course of that opinion Judge Lurton quoted with approval the following paragraph from a decision of the Court of Appeals of the State of New York:

"If agreements and combinations to prevent competition are or may be hurtful to trade, the only sure remedy is to prohibit all agreements of that character. If the validity of such an agreement was made to depend upon an actual proof of public prejudice or injury it would be very difficult in any case to establish the invalidity, although the moral evidence might be very convincing."

The concluding paragraph of Judge Lurton's opinion in this case contains the following significant sentences:

"It has been suggested that we should have regard to new commercial conditions and a tendency toward a relaxation of old common law principles which tend to prevent development on modern lines. This is an argument better addressed to legislative bodies than to the courts. Neither is it wise for the courts to countenance the introduction of artificial distinctions, dependent upon the variant economic views of various judges. Distinctions which are specious, analogies which are but apparent will but afford opportunities to whittle away broad economic principles lying at the bottom of our public policy; principles which have long received the sanction of statesmen and the approving recognition of a long line of jurists. A like argument is expected whenever some new method of circumventing freedom of commerce comes under the tests of the law. It was made in the Addyston Pipe case and answered by Judge Taft with a strength to which we can add nothing."

18. American Banana Company vs. United Fruit Co., 153 Fed. Rep., 943, and 160 Fed. Rep., 184, and 166 Fed.

Rep., 261, and 213 U. S., 347.   This was an action at law brought in the United States Circuit Court for the Southern District of New York to recover treble damages under Section 7 of the Sherman law for injuries inflicted by the United Fruit Company upon the American Banana Company.

The first judicial action taken in the case was the granting by Judge Lacombe on January 28, 1907, of a motion requiring the defendant to produce at the trial all the books and papers of the defendant which were enumerated with definiteness in the motion and which related to the case.

The next step taken in the case consisted in the granting by Judge Hough at the trial of the defendant's motion to dismiss the case on the pleadings, which event occurred on March 9, 1908.

Thereupon the case was taken to the Circuit Court of Appeals for the Second Circuit by means of a writ of error and was argued and decided in that tribunal in 1908.   The opinion of that court was delivered by Judge Noyes and resulted in affirming the judgment of the Circuit Court.

The case was finally taken to the Supreme Court of the United States by means of a writ of error and was decided by that tribunal early in 1909.   That decision was an affirmance of the judgment of the Circuit Court of Appeals in pursuance of an opinion delivered by Justice Holmes.

The facts which are set forth in that opinion were essentially as follows:

The plaintiff was an Alabama corporation, while the defendant was a New Jersey corporation.   Those doings of the defendants which were complained of as violative of the Sherman law, were all performed in Central America, near the dividing line between the Republic of Costa Rica and the Republic of Panama, or in one or the other of those republics. Justice Holmes stated that those doings did include restraint and monopolization of trade in bananas, but that they were not violative of the Sherman law, because they were not committed within any territorial limits over which the United States has any jurisdiction, although they were committed by a corporation which had been created by one of the United States. In support of this conclusion of law, Justice Holmes wrote the following sentences:

"No doubt in regions subject to no sovereign, like the high seas, or to no law that civilized countries would recognize as adequate, such countries may treat some relations between their citizens as governed by their own law, and keep alive to some extent the old notion of personal sovereignty. They go further, at times, and declare that they will punish any one, subject or not, who shall do certain things, if they can catch him, as in the case of pirates on the high seas. In cases immediately affecting national interests, they may go further still and may make, and if they get the chance, may execute, similar threats as to acts done within another recognized jurisdiction. An illustration from our statutes is found with regard to criminal correspondence with foreign governments. But the general and almost universal rule is that the character of an act, as lawful or unlawful, must be determined wholly by the law of the country where the act is done."

It was in this one of the characteristically brilliant judicial opinions of Justice Holmes, that he inserted his own original definition of law in the following twenty-two words: "Law is a statement of the circumstances in which the public force will be brought to bear upon men through the courts."

19. Pennsylvania Sugar Refining Co. vs. American Sugar Refining Co. and others, 160 Fed. Rep. 144, and 166 Fed. Rep. 254. This was an action at law, brought in the United States Circuit Court for the Southern District of New York to recover $30,000,000, as triple damages inflicted by the American Company and its co-conspirators upon the Pennsylvania Company, by means of a violation of the Sherman law.

The complaint was dismissed on March 20, 1908, by Judge Holt, a United States District Judge, who was then holding the United States Circuit Court for the Southern District of New York, on the ground that in his opinion the facts of the case were so nearly like those in the Knight case, that according to the view of the law taken in that case, those facts did not constitute a violation of the Sherman law. Thereupon, the case was taken to the United States Circuit Court of Appeals for the Second Circuit, by means of a writ of error; which court, on December 15, 1908, reversed the judgment of Judge Holt, and sent the case back to the Circuit Court for a trial of the questions of fact involved therein, including the amount of damages which had been incurred by the plaintiff. This reversal of the judgment dismissing the complaint was based, as that judgment had been, upon the temporary assumption that the statements of facts in the complaint were true. Those facts were essentially as follows:

The Pennsylvania Sugar Company, from the year 1883 to the year 1898, had been engaged in the business of importing raw sugar from other states, and from foreign countries, and manufacturing it there into refined sugar, and exporting that product to other states and countries. The plaintiff suspended that business in 1898, on account of the Spanish War, but in 1901 it commenced the erection of a new and enlarged refinery, which was

completed in 1903.   When the plaintiff was about to resume and continue its former importation of raw sugar,
manufacture of refined sugar and exportation of refined
sugar, the defendants conspired to prevent such re-en-
gagement in that business; and they accomplished that
object by inducing Mr. Segal, who indirectly held a majority of the stock of the Pennsylvania Sugar Company,
to accept a loan of a large sum of money, and to secure
that loan by transferring to the defendants that stock
with its voting power attached thereto.   Thereupon the
defendants elected new directors to manage the business
of the Pennsylvania Sugar Company, and caused those
directors to prevent any renewal of business by that
company.

On the basis of these facts, the complaint took the
ground that the doings of the defendant had restrained
interstate and international commerce in sugar, as well
as restraining the refining of sugar in Pennsylvania, and
that the Pennsylvania Sugar Company was entitled to
recover as damages, under Section 7 of the Sherman
law, the amount of the profits which it would have made
in that business, if the defendants had not prevented any
such business from being done; and that those profits
during the years through which the defendants prevented the Pennsylvania Sugar Company from doing any
sugar business amounted to $10,000,000.

The defendants contended, in the Circuit Court and in
the Circuit Court of Appeals, that the complaint stated
restraint of manufacture of refined sugar in Pennsylvania, but did not allege restraint of international or
interstate commerce in sugar; and on the basis of that
contention, the defendants took the ground that according to the Knight case they had not violated the Sherman law.   But the Circuit Court of Appeals decided
that whereas, there was nothing in the Knight case to
prove that the defendants in that case had any intention

to restrain trade or commerce, the statements of fact in this Pennsylvania Sugar case showed a conspiracy which must necessarily result in putting a direct restraint upon interstate commerce.

The defendants also contended that the complaint did not state any case of restraint of interstate or international commerce, because the plaintiff was not engaged in any such commerce at the time of the alleged conspiracy. But that contention was overruled by the Circuit Court of Appeals on the ground that interstate commerce may be restrained by preventing particular persons from engaging therein, as truly as by preventing them from continuing therein when thus engaged already.

And finally, the defendants contended, that if the conspiracy was illegal, the plaintiff corporation was a party thereto, and therefore could not maintain an action against the other parties, for damages resulting therefrom.

In reply to this contention, Judge Noyes, who wrote the opinion of the Circuit Court of Appeals, said that a corporation is not responsible for any conspiracy entered into by its own directors, for the purpose of injuring the interests of the corporation, and thus inflicting damage upon its stockholders.

After this case was returned to the Circuit Court, in pursuance of the foregoing decision of the Circuit Court of Appeals, it came on for trial before a judge and a jury early in 1909, the leading attorney for the plaintiff being Frank S. Black, formerly Governor of New York, and the leading attorney for the defendants being John G. Milburn. As soon as the plaintiff's evidence was introduced, the defendants sought and obtained a settlement of the case, by paying a large sum of money, the precise amount of which was not published, but which is reported to have been more than $2,000,000.

20. Bigelow vs. Calumet & Hecla Mining Co. and others, 155 Fed. Rep. 869, and 167 Fed. Rep. 704, and 167 Fed. Rep. 721. This was an action in equity in the Circuit Court of the United States for the Western District of Michigan, in its Northern Division. The complainant was a citizen of Massachusetts, and was a large stockholder in the Osceola Company, a Michigan corporation, which corporation was one of the defendants, the principal defendant being the Calumet & Hecla Company. Both of these corporations were engaged as competitors in producing copper in Michigan, and in selling that copper in interstate commerce. Prior to the beginning of the suit, the Calumet & Hecla Company had purchased a large block of the stock of the Osceola Company, and had obtained voting proxies for an additional large amount of that stock; and the complainant feared that at a forthcoming stockholders' meeting of the Osceola Company, then appointed to be held on March 14, 1907, the Calumet & Hecla Company would obtain and would thereafter maintain complete control of the Osceola Company. On the basis of these facts, the bill of complaint charged that the programme constituted an attempt to violate the Sherman law, and also the Michigan anti-monopoly law, and also the common law; and thereupon the bill prayed that the Calumet & Hecla Company and the Osceola Company should both be restrained from carrying out the contemplated plans.

Thereupon a motion for an injunction in pursuance of that prayer was presented to Judge Knappen, who was then the United States District Judge for the Western District of Michigan, but who is now one of the United States Circuit Judges for the Sixth Circuit, and that motion was granted, and that injunction ordered, on April 12, 1907.

In the written opinion which Judge Knappen filed to support his decision to grant an injunction, he said that the bill plainly alleged a violation of the law, unless the alleged attempted monopoly is made lawful by the fact that it is proposed to be accomplished by means of getting and maintaining control of a competing corporation through purchasing its stock, instead of by previous agreement between two corporations. On this point Judge Knappen said that "It seems clear that under the decision in the Northern Securities case, the creation of a monopoly by way of stock purchase and control offends against the statute," and the context shows that the statute to which he referred was the Sherman law.

Judge Knappen also held that under the general jurisdiction of equity, relief by injunction may be granted to a private party against violations of the Sherman law; wherein he avowedly differed in opinion from those judges who had previously decided that the only remedy given to private parties by the Sherman law was an action at law for damages, under Section 7 of that statute.

The foregoing decision of Judge Knappen was provisional only, and not final, and the resulting injunction was only temporary. The final decision of Judge Knappen in the case was rendered on October 3, 1908. That decision was to the effect that the bill of complaint should be dismissed. That conclusion was reached in the light of the evidence which had been taken in the case since the temporary injunction was granted, and which evidence convinced Judge Knappen that the proposed acquirement by the Calumet & Hecla Mining Company of the control of the Osceola Company was not intended to restrain trade or create monopoly, and would not have a direct, immediate and necessary effect to accomplish any such result.

An appeal was taken by Mr. Bigelow, the complainant, from this final decree of Judge Knappen, to the Circuit

Court of Appeals for the Sixth Circuit, and that appeal was decided adversely to Mr. Bigelow by that court on February 18, 1909, when the court was being held by Circuit Judges Lurton and Severens, and District Judge Cochran of the Eastern District of Kentucky. All of those three judges concurred in the judgment of the court; and Judge Lurton wrote one opinion, while Judge Cochran wrote another opinion, in support of that conclusion.

Judge Lurton, after quoting Sections 1 and 2 of the Sherman law, wrote the following significant sentences in his opinion:

"We shall assume at the outset that the authoritative decisions of the Supreme Court have so construed this anti-trust act as to give it a broader application than the prohibition of contracts and agreements in restraint of trade at the common law. It is not essential that the restraint shall be unreasonable, within the well understood definition of an unlawful restraint before the statute. Under this act, the validity of an alleged combination or contract in restraint of trade, interstate or foreign, is to be determined by the terms of the statute which forbids any such contract or combination, without respect to its nature or beneficial results. But the power of Congress to legislate upon the subject, aside from the territories and the District of Columbia, is derived from its power to regulate commerce among the states and with foreign nations. It is therefore well settled that it does not apply to restraint or monopolies as such, but only to those which directly and immediately, or those which necessarily affect commerce among the states or with foreign nations. This limitation of the act to those contracts and combinations which directly or immediately or necessarily affect commerce among the states, is recognized in a long series of opinions. The Knight case, in its last analysis, is but a striking illustration of the rule that the monopoly or agreement, to come within the act, must directly and immediately affect interstate commerce. Confining the case to its facts, it establishes the proposition that a mere combination between manufacturers only, by which a monopoly of a product results, is not, without other special circumstances, sufficient to justify an active intervention under the act, to undo a contract by which such monopoly has been brought about. That the product thus monopolized by such a combination of mere manufacturers, may ultimately find itself into the stream of interstate commerce, is there held not to be such a special circumstance as to constitute the direct and immediate effect upon commerce among the states, as to bring the agreement within the act."

"The specific thing complained of in the case for decision, is that one Michigan mining corporation has obtained by purchase or proxy, a majority of the capital shares of another Michigan mining corporation, and purposes to exercise its voting power to place in the directory of the latter a majority of its own selection from its own board of officers. The specific relief sought is an injunction against the exercise of the voting power and a decree compelling a disposition of the shares so held under purchase or proxy. Confessedly the products of these two companies are in competition in the markets, and confessedly, the greater part of the product will, sooner or later, enter into the stream of interstate commerce, for the chief demand for the product is outside the state of production. But that is not enough. There was all this and more in the Knight case. If, indeed, such stock control results in monopoly, it is only a monopoly in manufacture in the same state, and we have again the conceded situation in the Knight case. Unless that monopoly of manufacture, in a single state of a product which goes into interstate commerce directly and immediately, or necessarily interferes with or restrains that commerce, the monopoly does not come under the act of Congress. But we are unable to conclude upon this record that mere stock control of such a company by another in the same state, either directly or necessarily destroys competition there, or if it did, that it results in any such monopoly as to directly or necessarily and immediately affect commerce among the states."

"The power of stock control which the Calumet Company has acquired may be exercised only in a legitimate and lawful way in the interest of an economical management of both companies, in that case it has done nothing directly affecting commerce among the states."

"On the other hand, that power may be a mere preparation for the doing of acts which will directly and necessarily interfere with the freedom of that kind of commerce which it is the purpose of Congress to protect. When this unlawful use of the power shall result in an unlawful restraint, or further steps shall point to results directly affecting such commerce, there may be interference by the courts."

The concurring opinion of Judge Cochran was devoted mainly to a long and elaborate exposition of the Supreme Court decision in the Knight case, because he thought that decision, when correctly construed, was exactly applicable to this Calumet case, and necessitated a decision thereof, in favor of the Calumet & Hecla Company. His analysis of the decision in the Knight case resulted in his conclusion that that decision was confined to a negative answer to the question whether the purchase by the American Sugar Refining Company of the capital stock of four Pennsylvania corporations which owned sugar refineries in Philadelphia, constituted a violation of the Sherman law. In reaching that conclusion, Judge Cochran found that the decision in the Knight case did not include any decision of the question whether the Sherman law would

have been violated if it had been proved in the record
that after the purchase by the American Sugar Refining
Company of the capital stock of the four Pennsylvania
corporations, those corporations had entered into an
agreement among themselves concerning any external
commerce to be done by them.

During the fifteen years which have passed since the
Knight case was decided by the Supreme Court, no judicial expositions of the significance of the decision in that
case have been published which were more acute or more
astute than those of Judge Lurton and Judge Cochran
in this Calumet & Hecla case. The entire record in the
Knight case was printed in a pamphlet of 215 pages, and
that record contains no evidence that the American Sugar
Refining Company ever used its ownership and control
of the corporate stock of the four Pennsylvania sugar
refining companies to cause or to promote any agreement,
contract, combination or conspiracy to restrain any interstate commerce, nor any evidence that any such result
followed the acquirement of that stock, or that any sugar
thereafter refined in any of the four Philadelphia refineries was ever sent or shipped beyond the boundary
lines of Pennsylvania, or ever became in any way a subject of interstate or international commerce.

The Supreme Court necessarily decided the Knight case
upon the record in that case. But many counsel and some
courts have construed that decision as if it were based
upon all the facts which they supposed to be true, including the material facts which were not set forth in the
record. Those material facts included the fact that while
there was never any combination, contract or conspiracy
between any of the four Pennsylvania corporations,
either in respect of the sale of their corporate stock to
the American Sugar Refining Company, or in respect of

any business done by any of the four Pennsylvania corporations after those stocks were thus sold, there was a
combination between the American Sugar Refining Company and each of the four Pennsylvania corporations, to
restrain interstate and international commerce in sugar.

The absence from the record of any admission or any
evidence of any combination between any two parties to
restrain any interstate or international commerce, was
what resulted in a decision of the Knight case against
the United States. That result was an unfortunate defeat of justice in that case at that time. And justice
has been many times delayed, if not defeated, in other
cases during the last fifteen years, as a result of that
misconstruction of the decision of the Supreme Court
in the Knight case, which followed from the general assumption that the record in that case included some
evidence of restraint of interstate commerce, as an incidental result of restraint of local manufacture.

21.   Meeker et al vs. Lehigh Valley Railroad Company 162 Fed. Rep. 354.   This was an action at law, in
the United States Circuit Court for the Southern District
of New York, brought by Meeker & Co., a partnership
engaged in buying anthracite coal at the anthracite coal
mines in Pennsylvania, shipping that coal therefrom over
the Lehigh Valley Railroad to tide water at Perth Amboy,
New Jersey, and thence on boats to the City of New
York, and in selling that coal in that city.   The complaint
stated that the transportation of anthracite coal from the
anthracite mines in Pennsylvania to tide water adjacent
to the City of New York, was necessarily conducted by
one or another of eight different railroad companies, including the Lehigh Valley Railroad Company, the Philadelphia & Reading Railway Company and the Pennsylvania Railroad Company; and that all these eight railroad
companies, directly or indirectly owned coal lands and

were engaged in mining and selling coal, in addition to being engaged in transporting their own coal and the coal of other miners from the anthracite region, to tide water adjacent to New York. Thereupon the complaint stated that all of the said eight companies except the Pennsylvania Railroad Company, conspired and combined together in or about the year 1899, to raise the charges for transporting anthracite coal between the mines in Pennsylvania and tide water in New Jersey and New York, and agreed to fix those prices at a uniform schedule, ranging from $1.10 to $1.55 per ton, for the four different classes of anthracite coal, respectively; and that those rates had ever since been enforced by all of the seven railroad companies, and were far in excess of the value of the transportation to the plaintiffs, who had been compelled to pay those rates as a result of the combination between all the railroad companies to transport coal at those rates only. The complaint asked a judgment for triple damages, under Section 7 of the Sherman law.

The complaint was defective in not stating the facts which showed that the rates thus agreed to be charged by the seven railroad companies were extortionate, as compared with what fairly compensatory rates would have been. Those facts, if they had been stated in the complaint, would have shown that the rates agreed to be charged and charged by the seven railroad companies, were thus extortionate to the extent of at least one-half of each rate. And those facts must have been well known to Mr. Meeker, for they have long been notorious and are undeniable. But through some error, those facts were not stated in the complaint, and therefore could not be considered by the court, when deciding the case, as it was decided upon a demurrer to the complaint.

That decision was rendered on June 6, 1908, by Judge Ray, the United States District Judge for the Northern

District of New York, when temporarily holding the
United States Circuit Court for the Southern District of
New York. Judge Ray held that "a resort to the Interstate Commerce Commission is a condition precedent to
the maintenance of an action, in the Circuit Court of the
United States, to recover damages solely occasioned by
the payment of excessive, unjust or unreasonable rates
for the transportation of interstate commerce, even when
the exaction of such excessive rates was the result of a
combination or conspiracy made unlawful by the Sherman
anti-trust law." This decision was equivalent to holding
that a Circuit Court of the United States, when entertain-
ing an action at law for the purpose of ascertaining the
amount of damage which a particular combination or conspiracy violative of the Sherman law, has inflicted upon
a plaintiff claiming to have been injured thereby, will not
receive evidence proving the bottom facts, but will be
governed entirely by whatever declaration relevant to the
question, may have been made by the Interstate Commerce
Commission, and that in the absence of any such declaration, no damage whatever can be recovered in any United
States Circuit Court.

It does not appear that the plaintiffs in this case have
ever prosecuted the case in court since that adverse decision of Judge Ray was rendered; for the published reports of the United States courts do not contain any
report of any review of Judge Ray's decision. Whenever
hereafter the same question arises between other parties
before another judge, it is to be expected that that judge
will decide that Section 7 of the Sherman law does not
express or imply any necessity for any resort to the Interstate Commerce Commission, as a condition precedent
to the enforcement of that section by any Circuit Court
of the United States, in any case where the bottom facts
are found by legal evidence, to require such an enforcement.

22. Monarch Tobacco Works vs. American Tobacco
Co. and others, 165 Fed. Rep. 774. This was an action
at law brought in the United States Circuit Court for the
Western District of Kentucky, under Section 7 of the
Sherman law to recover damages for injuries claimed
to have been inflicted upon the plaintiff by the American
Tobacco Company and the Nall & Williams Tobacco
Company, and the Mengel Box Company. The complaint
stated that the plaintiff was organized in 1901, and had
by the expenditure of a large sum of money built up a
good trade in tobacco by the beginning of 1903; and that
in 1903 the American Tobacco Company acquired secret
control of the Nall & Williams Tobacco Company by
secretly purchasing a large majority of its capital stock,
and thereupon falsely pretended that the Nall & Williams
Tobacco Company was an independent corporation, while
so controlling that corporation, as to greatly injure the
plaintiff's interstate business. The complaint also stated
that the plaintiff had formerly made a still outstanding
contract with the Mengel Box Company to furnish the
plaintiff with boxes for all the tobacco put up by the plaintiff, which contract contained a stipulation that the Mengel
Box Company should not disclose to any other party the
number of boxes delivered to the plaintiff; but that the
American Tobacco Company had acquired a controlling
interest in the Mengel Box Company and thus acquired
knowledge of the plaintiff's secret, and had used that
knowledge to aid it in executing the injurious combination and conspiracy of which the plaintiff complained.

In response to this complaint, each of the defendants
filed a general demurrer, and also filed a motion to require the plaintiff to make its allegations of damages
more definite; and the American Tobacco Company and
the Mengel Box Company moved the court to require
the plaintiff to drop from the suit either the Nall & Williams Tobacco Company or the Mengel Box Company,

upon the ground that the complaint did not state that either of those two defendants had done anything in combination with each other.

The demurrer and the motions were argued before Judge Evans, the District Judge for the Western District of Kentucky, and on December 21, 1908, he overruled them all on the ground that the sufficiency of the complaint, when judged by the generality of the language of the Sherman law and by the Civil Code of Practice of Kentucky, was sufficient, and was sufficiently specific to jointly charge all the defendants with having combined to violate the Sherman law, and to lay the foundation for evidence of the extent of the injury which had been inflicted upon the plaintiff as a result of that combination.

23. Blount Manufacturing Co. vs. Yale & Towne Manufacturing Co., 166 Fed. Rep. 555. This was an action in equity, in the United States Circuit Court for the District of Massachusetts, brought for an accounting in accordance with the terms of a contract concerning the profits arising from the manufacture and sale of patented liquid door checks. The defendant filed a demurrer, in pursuance of which it claimed that the complainant was not entitled to recover, because the contract was void under the Sherman law. The demurrer was argued before Judge Brown, the United States District Judge for the District of Rhode Island, when temporarily holding the United States Circuit Court for the District of Massachusetts, and the demurrer was sustained by him on January 14, 1909. In order to sustain the demurrer, Judge Brown had to distinguish the case from the Supreme Court decision in the case of Bement vs. National Harrow Co., 186 U. S. 70; for the complainant contended that the demurrer should be overruled in pursuance of that precedent.

The following was how Judge Brown distinguished this Blount case from the Bement case:

In the Bement case the National Harrow Company was the absolute owner of all the letters patent covered by the contract which was involved in that case; and therefore that contract did not create any restraint of trade or any monopoly beyond the monopoly which the National Harrow Company already had under the patent law. But in the Blount case, some of the patents involved in the contract were the property of the complainant, and some of them were the property of the defendant, and the contract operated to restrain all competition between the parties in regard to their respective patented inventions; and inasmuch as that competition included interstate commerce, the contract therefore operated to restrain such commerce. In the Bement case, there was no competition between the patents before the contract was made, and therefore that contract did not restrain any competition. But in the Blount case before the contract was made there was competition between the patents owned by the plaintiff and those owned by the defendant, and that competition was ended by the contract, which ending made the contract violative of the Sherman law.

24. Ames vs. American Telephone & Telegraph Co., 166 Fed. Rep. 820. This was an action at law, brought in the United States Circuit Court for the District of Massachusetts, to recover triple damages under Section 7 of the Sherman law, for injuries claimed to have been inflicted upon the plaintiff, by the defendant, when violating that law. The declaration stated that the plaintiff was the owner of some shares of the capital stock of the Telephone, Telegraph & Cable Company of America, which had been organized to operate telephones throughout the United States in competition with the defendant company; and that thereupon the defendant company had purchased a majority of the shares of the stock of the Telephone, Telegraph & Cable Company, and had used the power thus acquired to diminish and suppress the business of that theretofore competing company, until the value of the complainant's stock, which prior to the defendant's doings was $15 a share, had as a result of those doings, been reduced to nothing.

The defendant filed a demurrer to this bill of complaint; and that demurrer, on January 14, 1909, was sustained by Judge Brown, on the ground that the injury complained of was inflicted upon the Telephone, Telegraph & Cable Company, and that according to Sections 7 and 8 of the Sherman law, that corporation was the only "person" to maintain an action to recover triple damages alleged to have been caused by the doings of the defendant.

The foregoing twenty-four cases of litigation between private parties, which occurred during Roosevelt's administration and which related to the Sherman law, may be classified as follows:

Those of the twenty-four cases which are designated by the numerals 3, 12, 13 and 23, relate to the relations which the patent law bears to the Sherman law, and to the circumstances under which commodities which are covered by patents, are exempt from those provisions of the Sherman law which prohibit restraint and prohibit monopolization of certain kinds of trade or commerce.

Those of the twenty-four cases which are designated by the numerals 2, 7, 9, 15, 19 and 22 were successful actions at law, brought under Section 7 of the Sherman law, to recover triple damages from the defendants on account of injuries which they had inflicted upon the plaintiffs by their violations of the Sherman law.

The cases which are designated by the numerals 5, 18, 20, 21 and 24, were unsuccessful attempts to enforce the Sherman law against the defendants in those cases, respectively.

The cases which are designated by the numerals 4, 6, 8, 11 and 16, were cases in which the defendants unsuccessfully invoked the Sherman law to protect them from meritorious suits.

The cases designated by the numerals 10, 14 and 17 were cases in which the defendants successfully invoked the Sherman law to protect them against suits in which they had no other defense.

The case designated by the numeral 1, was a case in which the petitioner for a writ of habeas corpus sought and secured liberty to refrain from giving testimony before a Grand Jury, which if given, would have tended to incriminate him as a violator of the Sherman law.

The only one of the sixteen cases, wherein the Sherman law can possibly be claimed to have produced an unjust result, was the case of the Continental Wall Paper Company against Voight & Sons Company, which in the foregoing pages is designated by the numeral 14. And Justice Harlan, in delivering the opinion of the Supreme Court in that case, held that its result was not unjust because that result consisted in the non-recovery of money, which if recovered, would have rewarded the plaintiff for violating the Sherman law. On the other hand, Justice Holmes, who dissented from the decision of the Supreme Court in that case, held that that result was unjust, because it enabled the defendant to avoid paying for merchandise which it had purchased.

CHAPTER IX.

The administration of President Taft at this writing has covered nearly a year and a half, extending from March 4, 1909, to August 31, 1910. The Attorney General during that time has been George W. Wickersham, of New York. The public cases and the private cases, relevant to the Sherman law, which have been pending during a part or all of that time, include many which were brought but not adjudicated prior to March 4, 1909, and many others which have been brought since that day, and which have not yet been adjudicated. Those public Sherman law cases which having been brought by the United States to restrain or punish violations of the Sherman law, and which were adjudicated after the beginning of Taft's administration, and before September 1, 1910, were the following:

1. United States vs. American Naval Stores Co. and others, 172 Fed. Rep. 455. This was a trial in the United States Circuit Court for the Southern District of Georgia, in its Eastern Division, of two corporations and six men, upon an indictment having two counts, one of which charged the defendants with having violated Section 1, and the other of which charged them with having violated Section 2, of the Sherman law. Upon that trial, on May 12, 1909, the charge to the jury was delivered by Judge Sheppard, the United States District Judge for the Northern District of Florida, who was temporarily holding the United States Circuit Court for the Southern District of Georgia. In the course of that charge, Judge Sheppard stated to the jury, for their guidance, the following points of law:

"To constitute the offense of monopolizing or attempting to monopolize, under the act of Congress (the Sherman law) it is necessary to acquire, or attempt to acquire, an exclusive right in such commerce, by means which will prevent others from engaging therein."

"As to what constitutes a restraint of trade under the statute, the act prohibits any combination which obstructs the free flow of commerce between the states, or restricts in that regard, the liberty of a trader engaged in business. This includes restraints of trade aimed at compelling third parties and strangers, involuntarily, not to engage in the course of interstate trade or commerce, except on conditions that the combination imposes."

"A conspiracy is defined as a combination of two or more persons, by concerted action, to accomplish a criminal or unlawful purpose, or some purpose not in itself criminal or unlawful, by criminal or unlawful means."

"The prohibitory provisions of the act under consideration, apply to all monopolies, combinations, or conspiracies in restraint of interstate or foreign trade or commerce, without exception or limitation, and are not confined to those in which the restraint is unreasonable. The government need not show that a conspiracy is entered into for the direct purpose of restraining trade or commerce, if such restraint is its necessary effect."

"A corporation, although an artificial being, existing only in contemplation of law, is held to the same measure of liability as an individual, and is entitled to the same rights of protection as an individual. While a corporation may not conspire with its own officers, directors or agents, it may conspire with another corporation. Corporations may conspire with individuals. But a corporation is only responsible for the acts of its agents while acting within the scope of their employment, or for such acts only as may have been authorized."

Having heard this excellent charge, the jury after deliberation, returned a verdict of guilty as to five individual defendants; whereupon the court sentenced two of those defendants to be imprisoned in jail three months and imposed upon all five of them fines aggregating $17,500.

2. United States vs. Kissel and others, 173 Fed. Rep. 823. This was an indictment in the United States Circuit Court for the Southern District of New York, of the American Sugar Refining Company and others, which was based upon the same violation of the Sherman law as that which was the subject of the civil suit of the Pennsylvania Sugar Refining Company against the American Sugar Refining Company and others, and which civil suit is No. 19 of the private litigations which are explained in Chapter VIII of this book.

The question relevant to this indictment which was decided in this case, was decided by Judge Holt, one of the United States District Judges for the Southern District of New York, on October 26, 1909. That decision consisted in overruling a demurrer which had been filed by the United States, in response to certain pleas in bar to the indictment, which had been filed by two of the defendants, namely G. E. Kissel and T. B. Harned. Those pleas in bar were based upon Section 1044 of the Revised Statutes of the United States, which provides that no persons shall be prosecuted, tried or punished for any offense not capital, nor arising under the revenue laws, or the slave trade laws of the United States, unless the indictment is found or the information is instituted within three years next after such offense shall have been committed.

In overruling the demurrer to these pleas in bar, Judge Holt held that Section 1044 of the Revised Statutes of the United States was a bar to the indictment, because the original conspiracy of the defendants to violate the Sherman law, and their first overt act in pursuance of that conspiracy occurred more than three years before the indictment was filed on July 1, 1909.

3. Union Pacific Coal Company and others vs. United States, 173 Fed. Rep. 737. This was an indictment in the District Court of the United States for the District of Utah, which was followed by a conviction of the defendants for violation of the Sherman law. Those convicted defendants were The Union Pacific Coal Company, the Union Pacific Railroad Company, the Oregon Short Line Railroad Company, and two men, one of whom was an agent of the coal company, and the other of whom was an agent of the two railroad companies.

The charge in the indictment was that about July 20, 1906, the defendants combined to compel Mr. Sharp, who was a purchaser of coal from the coal company and a retail dealer in coal in Salt Lake City, to quit his coal business, unless he would discontinue an advertisement which he had published, to the effect that he would sell storage coal at a reduction of 50 cents a ton from the regular retail price theretofore prevailing in Salt Lake City; which effort to force Sharp out of his business consisted in the refusal of the coal company, and its agent Moore, to sell any coal to Sharp, and of the refusal of the railroad companies, and their agent Buckingham, to transport any coal for him after July 22, 1906.

The trial having resulted in conviction of the defendants, they took the case to the Circuit Court of Appeals for the Eighth Circuit, by means of a writ of error. On November 19, 1909, Judge Sanborn, the Chief Judge of that court, delivered the opinion of that tribunal, re-

versing the judgment of the court below, with directions
to set aside the verdict and grant a new trial. That reversal was based upon the opinion of the Circuit Court
of Appeals that there was no substantial evidence of
any combination between any two of the defendants,
either to refuse to sell coal to Sharp, or to refuse to
transport coal for him; and that in the absence of any
such combination, the coal company had a right to refuse
to sell coal to Sharp; and that there was no evidence that
either of the railroad companies, or Buckingham their
agent, had ever failed or refused to transport any coal
or other merchandise which Sharp had requested any of
them to carry.

4. United States vs. Standard Oil Company of New
Jersey and others, 173 Fed. Rep. 177. This was a bill in
equity, filed November 15, 1906, in the United States
Circuit Court for the Eastern District of Missouri, under
the direction of Attorney General Moody, against the
Standard Oil Company of New Jersey, and about seventy
subsidiary corporations and seven individual defendants.
The decisions of the court, overruling the dilatory defenses which were originally interposed by the defendants, are stated and explained in Chapter VIII of this
book, wherein it is also stated that after those defenses
were overruled by the court, the defendants filed their
answers to the bill of complaint, whereupon the taking
of evidence in the case occupied more than a year, and
continued until nearly the end of President Roosevelt's
administration.

The argument of the case on its merits and demerits,
occurred in April 1909, and was conducted orally and
in print by Frank B. Kellogg of Minnesota and five other
lawyers for the United States and by John G. Johnson
of Pennsylvania and twelve other lawyers for the defendants.

The judges who composed the court at the time of the argument of this case, included all of the four judges of the Eighth Circuit, namely: Judges Sanborn, Van Devanter, Hook and Adams. All of those judges concurred in deciding the case in favor of the United States, and when they rendered that decision on November 20, 1909, Judge Sanborn filed an opinion expressing views of all four of the judges in support of that decision, and Judge Hook filed a concurring and supplemental opinion, in support of the opinion filed by Judge Sanborn.

The elaborate opinion of Judge Sanborn is printed on pages 179 to 193 of Volume 173 of the Federal Reporter. Several of those pages are devoted to stating the history of the Standard Oil combination from 1865, when John D. Rockefeller controlled a single oil refinery, until 1908, when the par value of the capital stock of the corporations which belong to the combination complained of in the suit was more than $150,000,000, and when the market value of that stock was four or five times greater than its par value. The first stage of that history continued from 1865 to 1870, during which five years the business was owned by a partnership, of which John D. Rockefeller was the principal partner, and which in 1870 owned two oil refineries. That stage was terminated in 1870, by the organization of a corporation to take the business from the partnership, which corporation was the Standard Oil Company of Ohio, having a capital stock of $1,000,000. The next stage of the history extended from 1870 to 1879, in the latter of which years the control of that corporation and more than thirty other corporations engaged in the oil business, was conveyed to three trustees, who operated all the corporations and refineries belonging to the combination until 1882, when the trust property which they held had accumulated to the value of more than $55,000,000.

10

In January, 1882, all the three trustees and everybody else interested in the combination, conveyed the control and management of all the corporations and all the property in which they were interested, to nine trustees to hold during their lives and the life of the last survivor of them, and for twenty-one years thereafter; unless the trust would somehow be sooner dissolved. The written opinion of Judge Sanborn does not state the names of those nine trustees, but their names were John D. Rockefeller, William Rockefeller, John D. Archbold, H. M. Flagler, O. H. Payne, J. A. Bostwick, William G. Warden, Charles Pratt and Benjamin Brewster. These nine trustees, when receiving the control of all the corporations and all the property belonging to the numerous persons and corporations who had conveyed it to them, issued to those persons and corporations, trust certificates of 700,000 shares in the trust, each of which shares had a par value of $100, and all of which had a par value of $70,000,000. During the next ten years, those trustees issued 272,500 additional shares of trust certificates, so that on March 21, 1892, the outstanding certificates represented 972,500 shares, having a par value of $97,-250,000.

Early in March, 1892, the Supreme Court of Ohio decided that the Standard Oil Trust of 1882 was contrary to the laws of Ohio and contrary to the common law, and must be enjoined from continuing its operations. At that time the trustees held stocks in eighty-four corporations. Thereupon they distributed the stocks which they held in sixty-four of these corporations, among ten other corporations, including the Standard Oil Company of New Jersey, but they retained the stock of those ten corporations and also the stock of ten other corporations, and thus continued to directly control twenty of the eighty-four corporations, and to indirectly control the other sixty-four, for seven years more, and until 1899.

Thus it came about that in 1899 the Standard Oil Company of New Jersey was one of twenty corporations, among which the ownership of the whole Standard Oil business was distributed, but all of which were still controlled by the nine trustees. But in that year the charter of the Standard Oil Company of New Jersey was amended to empower it to do all kinds of mining, manufacturing, trading and transportation business in all parts of the world, and also to acquire, hold, vote, sell and assign shares of capital stock of other corporations. At the same time its own capital stock was increased to 1,000,000 shares of $100 each, and the stock of the other nineteen companies was exchanged for the stock of the Standard Oil Company of New Jersey, so that the latter company succeeded to the legal title to the majority of the stock of the nineteen companies, and thereby succeeded to the management and control of those corporations, and of all the corporations which they controlled.

Thus it resulted that step by step, from 1892 to 1899, the control and management of all parts of the great Standard Oil combination was transferred from the nine trustees holding under the Standard Oil Trust, to the Standard Oil Company of New Jersey, as a holding corporation; but inasmuch as that holding corporation was then and thereafter controlled and managed by substantially the same cluster of men who were formerly the nine trustees, the corporate organization of New Jersey was substantially the same in respect of its control of the petroleum business, as the Standard Oil Trust of Ohio had been, before it was found illegal, and was dissolved in pursuance of a decision of the Supreme Court of that state.

After the entire control of the Standard Oil business was combined, in the form of the Standard Oil Company of New Jersey, in 1899, and until 1906, the affairs of the principal company and of the subsidiary companies

were managed by the Standard Oil Company of New
Jersey, with unity of purpose and absolute control. The
filing of the bill of complaint in this case in 1906 did
not cause any change in the Standard Oil organization;
and, indeed, its business continued to grow from that
time until the case was decided in November, 1909.
Midway between those periods, in 1907, the Standard
Oil Company of New Jersey and its subsidiary companies manufactured more than three-fourths of all the
petroleum refined in the United States, marketed more
than four-fifths of all the illuminating oil sold in the
United States or exported from the United States, sold
more than four-fifths of all the naphtha sold in the
United States, and sold more than nine-tenths of all the
lubricating oil purchased by railroad companies in the
United States.

After thus stating the history and the magnitude of
the Standard Oil combination, Judge Sanborn inserted
in his written opinion the following statement of facts
relevant to the resulting restraint of interstate and international commerce:

"The principal company, by means of this trust and
the commanding volume of the oil business which it
acquired thereby, secured, and has since exercised and is
using, the power to prevent competition between the
companies it controls, to fix for them the purchase price
of the crude oil, the rates for its transportation, and the
selling prices of its products. It has prevented, and is
preventing, any competition in interstate and international
commerce in petroleum and its products, between its subsidiary companies, and between those companies and
itself."

It was upon the basis of the facts which were stated
by Judge Sanborn in the last paragraph, that the opinion
written by him reached the conclusion that the Standard

Oil Company of New Jersey, and the seven individual defendants who exercised its power, and the subsidiary corporations, who knowingly submitted to and assisted that exercise, were all guilty of violating Section 1 of the Sherman law. That conclusion involved and implied that construction of that section which ascribes to the word "restraint" a meaning broad enough to cover mutual restraint between the members of a combination, regardless of the question whether the combination as a whole is guilty of exercising extraneous restraint upon one or more other parties.

Having reached these conclusions relevant to the violation by the Standard Oil combination of Section 1 of the Sherman law, the written opinion of Judge Sanborn proceeds to ascertain and state whether that combination was also guilty of violating Section 2 of that law. On that point Judge Sanborn stated that the bill of complaint alleged that the defendants had secured from common carriers preferential rates and rebates and had operated some subsidiary corporations while representing them to be independent and had procured from employees of railroad companies information of the trade of competitors and had used that information to secure interstate commerce for themselves and to injure and destroy the interstate commerce of those competitors and had sold their products in special cases below remunerative prices in order to crush competition at those particular times and places and had recouped the resulting losses by selling such products at high prices at other times and places. But Judge Sanborn's opinion also states that it was unnecessary for the court to express any opinion upon the question of the truth of these charges in the bill of complaint, because the court was of opinion that the combination and conspiracy in restraint of trade contrary to the first section of the Sherman law, which had been found to exist in the case, constituted illegal means by which the conspiring defendants combined to monopolize a part of interstate and international commerce and by which they had secured an unlawful monopoly of a substantial part of such commerce and that the defendants had thus violated and were violating not only the first section of the Sherman law, but also the second section of that act.

The concurring opinion of Judge Hook in this Standard Oil case is printed on pages 193 to 197 of Volume 173 of the Federal Reporter. That opinion contains the following pivotal statements as being propositions to which all the four judges of the court were agreed:

"A holding company owning the stocks of other concerns whose commercial activities, if free and independent of a common control, would naturally bring them into competition with each other is a form of trust or combination prohibited by Section 1 of the Sherman antitrust act. The Standard Oil Company of New Jersey is such a holding company. The defendants, who are in the combination, are enjoined from continuing it and from forming another like it."

"The defendants in the combination are also monopolizing interstate and foreign commerce in petroleum and its products contrary to Section 2 of the act. A wrongful method employed to gain the monopoly is found to exist in the unlawful combination above mentioned, and it therefore becomes unnecessary to determine the other charges upon that subject in the petition of the Government."

"The true test to apply to a case under the first section is not whether the restraint upon competition imposed by the contract or combination in question should be regarded as reasonable or as unreasonable, but whether it is direct and appreciable. Conceptions of the reasonable and unreasonable are much too diverse to afford a stable, uniform rule for construing a law which contains no mention of those terms. So much depends upon the point of view that it frequently happens that what appears to one to be wholly unreasonable is thought entirely reasonable by another. But if the restraint is direct and appreciable, and not merely incidental to some contract having a lawful purpose, it falls clearly within the prohibition of the statute, and there is no room for further construction. There are many contracts which, in the days when the common law was forming, would have been adjudged contrary to public welfare, as being in restraint of the narrow trade of those times, but which in a commercial age like the present have such a negligible effect in that direction as to be no longer evil within the meaning of the law. Their effect is so indirect and inappreciable that it is properly referable to the class *de minimis,* and it is not to be supposed Congress had them in view when it legislated to preserve freedom of competition in the broad field of interstate and foreign commerce."

"Manifestly the second section is quite distinct from the first, and was not intended to cover precisely the same ground. Though the natural tendency of a combination in restraint of trade, declared illegal by Section 1, may be and generally is toward monopoly denounced by Section 2, and may even accomplish it, yet the scope of the latter section is far broader and was designed to extend also to monopolies secured by other means than by contracts, combinations and conspiracies in restraint of trade, which, as those terms necessarily imply, require concert between two or more persons or corporations. What is monopoly in contravention of the statute? Magnitude of business does not alone constitute a monopoly, nor effort at magnitude an attempt to monopolize. To offend the act the monopoly must have been secured by methods contrary to the public policy as expressed in the statutes or in the common law. Success and magnitude of business, the rewards of fair and honorable endeavor, were not among the evils which threatened the public welfare and attracted the attention of Congress. But when they have been attained by wrongful or unlawful methods and competition has been crippled or destroyed, the elements of monopoly are present."

The decree which was made by the Circuit Court for the Eastern District of Missouri in pursuance of the unanimous opinions of the four judges in this Standard Oil case, is printed in full on pages 197 to 200 of Volume 173 of the Federal Reporter. That decree states the names of the numerous corporations and of the seven men who were the defendants against whom it was made; which men were John D. Rockefeller, William Rockefeller, John D. Archbold, Henry M. Flagler, Oliver H. Payne, Charles M. Pratt and Henry H. Rogers. All of these men, except Henry H. Rogers, were six of the nine trustees who had managed the Standard Oil Trust of Ohio before that trust was dissolved in pursuance of a decision of the Supreme Court of Ohio in 1892. Three of those nine trustees, namely, J. A. Bostwick, William G. Warden and Benjamin Brewster, were not defendants in this Standard Oil case, nor mentioned in the decree of the court therein.

That decree adjudged that the defendants had made a combination in restraint of trade and commerce in petroleum and its products among the several states and territories, and with foreign nations, in violation of Section 1 of the Sherman law, and that, by means of that combination, the defendants had combined and conspired to monopolize and had monopolized, and were continuing to monopolize, a substantial part of the commerce among the states, in the territories and with foreign nations in violation of Section 2 of the Sherman law, and that the defendants were enjoined and prohibited from continuing or carrying into further effect that combination and from entering into or performing any like combination, and were also enjoined and prohibited, until the discontinuance of the operation of the said combination, from engaging or continuing in commerce among the states or in the territories of the United States.

The decree also provided that it was to take effect thirty days after its entry in case no appeal was taken from it, but if an appeal would be taken from it within those thirty days, then the decree, unless reversed or modified by the Supreme Court, was to take effect thirty days after the final decision of the case by the Supreme Court in pursuance of such an appeal.

The Standard Oil Company of New Jersey and its subsidiary corporations and all the other defendants, did take an appeal from the decision of the Circuit Court in this case. That appeal was argued in March, 1910; the appeal of the defendants in the case against the American Tobacco Company having been argued in January, 1910. At both those hearings the sitting justices consisted of Chief Justice Fuller and Associate Justices Harlan, Brewer, White, McKenna, Holmes, Day and Lurton. Justice Moody was absent on account of severe illness and was also disqualified to sit as one of the justices of the court to decide either of these two cases, because they had been brought by the United States under his direction as Attorney General.

After the two cases had been argued and submitted to the Supreme Court for decision and while they were being held under advisement by that tribunal, Associate Justice Brewer died on March 28, 1910. And in April, 1910, Chief Justice Fuller announced that both cases were restored to the calendar for reargument at some future time, and on a later day he announced that that time would be in November, 1910. But on July 4, 1910, Chief Justice Fuller himself departed this life, and now, at the end of August, 1910, there are only six justices of the Supreme Court who are able and qualified to sit in that tribunal to hear and decide either the Standard Oil case or the American Tobacco case.

It is true that Governor Hughes, of New York, has been appointed to succeed Justice Brewer as one of the associate justices of the Supreme Court, but he has not yet assumed that office, though he is expected to do so at the beginning of the next term of the court on October 10, 1910. But it is also expected that only seven justices of the court will be sitting at that time, or at any time thereafter, prior to the filling of the bench by appointment in the following winter and therefore it is not expected that this Standard Oil case or the American Tobacco case will be argued soon enough to be decided until some time in the year 1911.

Cases of litigation between private parties relevant to the Sherman law which have thus far been adjudicated during Taft's administration were the following:

1. People's Tobacco Co. vs. American Tobacco Co. and others, 170 Fed. Rep. 396. This was an action at law in the Circuit Court of the United States for the Eastern District of Louisiana to recover triple damages from the defendants under Section 7 of the Sherman law, alleged to result from injuries which had been inflicted upon the plaintiff on account of certain violations by the defendants of Sections 1 and 2 of the Sherman law. The action was begun by filing an elaborate petition, which is printed on pages 396 to 406 of volume 170 of the Federal Reporter. The defendants filed an exception to that petition, alleging that it did not disclose any

right of action. The Circuit Court sustained that exception and dismissed the suit. Thereupon the plaintiff took
the case to the Circuit Court of Appeals for the Fifth
Circuit by means of a writ of error.

The case was decided by the Circuit Court of Appeals
on May 3, 1909, when that court was held by all three
of the Circuit Judges for the Fifth Circuit. That decision reversed the judgment of the Circuit Court on the
ground that the petition was found by the Circuit Court
of Appeals to disclose a right of action. To reach that
conclusion the Circuit Court of Appeals stated that such
a petition need only aver and state facts to show that
the defendants had committed one or more of the offenses
condemned by the first and second sections of the Sherman law, and that the plaintiff had been injured in his
business or property by that conduct, and that the plaintiff had sustained some specified amount of damages as
a result of that injury.

2. Fonotipia, Limited, and others vs. Bradley, 171
Fed. Rep. 951. This was an action in equity in the
United States Circuit Court for the Eastern District of
New York, the purpose of which was to get an injunction to restrain the defendant from infringing an
alleged trademark belonging to the complainants and
from conducting unfair competition with the complainants by imitating their commodities.

The defendant made a number of defenses, one of
which was based upon the allegation that one of the
complainants had combined with the complainant in another similar case against the defendant to control the
retail prices at which their competing commodities were
to be sold and that that combination was violative of Section 1 of the Sherman law in being a restraint of trade
and commerce. This defense was plainly unsound, as
being contrary to the principle of the decision of the

United States Supreme Court in the case of Connolly vs. Union Sewer Pipe Company, 184, U. S. 540; because that case established the doctrine that a stranger to a combination which is violative of the Sherman law is not entitled to invoke the fact of that violation as a defense to a suit brought against him by a member of the combination to enforce some legal liability which he owes to the plaintiff.

But Judge Chatfield, the District Judge for the Eastern District of New York, who decided this Fonotipia case, instead of placing his decision against the defendant on that ground, did place that decision on another ground, which can hardly be reconciled with any of the repeated decisions of the Supreme Court and of other Federal courts, wherein it was held that Section 1 of the Sherman law prohibits all restraint of interstate commerce, whether they may be thought to be inherently reasonable or unreasonable. That other ground was the opinion of Judge Chatfield that Section 1 of the Sherman law is not violated by a combination to restrain interstate commerce where that combination was only a fair and reasonable attempt to avoid losses which otherwise might result from the members of the combination cutting rates and prices below the reasonable expense of production and a reasonable profit thereon. But that opinion is not a precedent to be followed by any other court because it is inconsistent with the decisions of the Supreme Court in a number of cases, including the Trans-Missouri case in 166 U. S. 290, and the Joint Traffic Association case in 171 U. S. 505.

3. Arkansas Brokerage Co. and others vs. Dunn & Powell Co., 173 Fed. Rep. 899. This was an action at law brought in the Circuit Court of the United States for the Eastern District of Arkansas to recover threefold damages under Section 7 of the Sherman law for injuries claimed to have been inflicted upon the Dunn & Powell Company by the Arkansas Brokerage Company and others. On the trial of the case in Arkansas the defendants requested the trial judge to instruct the jury that the plaintiff corporation was not entitled to recover. But that judge declined to give that instruction and the result of the trial was a judgment for the plaintiff.

Thereupon the defeated defendants took the case to the Circuit Court of Appeals for the Eighth Circuit by means of a writ of error. The case was decided by that tribunal on October 25, 1909, when that court was being held by Circuit Judge Adams and District Judges Riner and Amidon. The opinion of the Circuit Court of Appeals was delivered by Judge Adams. He stated in that opinion that for many years prior to 1906 the Dunn & Powell Company had conducted in Pine Bluff, Arkansas, a commercial brokerage business by negotiating sales of merchandise between manufacturers and wholesale dealers of other states and merchants doing business in and about Pine Bluff, but that in the year 1906 the five defendant Arkansas corporations organized the Arkansas Brokerage Company to enter into competition with the Dunn & Powell Company, relevant to such brokerage business as that company had long been doing, and that the Arkansas Brokerage Company had, without the use of any unfair means, acquired so nearly all of such brokerage business that could be done in Pine Bluff that the Dunn & Powell Company ceased doing business there, while continuing to do brokerage business in Little Rock, Arkansas.

On the basis of these facts Judge Adams announced it to be the opinion of the Circuit Court of Appeals that the combination of the five defendant Arkansas corporations to organize the Arkansas Brokerage Company, followed by the doings of that company, did not constitute any combination in restraint of interstate commerce, though that combination did result, through competition, in transferring a considerable amount of interstate commerce from the Dunn & Powell Company to the Arkansas Brokerage Company.

4. Northwestern Consolidated Milling Co. vs. William Callam & Son, 177 Fed. Rep. 786. This was an action in equity in the United States Circuit Court for the Eastern District of Michigan in its Northern Division, which action was based upon alleged infringement of a trademark used to designate the best grade of flour manufactured and sold by the complainant.

The defendants, having set up other defenses in their answer, requested the court to grant permission to amend that answer by pleading that the complainant was organized and was operating in violation of the Sherman law. Judge Swan, the District Judge for the Eastern District of Michigan, when deciding the case, held that the facts proposed to be stated in support of that defense did not constitute any violation of the Sherman law and that even if those facts had constituted such violation it was contrary to the decision of the Supreme Court in the case of Connolly vs. Union Sewer Pipe Company, 184 U. S. 540, for the defendant to invoke that law as a defense to his own liability arising from his infringement of a trademark belonging to the complainant.

5. Ware-Kramer Tobacco Co. vs. American Tobacco Co. and others, 178 Fed. Rep. 117. This was an action at law in the United States Circuit Court for the Eastern District of North Carolina, brought against the American Tobacco Company and the Wells-Whitehead Tobacco Company to recover $3,600,000, in pursuance of Section 7 of the Sherman law, on account of injuries claimed to have been inflicted by the defendants through their violations of that law, upon the business and property of the plaintiff.

On March 8, 1910, the case was presented to Judge Connor, the District Judge for the Eastern District of North Carolina, on a motion of both defendants to strike out many of the statements in the complaint as being irrelevant or at least redundant. In deciding that motion, Judge Connor said that "While the courts will, in proper cases, grant such motion, they usually permit a plaintiff to state his cause of action in his own way, providing he avoids scandalous and indecent matter," and that "It is very difficult to analyze a complaint and eliminate all matter which may, upon the trial, prove to be immaterial or irrelevant without unduly restricting the plaintiff's right to tell a connected story of his grievance," and that "If the complaint sets out no more than is required to sustain the action, such matter cannot be said to be irrelevant or redundant, although there may be intermingled with the essential allegations, expressions and language not, strictly speaking, necessary," and that "The plaintiff must allege that the defendants had formed a conspiracy, or combination, in restraint of trade or, if there be but one defendant whose acts are made the basis of the action, that it is of itself such a combination, within the purview of the act." And that "To do this it is not only proper, but necessary to set forth fully the origin, character of the defendant, its history in regard to the alleged unlawful conduct, growth, methods of business in the respect complained of, and its combination with the other persons or corporations involved, and so forth." And that "The plaintiff must set forth its own origin, character of business, and other relevant matter, so that the court may see that its business bears such relation to the alleged unlawful character and conduct of the defendants, as brings it within the provisions of the statute." And that "The final and essential allegation is that by reason of the conduct of the defendant in doing the things forbidden, or declared to be unlawful, the plaintiff has been injured in his business or property and the character and extent of the damage."

6. Virtue and others vs. Creamery Package Manufacturing Co. and others, 179 Fed Rep. 115. This was an action at law in the Circuit Court of the United States for the District of Minnesota, which was brought to recover triple damages, under Section 7 of the Sherman law, for injuries claimed to have been inflicted, through a violation of that law, by the Creamery Package Manufacturing Co. and others upon the plaintiffs. On the trial of the case in Minnesota, the trial judge directed the jury to return a verdict for the defendants, which being done, that judge rendered a judgment for the defendants.

Thereupon the plaintiffs took the case to the Circuit Court of Appeals for the Eighth Circuit, by means of a writ of error; and the case was decided by that tribunal on March 23, 1910, when that court was held by Circuit Judges Sanborn and Adams, and District Judge Riner. The decision of that court was announced in an opinion delivered by Judge Riner, and was to the effect that the plaintiff was not entitled to recover, because that contract and that combination between the defendants which were complained of were not really violative of the Sherman law. That contract simply provided that the Creamery Package Manufacturing Company was to be the exclusive selling agent of the combined churns and butter workers and other machines and implements used in dairies and creameries, which it was the business of the Owatonna Manufacturing Company to manufacture. On this point the court held that the manufacturing company had a right to select its customers, and to sell and refuse to sell to whom it chose, and to that end, to select one particular selling agent, and that such a selection did not constitute any violation of the Sherman law, as being in restraint of commerce.

The combination between the Creamery Package Manufacturing Company and the Owatonna Manufacturing Company, which was complained of in the suit, consisted in their alleged agreement to separately sue the plaintiffs for alleged infringements of certain patents for inventions, which were separately owned by the Owatonna Manufacturing Company, and the Creamery Package Manufacturing Company. But the only evidence in support of the theory that those separate suits were brought in pursuance of any agreement between the two complainants therein, was to be deduced, if at all, from the fact that those suits were brought on the same day, and by the same lawyer, on behalf of the separate complainants. And the Circuit Court of Appeals found that those two facts fell far short of proving an agreement between those two complainants to attempt to drive out of business the party thus sued.

The four public cases and the six private cases relevant to the Sherman law, which were adjudicated during the first eighteen months of Taft's administration, included six cases in which the Sherman law was invoked in vain, and two cases in which it was invoked with preliminary success only, and one case which resulted in a verdict of guilty and in a judgment imposing punishment by fines and imprisonments; and included also the great Standard Oil case, which resulted in a final decree of the United States Circuit Court for the Eastern District of Missouri, in favor of the Sherman law and its enforcement.

Some other cases have been brought by the United States to enforce the Sherman law, which have not been adjudicated at the present writing, in September, 1910. The most noteworthy of those cases are the following:

United States vs. Terminal Railroad Association of St. Louis. This case was brought in the United States Circuit Court for the Eastern District of Missouri on November 25, 1905, to dissolve a monopoly of terminal facilities at St. Louis, Missouri.

United States vs. American Ice Co. and others. This was an indictment in the Supreme Court of the District of Columbia, which was returned by the Grand Jury on July 12, 1906, and which charged the defendants with an agreement to control prices and restrict competition in ice, contrary to the Sherman law. The indictment in this case is still pending, as it has been pending more than four years.

United States vs. The Reading Company and others. This is an action in equity in the United States Circuit Court for the Eastern District of Pennsylvania, which was brought June 12, 1907, to dissolve the long existing combination between the corporations which are engaged in transporting anthracite coal from the anthracite mines in Pennsylvania to the eastern shores of New Jersey. All the evidence in the case has been taken, and the case has been argued, and is now, at the end of August, 1910, being held under advisement by the Circuit Court.

United States vs. du Pont, de Nemours Co. This is an action in equity which was brought in the United States Circuit Court for the District of Delaware, July 30, 1907, to dissolve the so-called Powder Trust. The evidence in the case has been completed, but the case has not yet been argued.

United States vs. Union Pacific Railroad Co. and others. This is an action in equity, which was brought

February 1, 1908, in the United States Circuit Court for the District of Utah, to dissolve the combination between the Union Pacific Railroad Company and the Southern Pacific Railroad Company, which combination consists in the exercise by the Union Pacific Railroad Company, of its function as a holding company, in connection with its function as a railroad company. All the evidence in the case has been taken, and the case has been set for argument in October, 1910.

United States vs. National Packing Co. and others. This is a bill in equity, filed in the United States Circuit Court for the Northern District of Illinois, March 21, 1910, to procure a dissolution of the so-called Meat Trust. This case is still pending, and may be expected to be vigorously prosecuted and duly decided in the near future.

United States vs. Armour Packing Co. and others. This is an indictment, which was returned April 30, 1910, by the Grand Jury of the United States Circuit Court for the Southern District of Georgia, and which indictment charges the defendants with a combination to control prices and restrict competition in meat. The indictment is still pending, and may be expected to be tried in the near future.

United States vs. Missouri Pacific Railroad Co. and twenty-four other railroad companies. This was an action in equity which was begun May 31, 1910, in the United States Circuit Court for the Eastern District of Missouri, to enjoin twenty-five railroad companies from violating the Sherman law, by means of a mutual contract to restrain themselves, in respect of fixing prices for transportation of freight over their respective railroads. A temporary restraining order was issued by the court, in pursuance of the prayer of the bill; whereupon the defendants sought and secured from the President of the United States a promise to cause the bill to be dismissed, in consideration of their promise to cancel their mutual contract and to abandon their illegal combination. And the bill was dismissed, under the direction of the Attorney General, in pursuance of that promise.

United States vs. Southern Wholesale Grocers' Association. This is an action in equity, which was begun June 9, 1910, in the United States Circuit Court for the Northern District of Alabama. The bill prays for a dissolution of the defendant association, as violative of the Sherman law and the case being less than three months old, is still pending.

United States vs. Frank Hayne, James A. Patten and others. This is an indictment returned June 17, 1910, in the United States Circuit Court for the Southern District of New York, which indictment charges the defendants with a combination and conspiracy in restraint of interstate commerce in cotton, which restraint is claimed to have resulted from the operations of the defendants as a "pool," speculating in cotton in a method and with a result injurious to legitimate interstate commerce therein.

United States vs. Great Lakes Towing Company and others. This is an action in equity, which was begun June 18, 1910, in the United States Circuit Court for the Northern District of Ohio, to dissolve a combination of tug owners on the Great Lakes.

United States vs. Standard Sanitary Manufacturing Co. and others. This is an action in equity, which was begun July 22, 1910, in the United States Circuit Court for the District of Maryland, against a combination of manufacturers and sellers of bathing and other sanitary apparatus.

CHAPTER X.

Chapter III of this book is devoted to construing the Sherman law upon its face in the light of its language, and in the light of the Congressional debates and votes which resulted in its enactment. The statements and arguments of that chapter conducted to the conclusion that the meaning of the first sentence of Section 1 of the Sherman law can be fully and precisely expressed by the following paraphrase of that sentence, namely: "Every combination in mutual or extraneous, direct and material restraint of interstate or international commerce, is hereby prohibited;" and that the second sentence of Section 1 of the Sherman law is so plain in all its parts, as to require no interpretation or explanation or paraphrase to express its entire and precise signification; and that Section 2 of the Sherman law is so plain in all its language as to require no explanation or interpretation, except to define the word "monopolize;" and that that word has a meaning in the law which includes the idea that the monopolist, in making a complete acquirement of the thing monopolized, did something to prevent others from competing with him in reaching that complete acquirement; and that Sections 3, 4, 5, 6, 7 and 8 of the Sherman law are so plain in all their parts, that they require only to be attentively read by lawyers and judges to be uniformly understood by men accustomed, like them, to read statutory enactments.

The twenty years which have passed since the Sherman law was enacted, and the numerous judicial decisions relevant to that law which have been made during those twenty years have, with a close approach to unanimity, conducted to the conclusion that the *prima facie* construction of the Sherman law, which Chapter III of this book deduced from the face of that law, is also its true construction. Indeed, the only noteworthy deviations from that unanimity, which are to be detected in those judicial decisions, are the following:

Judge Lacombe, in delivering one of the three opinions of the United States Circuit Court for the Southern District of New York, in the American Tobacco case, held that the word "restraint" in Section 1 of the Sherman law is indicative of all direct restraint, however slight, and is not confined to such restraint as is extensive enough to be materially injurious to public or to private welfare.

To illustrate his construction of the statute upon that point, Judge Lacombe held that the statute would be violated by "two individuals who have been driving rival express wagons between villages in two contiguous states, and who enter into a combination to join forces and operate a single line."

The prevailing view of the Federal judges and courts upon this question was expressed by Judge Hook in the Standard Oil case, on page 194 of Volume 173 of the Federal Reporter, in the following language:

"There are many contracts which, in the days when the common law was forming, would have been adjudged contrary to public welfare, as being in restraint of the narrow trade of those times, but which in a commercial age like the present have such a negligible effect as to be no longer evil within the meaning of the law. Their effect is so indirect and inappreciable that it is properly referable to the class *de minimis,* and it is not to be supposed Congress had them in view when it legislated to preserve freedom of competition in the broad field of interstate and foreign commerce."

Several judges have held that the word "monopolize" in Section 2 of the Sherman law should be construed to cover any complete acquirement of a particular business, whether the monopolist in making that complete acquirement, did or did not do something to prevent others from competing with him in achieving that end. But the prevailing view, which has been held by the courts on this point since the enactment of the Sherman law, is that which was held in Congress when that law was about to be enacted; and which view was expressed in the Senate by Senator Edmunds and also by Senator Hoar, when they stated that the word "monopolize" has a meaning in the law which includes the idea that the monopolist, in making a complete acquirement of the thing monopolized, did something to prevent others from competing with him in reaching that complete acquirement.

No Federal court has ever held, in any reported adjudicated case, that the first sentence of Section 1 of the Sherman law, in prohibiting "every contract, combination in the form of trust or otherwise, or conspiracy in restraint of trade or commerce among the several states or with foreign nations," is not broad enough to cover such a combination in the form of a "holding company." And the Supreme Court of the United States has decided in the Northern Securities case, that a holding company, which is only a holding company, is covered by that prohibition.

The Standard Oil Company of New Jersey, and the American Tobacco Company are each a combination of holding company and operating company; and the United States Circuit Courts for the Eastern District of Missouri and the Southern District of New York, respectively, decided in the Standard Oil case and the American Tobacco case, respectively, that a combination in the form of such a combined holding and operating company is a "combination in the form of trust or otherwise" within the meaning of the first sentence of Section 1 of the Sherman law, and that, when such a combination is engaged in restraint of trade or commerce among the several states or with foreign nations, it is illegal to the extent in which it is thus engaged; even if it is also engaged in operating some business which is not illegal.

The question whether that construction of the Sherman law which is stated in the last paragraph, and which was placed upon that law by the two Circuit Courts mentioned in that paragraph, is right or is wrong, is believed to be the only great question relevant to the construction of the Sherman law, which remains to be decided by the Supreme Court of the United States. And that is the pivotal question of law, and is probably the only great question of law which the Supreme Court will find it necessary to decide, or will decide, in the Standard Oil Case or in the American Tobacco case.

CHAPTER XI.

It is not the purpose of this chapter to prophesy, whether the nearly identical decisions of the two circuit courts of the Unitetd States, which decided these two cases, respectively, will be affirmed or will be reversed by the Supreme Court. But it is the purpose of this chapter to forecast those decisions, by stating and explaining whatever relevant views and opinions have heretofore been expressed in other cases, by the six justices of the Supreme Court who are now upon the bench of that tribunal, and who will probably constitute two-thirds of the members of the court, when in the year 1911 those two great cases come to be argued and to be decided.

Inasmuch as the Supreme Court has already decided, in the Northern Securities case, that a combination in the form of a holding company which is only a holding company, violates the Sherman law whenever it engages or is even organized to engage, in restraint of trade or commerce among the several states or with foreign nations, it is proper to infer that that tribunal will render a similar decision in any case wherein the combination is in the form of a corporation, which is a holding company and is also an operating company, unless some controlling distinction can be detected between those two forms of combinations.

The brief and argument for the American Tobacco Company and its subsidiary corporations, which was on file in the Supreme Court, when that case was argued in that tribunal in January, 1910, is a printed book of 275 pages, which appears to have been prepared by five distinguished lawyers, including ex-Judge William J. Wallace of New York, and John G. Johnson of Philadelphia. The pivotal part of that elaborate brief and argument is printed on pages 176 to 196, inclusive. The statements and arguments which are there set forth, are to the effect that the Northern Securities Company and the Continental Wall Paper Company were both organized and maintained for the sole purpose of restraining competition between the operating companies, to combine which they were organized; whereas, the American Tobacco Company is engaged in operating the tobacco business itself, and is engaged in holding the stock of other tobacco companies, only as incidental to its business as an operating company.

If this distinction is found by the Supreme Court to be material, and to be important enough to require a decision contrary to those which were rendered by that tribunal in the Northern Securities case, and in the Continental Wall Paper case, it will result in a reversal of the decision of the Circuit Court in the American Tobacco case. But if this distinction is found by the Supreme Court not to be material, or if material, not important enough to require a decision contrary to those rendered in the Northern Securities case and in the Continental Wall Paper case, then the decision of the Circuit Court in the American Tobacco case may be expected to be affirmed; for there is no other distinction between the Northern Securities case and the Continental Wall Paper case on the one hand, and the American Tobacco case on the other hand, which has any controlling significance.

The statements in the last paragraph are equally applicable to the Standard Oil case, for the Standard Oil Company of New Jersey is like the American Tobacco

Company in being primarily an operating company, and in being engaged in holding the stock of other oil companies, as incidental to its business as an operating company.

Now, having ascertained precisely on what pivotal point the decisions of the Supreme Court in the American Tobacco case and in the Standard Oil case, must evidently turn, it is proper to set forth all the available public information which when stated, may indicate which way, upon that pivotal point, those decisions will turn.

The senior Associate Justice of the Supreme Court is Justice Harlan, who has been an eminent member of that tribunal nearly thirty-three years. He has participated in the hearing of every one of the seventeen cases relevant to the Sherman law which have yet been decided by the Supreme Court, except the Bement case. He delivered the opinion of the Supreme Court in the Northern Securities case and in the Continental Wall Paper case, in each of which the accused combination was held to be illegal; and he concurred in each of the other eight cases in which similar decisions were rendered; and he dissented from the decision which was rendered by a majority of the Supreme Court in favor of the defendants, in each of four of the seven cases in which the defendants, though accused thereof, were not found guilty of violating the Sherman law. His contributions to the literature of the Sherman law, in the two cases in which he delivered the opinion of the Supreme Court, and in the four cases in which he dissented, are extensive and learned and eloquent arguments in support of the validity and value and comprehensive scope of that statute. No one who is acquainted with the general subject, and who reads those contributions, can fail to conclude that Justice Harlan may be expected to give his vote in the Supreme Court in favor of deciding the Standard Oil case and the American Tobacco case against those defendants.

The second Associate Justice of the Supreme Court is Justice White, who has been a member of that tribunal nearly seventeen years. He has participated in the hearing of each one of the seventeen Sherman law cases which have thus far been decided by that tribunal, except the Bement case; but he did not deliver the opinion of the court in any of those cases. He concurred with the majority of the court in each of the seven cases, except the Bement case, in which the defendants were not found guilty of violating the Sherman law; and he dissented from the decision of the majority of the court in each of four of the ten cases in which that tribunal held the accused combinations to be illegal; and in two of those four cases he delivered elaborate dissenting opinions.

His dissenting opinion in the Trans-Missouri case was mainly founded upon his view that the Sherman law should be construed as if the word "unreasonable" had been inserted before the word "restraint" in the first sentence of Section 1 of that statute, and upon his judgment that the restraint of interstate trade and commerce which was proved in that case, was not unreasonable. His dissent in the Northern Securities case was chiefly based upon the fact that no overt act was proved to have been committed by the combination in that case, in pursuance of that plan of that combination, which if it had been executed, would have operated to restrain interstate commerce. Neither of these reasons for deciding in favor of the defendants can be applied to the Standard Oil case or to the American Tobacco case, for many, if not all, of the restraints of interstate commerce, which are proved in the records of those cases, were undeniably unreasonable. And the evidence in those cases also proves the performance of many overt acts, during many years, by the American Tobacco Company combination and the Standard Oil combination, respectively.

For these reasons it is quite safe to entertain and express the expectation that Justice White will analyze and consider the American Tobacco case and the Standard Oil case on the records in those cases, with an open judicial mind, and without being even unconsciously influenced by the fact or by the purport of his dissenting opinion in the Trans-Missouri case, or his dissenting opinion in the Northern Securities case.

The third Associate Justice of the Supreme Court is Justice McKenna, who has been one of the associate justices of that court nearly thirteen years. He has participated in the hearing of eleven of the seventeen cases relevant to the Sherman law, which have heretofore been decided by the Supreme Court; but he did not deliver the opinion of the court in any of those cases, though he concurred in that opinion in all of them, except the Connolly case. His dissenting opinion in that case is printed . on pages 565 to 571 of Volume 184 of the United States Reports; but that dissenting opinion had no relevancy to the Sherman law.

The judicial views of Justice McKenna, relevant to the Sherman law, are to be deduced from the fact that he concurred with the elaborate written opinions of the court, which were delivered by Justice Harlan in the Northern Securities case and in the Continental Wall Paper case. The first of those great opinions is printed on pages 317 to 360, inclusive, of Volume 193 of the United States Reports; and the other one is printed on pages 254 to 267 of Volume 212 of the United States Reports.

Inasmuch as Justice McKenna has always agreed with Justice Harlan relevant to every Sherman law question which they have both participated in hearing in the Supreme Court, and inasmuch as those questions include those which are most analogous to the questions involved in the Standard Oil case and the American Tobacco case, no better forecast can be made of the view which Justice McKenna will take in those cases, than to assume that he will concur with Justice Harlan therein.

The fourth Associate Justice of the Supreme Court is Justice Holmes, who has been upon that bench nearly eight years. He has participated in the hearing of eight of the seventeen cases relevant to the Sherman law, which have now been decided by that tribunal; and he delivered the opinion of the court in four of those eight cases; but he delivered elaborate dissenting opinions in two of the other four. His views relevant to the Sherman law are therefore to be collected from six separate official writings.

The first of those writings in his dissenting opinion in the Northern Securities case; which opinion is printed on pages 400 to 411 of Volume 193 of the United States Reports. The second of those writings is that which represents the unanimous opinion of the court in the case of Swift & Co. vs. the United States, which is printed on pages 390 to 402 of Volume 196 of the United States Reports. The third of those writings is that which represents the opinion of the court in the Chicago Board of Trade case, which opinion is printed on pages 245 to 253 of Volume 198 of the United States Reports. The fourth of those writings is that which represents the unanimous opinion of the court in the Cincinnati Packet Company case, which opinion is printed on pages 182 to

186 of Volume 200 of the United States Reports. The fifth of those writings is that which presents the opinion of the court in the Chattanooga Foundry case, which opinion is printed on pages 395 to 399 of Volume 203 of the United States Reports. And the sixth and last of those writings is the dissenting opinion of Justice Holmes in the Continental Wall Paper case, which opinion is printed on pages 267 to 272 of Volume 212 of the United States Reports.

That one of the official writings of Justice Holmes, which has the most relevancy of any of them, to the questions which are involved in the Standard Oil case and in the American Tobacco case, respectively, is his dissenting opinion in the Northern Securities case. In that dissenting opinion he expressed his judicial approval of the decisions of the court in the Trans-Missouri case and in the Joint Traffic Association case, both of which had been rendered before he had become a member of the United States Supreme Court. But he called attention to the fact that the contracts which were held to be violative of the Sherman law in those cases, were contracts between otherwise independent railroad companies, by which they restricted their respective freedom as to freight rates. Thereupon he distinguished between the facts in those cases and the facts in the Northern Securities case, by calling attention to the circumstance that in the Northern Securities case, competition, instead of being ended by a special contract made for that purpose only, was ended by a combination which established a community of interest between its members, in all respects whatever. According to this view of Justice Holmes, the first sentence of Section 1 of the Sherman law should be construed to mean that the only contracts, combinations or conspiracies in restraint of interstate or international commerce which it prohibits, are such as may be made between parties who are otherwise independent of each other.

Inasmuch as this view was repudiated by the majority of the Supreme Court in the Northern Securities case, and therefore has never been clothed with the sanctity of a judicial decision, there can be no impropriety in saying in this place that whoever entertains this view, must quite disregard the voluminous evidence in the Congressional Record for the first session of the Fifty-first Congress, which proves that the Sherman law was intended by both houses of the Congress which enacted it, to prohibit all contracts, combinations and conspiracies in restraint of interstate or international commerce, whether the parties to those contracts had any other mutual relations or not. And there can be no impropriety in pointing out that the Holmes construction of the first sentence of Section 1 of the Sherman law cannot be expressed in words without amending the language of that sentence at least to the extent of inserting therein the words "between parties otherwise independent" after the word "conspiracy." Furthermore, there can be no wrong done by saying and showing that the Holmes construction of Section 1 of the Sherman law would exclude from its prohibitions so nearly all of the combinations, contracts and conspiracies in restraint of interstate or international commerce at which that section was aimed by Congress, that it would be hardly worth while, and indeed, would be unjustly discriminatory, to retain that section upon the statute books any longer if that construction were to prevail.

The fact that Justice Holmes in his dissenting opinion in the Northern Securities case took the ground that he did take, does not prove that he will take the same ground in the Standard Oil case or in the American Tobacco case. For even if he has not changed, and may never change his own opinion upon the point, he knows that

that opinion is contrary to what the Supreme Court decided in the Northern Securities case, and he realizes that what the court decided in that case in 1904, is as binding upon him now, as he then said the still earlier decisions of the Supreme Court in the Trans-Missouri case and the Joint Traffic Association case were binding upon him then.

The fifth Associate Justice of the Supreme Court is Justice Day, who has been a member of that tribunal more than seven years. He participated in hearing the same eight Sherman law cases, in the hearing of which Justice Holmes also participated, but he did not deliver the opinion of the court in any of those cases, though he concurred in the decision of the court in all of them except one. That one was the Chicago Board of Trade case, in which he dissented from the opinion of the court which was delivered by Justice Holmes without stating on what ground he dissented.

The opinions of Justice Day relevant to the Sherman law, so far as they can be collected from the reports of the Supreme Court, must therefore be collected from the written opinions of that court in seven cases in which he concurred, though he did not himself write any of those opinions. Among those seven cases, those which are most analogous to the Standard Oil case and the American Tobacco case, are the Northern Securities case and the Continental Wall Paper case, in both of which the opinion of the court was delivered by Justice Harlan. Those two elaborate and learned opinions may therefore be considered as representative of the relevant opinions of Justice Day.

But Justice Day was one of the judges of the Circuit Court of Appeals for the Sixth Circuit for several years prior to his appointment to the Supreme Court, and as such he delivered an elaborate opinion of that tribunal

11

relevant to the Sherman law in the case of the United States vs. Chesapeake & Ohio Fuel Company and others, 115 Fed. Rep. 610. In that opinion, in speaking of the Sherman law, he said: "Congress has seen fit to prohibit all contracts in restraint of trade. It has not left to the courts the consideration of the question whether such restraint is reasonable or unreasonable, or whether the contract would have been illegal at the common law or not. The act leaves for consideration by judicial authority, no question of this character, but all contracts and combinations are declared illegal, if in restraint of trade or commerce among the states."

This luminous statement written by Justice Day himself to express his opinion of the Sherman law, when considered in connection with the great opinions of Justice Harlan in the Northern Securities case and in the Continental Wall Paper case, in both of which Justice Day concurred, will probably convince everybody who carefully considers them all, in connection with the facts in the Standard Oil case and in the American Tobacco case, that Justice Day, as well as Justice McKenna, may be expected to agree with Justice Harlan in respect of the proper decision to be rendered in those two cases; and that that agreement will constitute a joint opinion, that both those cases ought to be decided in favor of the United States and against the defendants.

The sixth active Associate Justice of the Supreme Court is Justice Lurton, who was appointed by President Taft in December, 1909, and who took his seat upon the Bench on January 3, 1910. He did not participate in hearing any of the seventeen Sherman law cases which have heretofore been decided by the Supreme Court, though he did participate in the first hearing of the American Tobacco case in January, 1910, and the first hearing of the Standard Oil case in March, 1910, both of which hearings, however, have been set aside and rendered non-effective by orders for rehearings.

The judicial opinions of Justice Lurton relevant to the Sherman law, so far as they have been recorded, are to be collected from certain decisions of the Circuit Court of Appeals for the Sixth Circuit, which were rendered when he was one of the judges of that tribunal from 1893 until 1910.

The first of those cases was the case of the United States vs. Addyston Pipe & Steel Company and others, 85 Fed. Rep. 271. That case was decided on February 8, 1898, by the Circuit Court of Appeals for the Sixth Circuit, when that court was being held by Justice Harlan and Judges Taft and Lurton. The elaborate opinion of that court in that case was written by Judge Taft, and is printed on twenty-five pages of Volume 85 of the Federal Reporter, beginning with page 278, and Judge Lurton concurred in that opinion. So also the decision of the Circuit Court of Appeals in that case was afterward affirmed by the Supreme Court of the United States in 1899, in an opinion delivered by Justice Peckham, and printed on twenty-three pages of Volume 175 of the United States Reports, beginning on page 226.

The written opinion of Judge Taft, in which Judge Lurton thus concurred, and which was thus approved by the Supreme Court, was and is strongly favorable to enforcement of the Sherman law against any and every association or combination or contract in restraint of interstate commerce, no matter what excuse the parties to such an association or combination may present to the court for its existence or for their participation therein. Moreover, the only noteworthy difference between the facts in the Addyston case on the one hand, and the facts in the Standard Oil case and the American Tobacco case on the other hand, which can be plausibly invoked by the attorneys for the defendants in those cases, as constituting a reason for an opposite decision, consists in the fact that the combination in the Addyston case was confined to restraint of interstate commerce, whereas the combination in the Standard Oil case and also that in the American Tobacco case, is far more complete, and covers much other business also.   But there is nothing whatever to be found in the judicial record of Justice Lurton which indicates that he will ever give any judicial adherence to the view that a guilty combination can be shown to be innocent, by proving that in addition to violating a certain law, it is also engaged in transacting some other business which does not violate that law.

The second of the Sherman law cases, in the decision of which Justice Lurton participated, when he was Judge of the Circuit Court of Appeals for the Sixth Circuit, was the case of Cravens vs. Carter-Crume Company, 92 Fed. Rep. 479, in which case the opinion of the court was delivered by Judge Severens, and was concurred in by Judge Lurton, and was to the effect that the combination whose doings were involved in the case, was violative of the Sherman law.

The third case in the Circuit Court of Appeals for the Sixth Circuit, which is representative of the view of Justice Lurton upon the Sherman law, is the case of the United States vs. Chesapeake & Ohio Fuel Company and others, 115 Fed. Rep. 610, wherein he concurred with the opinion of that court, which was delivered in that case by Judge Day, and which has lately been mentioned as a part of the judicial record of Justice Day.

The fourth Lurton Sherman law case was the case of the City of Atlanta vs. the Chesapeake Foundry & Pipe Works and others, 127 Fed. Rep. 23.   This was a case in which Judge Lurton himself delivered the opinion of the Circuit Court of Appeals for the Sixth Circuit, enforcing the Sherman law against a particular combination in restraint of interstate commerce; and that decision was afterward affirmed by the Supreme Court, in an opinion delivered by Justice Holmes in Volume 203 of the United States Reports, beginning at page 395.

A fifth significant record of the judicial views of Justice Lurton upon the Sherman law, is to be found in the opinion of the Circuit Court of Appeals for the Sixth Circuit in the Continental Wall Paper case, which opinion is printed on pages 946 to 953 of Volume 148 of the Federal Reporter, and the decision that resulted from which opinion was affirmed by the Supreme Court in the opinion delivered by Justice Harlan, and printed on pages 254 to 267 of Volume 212 of the United States Reports.

In each of the last-mentioned five cases, Judge Lurton either expressed or concurred in a judicial decision which enforced the Sherman law against a particular combination in restraint of interstate commerce.

The last case in the Circuit Court of Appeals wherein Judge Lurton rendered any decision relevant to the Sherman law was the case of Bigelow vs. Calumet & Hecla Mining Company, in which he delivered the opinion of the Circuit Court of Appeals on February 18, 1909, and which opinion is printed on twenty pages of Volume 167 of the Federal Reporter, beginning with page 722. In that case the court found that the defendants were not chargeable with any violation of the Sherman law, because their doings were not proved to relate to any interstate commerce.

Judge Lurton in that Calumet case explained that the mere fact that one manufacturing company, through stock ownership, controlled a competing manufacturing company in the same state, was not enough to prove that that control would be exercised in restraint of interstate commerce; but that if the acquirement of that stock control was a mere preparation for afterward doing acts in restraint of interstate commerce, the courts might be expected to interfere with the conduct thus resulting.

Governor Hughes of New York was appointed by President Taft in May, 1910, to be an Associate Justice of the Supreme Court of the United States; and he is expected to take the oath of that office, and to take his seat upon the bench of that court on October 10, 1910.

Mr. Hughes has never yet had any occasion to take any official action relevant to the Sherman law. But when he was first candidate for Governor in 1906, he made many speeches in which he frankly stated to the people of New York what were his opinions upon a great number of public subjects. Among the topics to which he thus attended was the Sherman law. And he attended to that subject, by saying that he believed in that law and was in favor of its enforcement.

The supreme power in the United States is the Congress of the United States. And the Congress of the United States, after months of profound study of the subject, enacted the Sherman law, with an approach to unanimity which was never equalled in any other case so complex and so important. That law has stood the test of twenty years of strenuous litigation in every part of the country, from one ocean to the other, and from the northern lakes to the southern gulf. It embodies the national will. It is "a rule of civil conduct prescribed by the supreme power in the States, commanding what is right and prohibiting what is wrong." The Supreme Court has no power to change that law. Its constitutionality is already established by that tribunal. Its construction was never difficult and will soon be quite completed by that court. Only its application to particular cases will then remain to be made.

INDEX

of

DECISIONS, OPINIONS AND SPEECHES.

314   INDEX.

CLEVELAND, PRESIDENT
    history of Sherman law during administration of, 87-123.
COCHRAN, JUDGE
    opinion of, in Calumet & Hecla case, 260-261.
CONNOR, JUDGE
    decision of, in Ware-Kramer Tobacco case, 289.
COXE, JUDGE
    opinion of, in American Tobacco case, 213-214.
    decision of, in Dueber Watch case, 115.
    decision of, in Pidcock case, 118.
    decision of, in Wisewall case, 121.
CULBERSON, REPRESENTATIVE
    speech of, on Sherman bill, 36-37.
DALLAS, JUDGE
    opinion of, in Harriman case, 195.
    opinion of, in Knight case, 91.
DAY, JUDGE
    opinion of, in Chesapeake & Ohio Fuel case, 140-142.
DAY, JUSTICE
    judicial attitude of, on Sherman law, 307-308.
EDMUNDS, SENATOR
    opinion of, on the word "monopolize," 33.
    reporting Hoar substitute from Judiciary Committee, 27.
    speech of, on Sherman bill, 25.
EVANS, JUDGE
    decision of, in Monarch Tobacco case, 265-266.
    decision of, in Otis Elevator case, 159.
FITHIAN, REPRESENTATIVE
    speech of, on Sherman bill, 41.
FOSTER, JUDGE
    decision of, in Hopkins case, 133.
FULLER, CHIEF JUSTICE
    opinion of, in Danbury Hatters case, 228-230.
    opinion of, in Harriman case, 195.
    opinion of, in Knight case, 92-95.
GRAY, JUDGE
    dissenting opinion of, in Harriman case, 195.
GEORGE, SENATOR
    speech of, on Sherman bill, 7-8.
GRIGGS, ATTORNEY GENERAL
    reports of, to Congress, 170-172.
    service of, 124.
GROSSCUP, JUDGE
    opinion of, in Case Threshing Machine case, 236.
    opinion of, in Rubber Tire Wheel case, 234-235.
    opinion of, in Swift case, 197.
HAMMOND, JUDGE
    decision of, in Jellico Mountain Coal case, 64.
HANFORD, JUDGE
    decision of, in Gibbs case, 156-157.

www.ingramcontent.com/pod-product-compliance
Lightning Source LLC
Chambersburg PA
CBHW020335270326
41926CB00007B/190